D1499609

THE PRINCIPLES
OF NATIVE
ADMINISTRATION
IN NIGERIA

Selected Documents

1900–1947

THE PRINCIPLES OF NATIVE ADMINISTRATION IN NIGERIA

Selected Documents

1900–1947

Edited and Introduced by
A. H. M. KIRK-GREENE, M.B.E.

Reader in Public Administration
Ahmadu Bello University
Northern Nigeria

Foreword by
MARGERY PERHAM

LONDON
OXFORD UNIVERSITY PRESS
1965

Oxford University Press, Amen House, London E.C.4

GLASGOW NEW YORK TORONTO MELBOURNE WELLINGTON
BOMBAY CALCUTTA MADRAS KARACHI LAHORE DACCA
CAPE TOWN SALISBURY NAIROBI IBADAN ACCRA
KUALA LUMPUR HONG KONG

Printed in Great Britain
by Billing & Sons Ltd., Guildford and London

FOR
MY COLLEAGUES AND STUDENTS
AT THE INSTITUTE OF
ADMINISTRATION
ESPECIALLY THE 'YAN DIPIYAI

ACKNOWLEDGEMENTS

The editor and the publishers wish to acknowledge permission to quote received from the following:—

Cape Argus Press, for excerpts from C. L. Temple, *Native Races and Their Rulers*.

Colonial Office, for excerpts from the Secretary of State's *Despatch* of February, 1947.

Department of Technical Co-operation, for excerpts from the *Journal of African Administration*.

Federal Ministry of Commerce and Industry, Lagos, for excerpts from *Minute by His Excellency the Governor*, 1934.

Government Printer, Kaduna, for excerpts from Publication No. 456/36.

Government Printer, Lagos, for excerpts from the *Annual Reports of Nigeria* and Publication No. 2489/1147.

Waterlow and Sons, for excerpts from *Political Memoranda*.

Wm. Blackwood and Sons, for excerpts from F. D. Lugard, *The Dual Mandate*.

Since it was not clear whether the copyright of certain of the documents cited is now vested in the Federal or Regional Government, the MS was submitted to the Regional Government, for whose generous permission to publish the editor is grateful. The editor also wishes to express his thanks to his stenographers, Jonah Z. Abbaya and Abdulkarim Jimoh, for their work on the typescript, and to his students, Sani S. Ameh and Wilson O. Aiyepeku, for their valued assistance with the proofs.

CONTENTS

FOREWORD

I assume that Mr. Kirk-Greene has paid me the compliment of asking me to write this Foreword because, like him, I have for many years been interested in the development of African administration. I can claim, however, a longer span of years than his in which to pursue this study and also that it brought me the good fortune, while Mr. Kirk-Greene was still practising the art of administration, of friendship with Lord Lugard and with Mr. Creech Jones, two of those contributing to this book. I had also the opportunity to observe native administration with the help of another contributor, Sir Donald Cameron, in both Tanganyika and Nigeria during his governorships of those territories. I have probably already written too much upon the subject and shall do no more here than comment in general terms upon the contents of this book. But I find that, as the years go by and our ex-African dependencies develop out of the system of administration in which Britain tried to mould the tribes she annexed, the retrospective light on the scene changes a little with time and old judgements have to be adjusted to the new vision.

Today the world resounds with opinions about British colonialism, mostly of a denunciatory tone. Anyone who wishes to make a serious contribution to this debate should try to get behind feelings and reach the facts. The most basic of these are the documents which governed the practice of British rule. Mr. Kirk-Greene has done an important service in bringing together some of the most important of these documents illustrating British rule with especial reference to the territory long regarded as a model, Northern Nigeria. Mr. Kirk-Greene's book should be indispensable not only to the student but to anyone who wants to form an opinion upon Britain's administration of Africa.

The material in this book, covering four decades, will provide valuable material for consideration in the sixth, the current period of African independence. For in the few years of his occupation and government of Northern Nigeria, Lugard created a system of administration which proved so effective that it not only rooted itself in its first *locus* but spread as a model or at least an influence over the rest of Nigeria and over most of British Africa. The documents in this book illustrate phases which might be entitled the establishment, distortion, correction and supersession of indirect rule. Each word demands some enlargement.

Even the critics of indirect rule are bound to admit that in his establishment of British power Lugard constructed well, too well, some might say, to allow of later reconstruction. The more deeply the work of those years is studied the more impressive does the achievement appear. Lugard brought to the task a wide and varied experience in dealing with Africa, immense self-confidence and the physical and mental strength to work almost round the clock. But, of course, in the emirates he had superb material upon which to work. Here was an immense region, taken over at a blow and almost undamaged physically and in morale by the process. Here, instead of the usual divisive tribalism, there was a high degree of cultural and religious uniformity, a much more developed system of administration than in most of the continent, and a docile people which was already under the overlordship of a conquering class with a suzerain at Sokoto. Nowhere was it easier administratively to impose a higher superiority.

Even so the articulation of the emirates with the British administration was not so perfect in action as it appeared to be in Lugard's voluminous exposition of it in his Memoranda. There were two potentially weak places in the system. It depended upon the continuing loyalty of the people to the emir. Lugard assumed that he could appropriate two or three essential and superior attributes of their power and still expect that power to function within its new limits as if unchanged, both in essence and in the eyes of the subjects. Furthermore, beside each emir was a Resident who had the desire to advise but the power to control. To keep the traditional machinery of administration working normally a certain degree of make-believe was therefore necessary, with the Resident standing behind the throne but keeping his head well down. A responsibility, at once heavy and complex, was thus thrown upon the Resident who had to decide when and at what point between his standards and those of his emir he should intervene, the degree of the intervention, and how to veil it from the public.

These considerations lead us to Temple and the period of a distortion which was partly an actuality but still more a dangerous doctrine. This able, imaginative and artistic man in some ways saw more deeply into the problems than Lugard. He asked more searching questions and to some of these, it must seem, he gave the wrong answers. He must be reckoned as both influential and typical among that important body, the northern Residents. This is especially true of his exaltation of the linked status of the Residents and the emirs. Lugard, on returning in 1912, had to combat the tendency of the Residents to be more royalist than their kings. As, during Lugard's absence, they had gained the support of the Colonial

Office, and as Lugard was almost crushed under the huge task of amalgamating the Nigerias and also dealing with a war, both in general and on his frontier, he was only partly successful in correcting the bias. The strange thing is that when he wrote the *Dual Mandate* in the tranquillity of his Surrey home he did not directly discuss this underlying issue which lay at the heart of indirect rule.

So much for the phases of inauguration and distortion. Sir Donald Cameron certainly saw himself as applying correction. His autarchic character made it difficult for him to acknowledge how much his far-reaching reform of native administration in Tanganyika owed to his experience in Nigeria under Lugard, both in general principles and in much of the content of his system. But he could claim to have introduced a realistic and reforming spirit both in Tanganyika and Nigeria. He recognized, for example, that some detribalized peoples offered no basis for the 'indirect' principle; that there must be no easy toleration of a wide margin of abuse; that council doors must be open to the bracing air of new ideas and to the educated element which believed in them. Above all he attacked the 'unhallowed' assumption, if no more, that emirates were potential states. I remember well the tension in some Northern Nigerian administrative circles soon after Cameron's return as the cold wind of criticism blew up from Government House in Lagos. Sir Bernard Bourdillon followed up this corrective line with his clear-cut minute on native administration finance which has been most suitably included in this book. It is probable that recognition has not yet been given to the important part played by this Governor in correcting the tendency of his Chief Commissioner in the northern provinces, Sir Theodore Adams, to exalt the emirs to the status of sultans in the Malaya where Adams had served.[1] Adams's view was that Cameron had departed from Lugard's indirect principles. Bourdillon therefore sought a ruling from Lugard himself. I was working with Lugard at the time and was able to see this correspondence and discuss it with him. Lugard, in his reply, was able to quote his own clear instruction in paragraph 16 of his chapter on native administration and also Cameron's endorsement of his view of the emirs' status as his 'wakils', or deputies. He was also able to refer to page 196 (et seq.), of the *Dual Mandate* in which he distinguished that status from that of Malayan sultans or Indian princes. When Lugard later received from Bourdillon the latter's minute on finance, reproduced in this book, he replied (June 13, 1939): 'I am in hearty agreement with every word of it.' It is significant that the one exception he made with regard to paragraphs 18 and 19 showed him even less of an 'indirect ruler' than Bourdillon!

[1] See note 103, p. 38.

The final document in this book may be regarded as the official supersession in Whitehall of indirect rule. The Labour Secretary of State viewed African government from a somewhat different standpoint from that of the public-school governors and officials who had developed indirect rule from, as it were, the underside of the ruled and with a mind alert to welcome the forces of change leading towards democracy and self-government. His despatch by no means led to the complete or universal supersession of the old order in Africa. By the 'forties, however, experience had accumulated to show that the Lugard model of indirect rule, though economical, humane and, in varying degrees, effective for many years in many territories, had rarely been *wholly* suited to African institutions outside Hausaland. It had also become clear that the rising tide of political consciousness was going to catch up and overflow the more leisurely advance of evolution through a local government system based upon chief and tribe. The new movement became an almost uncontrollable flood ten years after Mr. Creech Jones's despatch. But as the tide of nationalism races to its final limits in ex-'British' Africa the emirates of Nigeria are seen standing like some massive breakwater, barely affected by the storms which, even in the rest of Nigeria, have so changed the political landscape.

This is not the place to discuss this striking contrast, which raises deep questions about the proper pace of change, the value of stability and the character of Islam. This book may help us to answer these questions but only if we can reconstruct the contemporary situations with which Lugard and his successors had to deal. A book which may throw a clear light on the issue is the very revealing autobiography of Sir Ahmadu Bello, who might be called a super-emir, since he is not only the Premier of Northern Nigeria but belongs to the paramount dynasty of Sokoto. Mr. Kirk-Greene's introduction and the documents themselves throw light upon many other aspects. One is the immense practical and deliberative effort which British administrators devoted to their task in Nigeria. The other is that neither in fact nor in their own estimation were they potters moulding plastic human clay. They were more like tailors trying to make the garments of their administration fit the restless, heterogeneous and swiftly growing shapes of their African wards.

Nuffield College,   MARGERY PERHAM
Oxford.

INTRODUCTION

Of all the facets of colonialism that will continue to attract the attention of African scholars—and the aspects are legion, ranging from economic policies to cultural repression, from nationalism and *négritude* to localization of the public service and the alleged exploitation of tribalism, and the curious dichotomy of the mutual antipathy of 'the colonial' and the indigenous educated élite contrasted with the warm bond of affection between the same District Officer and 'his' hill peasants or forest folk—none is likely to hold the stage for political scientists and public administration researchers with the same challenging persistence as the total philosophy of native administration. And among the diverse doctrines of native administration, pride of place goes to the theory and practice of indirect rule.[1]

Over the years indirect rule has been many things to many people. It has at once been the principal feature of British imperial practice, the anathema of nationalists, the bulwark of paramountcy, and the basis of self-government. None can yet pronounce for certain whether indirect rule was the bane or the boon of colonialism in British tropical Africa. It has been written about, argued, condemned and praised. It has been the subject of countless seminars, theses, articles and books. And yet what has been said about the place of indirect rule in the history of native administration is barely half of what is still to be said.[2]

This is not just another book about indirect rule and native administration. Rather is it a bridge leading to the next phase in the literature on native administration. It is an academic tool for the new generation of African scholars. For I am of the opinion that in political institutions—especially in the colonial context—there is a certain regularity of rhythm in historical acceptance. The beat comes into prominence at times of intense nationalism such as self-government or a war of aggression or world condemnation. Earlier judgements are then dissected and re-examined, perhaps to be discarded, reinterpreted and reinstated, perhaps to be diluted or added to before restoration. But always the process must be the same: a critical re-examination and rethinking as part of a *soi-disant* sober evaluation of what have hitherto been accepted as the 'facts'. External objectivity must now have the amalgam of internal emotion, above all in the ex-colonial situation, in order to produce the pure alloy of the new scholarship.

Experience in African university circles has convinced me that the new generation of African scholars will not be content with studying, say, Perham or Hailey or Mair on native administration. True, they will, if they are genuine scholars, gladly return to these brilliant secondary sources and learn from their critical objectivity and perceptive judgements. In particular, they will learn that true scholarship calls for a readiness to move with the times, backwards as well as forwards, so as to avoid the common pitfall in the new nations of looking at 1900 through the spectacles of 1950 or judging 1910 by the standards of 1960. Nevertheless, today more than ever the new African intellectual, be he professor, public servant or politician, is going to insist on examining the primary sources; and examining them for himself. He wants the actual documents before he can express his views, before he can evaluate the past judgements and present assumptions of other commentators—most of whom have of necessity been European scholars. He does not want only the opinions of others; he wants to be able to make up his own mind and to come to his own conclusions based on the evidence in front of him. What the African scholar wants above all in order to make his effective contribution are the raw materials of research.

It is precisely these materials, the documents of government and the policy directives which, as it were, comprised the District Officer's Bible, that are so hard to come by. Research workers of the next century may ask, when the last of the pensioned 'Yesterday's Rulers'[3] are dead and buried, how the District Officer ever knew what his job was. Rarely was the cadet issued with any manual of procedure, although a corpus of instructions like financial and office guides gradually grew up. He learned his job by the traditional British Civil Service way of apprenticeship, deriving from the mediaeval crafts guilds—by, in modern parlance, on-the-job training: *c'est en forgeant qu'on devient forgeron.*[4] Nevertheless, at the top level, there was policy; and this policy was thoughtfully incorporated in colonial despatches, gubernatorial minutes, secretariat circulars and provincial directives. In many cases such doctrinal *dicta* were enlarged upon in the memoirs and autobiographical reflexions of retired colonial servants.[5] Such materials, in so far as they contain something approaching the unwritten code of the Nigerian administrative system, supplement the actual legislation and offer to the political scientist indispensable source material for a study of the theory and practice of imperial administration. A few of these have had but limited publication; many are within the Nigerian archives, subject to the rather unrealistic application of the Public Records' fifty year rule; for the rest, they figure too often among the growing list of scarce Africana, usually unobtainable by the majority of researchers and quite inaccessible to the student, who must count himself fortunate if his university library has even one copy among its holdings. In short, the most serious research workers are deprived of the most essential documentary materials.

It is largely to meet this twin situation, of unavailability of basic materials and of a persistent demand for the actual documents before turning to hitherto standard commentaries, that this book has been devised. Its genealogy as a project derives from an awareness of these urgent problems born out of my experience with undergraduate and post-graduate students of African and American universities confronted with the difficulty of obtaining source materials for reading assignments supplementary to lectures and tutorials.

It may be asked why this collection of documents limits itself to native administration in Nigeria. There are four reasons for this. First, the pedestrian one of practical publishing economics: a bigger book would at once price itself out of the range of the very pockets for which this is designed, the pockets of the African university student. Secondly, because my own experience, both as an administrator and as an academic, has been in Nigeria. Thirdly, because it is Nigeria that has been held up as a laboratory *sans pareil* of indirect rule,[6] and it is from Nigeria that the classic principles of native administration were exported, deliberately as an exemplar, to West, East and Central Africa.[7] Finally, though Tanganyika may claim to vie with Nigeria as the leading exponent of successful native administration, it must be remembered that her greatest philosopher was the scholar-administrator Sir Donald Cameron, who not only gained his political education in the Nigerian Secretariat under Lord Lugard but also returned to Nigeria to implement the significant reinterpretation of policy known as indirect administration. If half the book is devoted to the administrative ideas and ideals of Lugard— and over half of those pages in their turn to *Political Memoranda*— and a third of it to the writings of his successors Cameron and Temple, this proportion is but a just tribute to the supreme place held by these craftsmen in the fashioning of native administration.

In the hope that this work will be of value to students not only in Nigeria but also in other African universities, I have sought to assemble here basic documents that illustrate the historical evolution of native administration from 1900 to 1947; in brief, its origin and its spirit. This genesis and genius comprise the philosophy and policy of Lugard's indirect rule, an expedient hardening through the years into a dogma; its liberalization and restatement as Cameron's indirect administration; and its culmination in the emergence of the Colonial Office emphasis on local government as a prerequisite for ultimate self-determination.

If this introduction were to become yet another treatise on the nature of indirect rule, then it would defeat the very purpose I have set myself in the foregoing apologia. Therefore I have limited my role to that of selecting the basic documents on native administration in Nigeria during the colonial period, without commentary and, as far as space and would-be objectivity allow, without editing. No attempt is made to draw up a balance sheet of indirect rule, nor to make any total assessment of native administration policies. Deliberately—yet not without severe temptation, given the excellence of the documentation—I have in the text eschewed quoting from the abundant resources of commentaries and critiques on native administration, though I am of the opinion that no scholar worthy of the title can afford to overlook such works once he has had the opportunity now presented to him of examining the documents for himself. My introduction seeks simply to facilitate a fresh, inside study of Native Administration in Nigeria and to place the documents in perspective for the young African scholar and his fellow-students in other universities.

1903: THE SPEECH AT SOKOTO

Few would deny that it was the practical implementation rather than the theoretical idea of indirect rule that created for it its reputation in Nigeria. Instead of citing the pre-Lugardian practitioners in the I.C.S. and Fiji, or those of the Moghul empire[8] or Alexander the Great or even Jethro's counsel to Moses,[9] it would be more instructive to examine Goldie's directives to his District Agents on the Niger and Benue[10] with a view to determining the extent to which these men were the predecessors of the type District Officer. Goldie's own essay[11] on African administration is widely quoted to show him anticipating Lugard in his advocacy of the system later to be classified as indirect rule. Its key passage reads thus:

Central African races and tribes have, broadly speaking, no sentiment of patriotism, as understood in Europe. There is therefore little difficulty in inducing them to accept what German jurisconsuls term Ober-Hoheit, which corresponds with one interpretation of our vague term 'Protectorate'. But when complete sovereignty, or Landes-Hoheit, is conceded, they invariably stipulate that their local customs and system of government shall be respected. On this point they are, perhaps more tenacious than most subject races with whom the British Empire has had to deal; while their views and ideals of life are extremely difficult for an Englishman to understand. It is therefore certain that even an imperfect and tyrannical native African administration, if its extreme excesses were controlled by European supervision, would be, in the early stages, productive of far less discomfort to its subjects than well-intentioned but ill-directed efforts of European magistrates, often young and headstrong, and not invariably gifted with sympathy and introspective powers. If the welfare of the native races is to be considered, if dangerous revolts are to be obviated, the general policy of ruling on African principles through native rulers must be followed for the present. Yet it is desirable that considerable districts in suitable localities should be administered on European principles by European officials, partly to serve as types to which the native governments may gradually approximate, but principally as cities of refuge in which individuals of more advanced views may find a living, if native government presses unduly upon them; just as, in Europe of the Middle Ages, men whose love of freedom found the iron-bound system of feudalism intolerable, sought eagerly the comparative liberty of cities.

Flint, Goldie's definitive biographer, has neatly pointed up the continuity between Goldie and Lugard:

Perhaps Goldie's most significant historical contribution was in the sphere of administration: through the administrative system of the Royal Niger Company he laid down the theoretical basis for what was later to become known as indirect rule—the system of administration based on using the existing legitimate African rulers. It is true that Goldie's work was in the main, though not entirely, theoretical. The great practical task of establishing a really effective system fell to Lord Lugard. Nevertheless, if Goldie's contribution is not placed in perspective the entire history of indirect rule goes out of focus. . . . Goldie played a direct part not only in beginning effective indirect rule in the Emirates, but also in actually laying down the policy which Lugard was instructed to follow. At this point it is necessary to emphasize that Goldie's theories were not evolved at the end of the company's tenure of power, they were developed as early as 1886 on the basis of the trading company's experience since 1879. Indirect rule was not dreamed up in a historical vacuum, it was the logical consequence of British policy in the 1880's and of the protectorate system. The inspiration for the idea of ruling through the African chiefs and Emirs lay in the company's poverty both in men and money. Goldie's genius lay in fitting these limitations, which in other areas could lead to administrative chaos and nullity, into a consistent theory of administration.[12]

Since, however, our concern is with indirect rule as the official policy in Nigeria and not as an adjunct of chartered rule, our first document, appropriately enough, derives from Lugard.

Though there is evidence of Lugard's formative ideas on indirect rule in both his Ugandan narrative[13] and in his diaries written on the voyage out to Nigeria, it is the speech made at the installation of the Sultan of Sokoto on 21 March, 1903, that marks the first significant statement on the intended policy of native administration in

B

the emirates. An identical ceremony was repeated at Katsina, Kano and Zaria.[14] The bastions of the Fulani empire had fallen and the way lay clear for the incorporation of all the Hausa states into the Protectorate. New emirs had been selected by the *majalisar gargajiya* (the traditional councillors) to replace the fugitive Aliyu of Kano and Attahiru of Sokoto. The Moslem kingdoms were ready to hear what the policies of these new rulers were to be.

It is for this reason that Lugard's address at Sokoto, 'regarding the conditions of British rule', is, short as it is, so important a document. Many of the basic principles of indirect rule at its later apogee in the emirates are to be found in it, and some of the features have survived the colonial period and persisted through independence. Here are the legitimacy of alien overlordship by right of conquest, the very claim of the Fulani themselves a century before; the right of Government (be it that of 1900 or 1960) to extend or withdraw recognition of any chief; the principles of taxation as the acknowledgement of sovereignty, and of the native authorities being permitted to collect tax only on behalf of Government; the confirmation of the status of native courts through the issue of a warrant of appointment; and the vesting of certain land rights in Government. Here, too, is the significant promise that 'Government will in no way interfere with the Mohammedan religion', a promise subsequently invoked to keep out Western civilization,[15] with retardative results today frankly lamented by Northern leaders. The wide mandate of the Administrative Officers, confirmed in the Residents' Proclamation of 1900 and continuing supreme right down till the introduction of a ministerial system of government in 1951, derives from the finale: 'You must not fear to tell the Resident every thing and he will help and advise you.' The subsequent enthronement ceremony of every chief in Northern Nigeria owes much to this occasion, and the installation of the Emir of Kano by Sir Kashim Ibrahim in 1963 bore a strikingly close resemblance to that performed at Sokoto in 1903.

The fundamental concept of the role and status of the emirs, adumbrated in this speech, is repeated in Lugard's *Memorandum on Native Administration:* 'There are not two sets of rulers—British and Native—working either separately or in co-operation, but a single government in which the Native Chiefs have well-defined duties and an acknowledged status equally with the British officials'.[16] This relationship between the centre and its component parts is of no less importance to an independent government than it was to a colonial administration. It is therefore instructive to compare this early statement of policy by Lugard with that recently promulgated by the Government of Northern Nigeria on the same problem:

Within the field of Local Government, the Regional Government is ready to grant Native Authorities complete freedom of action provided always that certain essential conditions are observed. These conditions are that Native Authorities should retain the confidence of the great mass of their people, that they should discharge adequately the duties and responsibilities assigned to them, that they should conduct their financial affairs in a prudent and responsible fashion, and that they should maintain the standards of honesty and impartiality required in a country approaching independence. The Regional Government, which is ultimately responsible for law, order and sound administration, must however reserve to itself the right to intervene in local government matters if these conditions are not met. This right is recognized by the law which has provided certain over-riding powers. These are financial, executive and legal, and they vary in range from the ability to withhold a small grant to the power of the Governor in Council to annul the appointment of a Native Authority. . . . In particular it [Government] is resolved to treat all Native Authorities, irrespective of their political sympathies, with strict impartiality and scrupulously to refrain from any action which could be attributed to political bias. Native Authorities may therefore rest assured that, provided that they for their part discharge their statutory and moral obligations, they will not be subject to unjustifiable interference or undue influence by the Regional Government.[17]

1914: THE AMALGAMATION REPORT

One of the significant consequences of the amalgamation of the Protectorates of Northern and Southern Nigeria in 1914 (the Colony of Lagos had been merged with the Southern Protectorate in 1906) was the deliberate extension of the emirate philosophy of native administration to the south.[18] The northern emirates amply met the accepted criteria of a 'state': centralized authority, administrative machinery, and a recognized judicial system, with distinctions of wealth, privilege and status deriving from the distribution of power and authority.[19] Indeed, had it not been for the anachachronism, Lord Hailey might almost have had the formulation of a state in mind when he noted how in Northern Nigeria 'centralized authority carried on its administration through officers who were in effect fief-holders . . . there was a revenue system involving a number of taxes . . . tribunals were presided over by trained judges . . .'[20] Not so the South, where the very characteristics that made for government in the North were signally lacking. With the advantage of hindsight, it is easy for us to question the feasibility of imposing such 'state' concepts on essentially 'segmented' societies,[21] nor is it hard for us to say today that some of the difficulties into which indirect rule ran in such areas might well have been foreseen.[22]

But the fact remains that this projection of the successful Northern system of indirect rule to the South was Lugard's policy, and the amalgamation of the two Protectorates under him provided the opportunity. Hitherto the South, unlike the North with its 13 provinces under Residents, had been made up of three 'Divisions' in charge of Provincial and District Commissioners, while the courts were in the hands of puisne judges.[23] Following the Northern pattern, nine Provinces were now established, each under a Resident supported by a team of District Officers.[24]

But 'native administration' came south in more than administrative terminology alone. Explaining the reasons for the divergence in local administration in the North and South, Lugard pointed out that 'the problem of native policy and administration was one which forced itself upon the Northern Government at the very beginning, whereas in the South the trader and the missionary were the pioneers'.[25] Lugard then summarized his concept of indirect rule:

The first step is to endeavour to find a man of influence as chief, and to group under him as many villages or districts as possible, to teach him to delegate powers, and to take an interest in his Native Treasury, to support his authority, and to inculate a sense of responsibility.[26]

The system, he concluded, could be said 'to have worked with good results in the North, and I desired to introduce its principles in the South'.[27] Lugard was, however, aware that one of the essential ingredients was an accepted system of direct taxation—a feature conspicuously absent in the area to which he now proposed to extend indirect rule.

However, the process went ahead, first in the Western and later in the Eastern Provinces.[28] The Native Courts Ordinance of 1914 applied the judicial system of the North to the whole of the new Protectorate. A senior administrative officer from the North,[29] and one of the architects of indirect rule in all its emirate glory, was immediately appointed to report on the possibility of introducing indirect rule to the Southern Protectorate. Carried away by the apparent authority of Yoruba kingship and its promising resemblance to the Fulani emirates,[30] he enthusiastically recommended the northern pattern of native administration.[31] The Native Authority Ordinance of 1916 extended to the South the substance of the native administration legislation and the indirect rule principles of the North; a Native Revenue Ordinance, hitherto applicable only to the Northern Provinces, was introduced in the West (1916) and later in the East (1928),[32] with its corollary of Native Treasuries[33]; and Native Authorities were created on the Northern model, though often they were little more than the District Officer presiding over a handful of unpopular judges and a petty, bankrupt treasury. The grave disturbances at Oyo and Abeokuta in 1918, the riots at Aba in 1929, the plethora of unviable Native Authorities that sprang up,[34] and the rapid dissolution of the Native Administration system in preference for a full-scale conciliar one under the first Local Government Ordinances of 1950 (East) and 1953 (West)—in contrast to the affectionate consolidation of the Native Administration system in the North[35] (even Kaduna Capital Territory was converted into a Native Administration in 1962)—suggest that the 1916 imposition of indirect rule on the South simply because of its success in the North[36] may be held to have been an error of administrative judgement.[37]

1918: TEMPLE'S POLITICAL TESTIMONY

Charles Temple was the son of a distinguished and aristocratic member of the I.C.S., and spent five years in the Consular Service in Latin America before he obtained, thanks to Goldie pleading his case on behalf of Temple's father, one of the coveted Residentships in Northern Nigeria in 1901. His intellectual brilliance ensured him accelerated promotion, so that as early as 1910 he found himself appointed Chief Secretary. From 1914 to 1917 he was Lieutenant-Governor of Northern Nigeria,[38] whence he retired, partly on grounds of ill health (he was only 46) to live in South Africa with his wife, the former Olive Mcleod. Temple was one of that remarkable band of Lugard's aides, many of whom went on to gubernatorial fame (Burdon, Orr, Gowers, Palmer) or wrote important books on the North (Orr, Temple, Palmer) or brought with them the finest of the Royal Niger Company experience (Wallace, Burdon, Hewby, Moloney, Festing).

Temple's clash with Lugard on the latter's return from Hong Kong as Governor-General in 1912 has been well described in a recent revelation of this hitherto unpublicised quarrel.[39] The development—indeed, the initiation—of the Beit-el-Mal system, or Native Treasuries, was a phenomenon that post-dated Lugard's departure from Northern Nigeria in 1906, and it now became the principal bone of contention between Temple and Lugard.[40] Temple, abetted by the no less able Palmer, who had virtually created the first Native Treasury by persuading the Emir of Katsina to pay his emirate revenue into an official treasury and to work according to an elementary form of budgetary procedure with different votes of expenditure, encouraged a certain measure of self-determination in the emirates by allowing them to treat their accounts as separate from the government revenues. Lugard, on the other hand, was rigidly opposed to the idea of the Native Administrations assuming through their financial independence any false notions of political sovereignty, a situation representing to him the very antithesis of his insistence on there being not two sets of rulers but a single government. Thus Temple played a large—and somewhat uneasy—part in Lugard's years as Governor-General, when his opposition was scarcely veiled. Scholar, linguist, and man of affluent circumstances that he was, he also left, in Perham's words, 'his own very individual mark upon Northern Nigeria. He became expert in the Hausa language and regarded the African through the eyes not only of an artist[41] but also of an amateur psychologist, amused, affectionate, but without illusion.'[42]

It is perhaps the rarity of Temple's book that accounts for the fact that his views on indirect rule have not been more closely scrutinized by scholars, especially the modern generation of African researchers. Its sub-title at once defines its locus: 'Sketches and Studies of Official Life and Administrative Problems in Nigeria'. Anticipating the nationalistic effect of World War II,[43] Temple foresaw how

not the least effect of the employment in this 1914–18 war of large numbers of natives, fighting shoulder to shoulder with white men, in the white men's countries, and against other white men, will inevitably be a great stride in the development, or at all events attention, of the conception which the native mind has formed of the white man. If we gain in material prestige we shall certainly not retain the psychical prestige which we formerly enjoyed.[44]

Writing as he did from South Africa, he was at pains to point out that his advocacy of indirect rule for Africans was applicable only 'in the case of those native communities which are living in conditions, climatic or other, which preclude the entry among them of any large proportion of Europeans', a situation quite different from that obtaining in East, Central or South Africa. Temple may today be accused of recommending a form of apartheid, with his undeniable insistence on separate growth, 'the natural development of their race'. But, unlike Lugard, he was at least prescient enough to have given thought to the consideration of the eventual goal of self-governing colonies:

I hold strongly that fusion, extermination, or the reclamation of liberty of action must, sooner or later, be the destiny of the subject race. At the same time, I do not see why in due course, if proper use is made of native institutions, those races which are now subject should not take their places in the ranks of that group of allied nations . . . which forms the British Empire.[45]

Temple's contribution to the principles of native administration is especially important because he epitomizes the rigid school of thought of the 1920s, with its insistence on the rationale of indirect rule as the protection of the native against the disintegration that would, they sincerely believed, result from too rapid a contiguity with western civilization.[46] His book *Native Races and Their Rulers* thus becomes the voice of the ultra-conservative 'indirect rulers', oriented—but always from the very best of motives[47]—toward what Sir Andrew Cohen has recently called the woad policy[48]: sheltering the undeveloped peoples against the outside world and cushioning the impact of western civilization on their psyche.[49] Indirect rule became, we learn from one of Temple's closest colleagues, his religion, 'and at times he verged on the fanatical'.[50] It is because of Temple's central position and dominating influence on the post-Lugardian development of indirect rule that his book could benefit today from a much closer examination than it has hitherto received in critical analyses of the principles of native administration; for if Lugard was the founder of indirect rule in Northern Nigeria, certainly Temple, along with Palmer later, could claim to have been the leading spirit in the second, narrower, and perhaps fossilizing,[51] phase of indirect rule as a policy of imperial administration—a phase that was later to bring upon it vilification and discredit. If one feels called on to defend Lugard when he is attacked for his indirect rule policy on the evidence of the twisted form that his successors made of it, one can but recall the epigram of Leonard Woolf; 'Sometimes the good that men do is not interred with their bones, it lives after them to be turned into evil.'[52]

The extracts in this book are taken from two of the major 'ponderations'[53] and 'pochades', as Temple called his chapters. For all their richness, it is to be regretted that the value cannot be 100 per cent. complete without the utterly delightful vignettes with which Temple illustrated his text.

1918 (1906): LUGARD'S POLITICAL MEMORANDA

For an understanding of the principles of native administration there can be no more valuable documents than Lugard's *Political Memoranda*. It is the supreme source for a study of indirect rule. Together with Cameron's *Memorandum*, these are the core excerpts in this book. Small wonder that the foremost observer of colonial administration has declared that the *Memoranda* 'remain one of the most important and illuminating documents in the history of British Native Administration . . . .[54] There is nothing quite like them in the varied documentation of the empire.'[55]

These instructions were originally issued by Lugard when he was High Commissioner of Northern Nigeria and were, after revision,

published in book form in 1906 for the guidance of officers in the
Political Department—today's Administrative Service. The original
project may have come to Lugard's mind even before he reached
Nigeria; certainly we have an early note in his private correspondence that, 'In the organization I am codifying and memo-writing
and reducing all subjects to a set of general principles and rules of
policy. I will send you [Major E. Lugard, his brother] these—they
are of real interest and well epitomize my work here'. Later, when
the two Protectorates had been amalgamated into one administrative
organization, the instructions were further altered so as to be
applicable to the whole of Nigeria and were published in 1919 as
*Revision of Instructions to Political Officers on Subjects chiefly
Political and Administrative: 1913–1918.*

That Lugard ever found time to formulate and write up his
principles of native administration can be in part ascribed to his
indefatigable energy and in part to his pact with the Colonial Office
that he should, during his leaves, have an office there and so remain
in control of the administration of Nigeria[56] without being burdened
by the routine of daily government in Lagos. Since these *Political
Memoranda* are one of the very few handbooks of guidance ever
issued to administrative officers of the Nigerian Service, it is worth
noting Lugard's own estimation of their *raison d'être*:

Their intention is to promote continuity and uniformity of policy, and to
be a guide in the application of the Ordinances and Regulations. They
do not, of course, affect the legal interpretation of the Ordinances, but
they will serve to explain their intention, and the views of the Governor,
and may be of some use in suggesting the method by which the law can
be judiciously enforced and administrative problems solved. The procedure
which they lay down will be adhered to, and no departure from it will be
made without sanction.[57]

It is because the 1918 version applies to the whole of Nigeria that
I have used it in my extracts in preference to the 1906 edition, which
affected the North only. Though there is little modification in the
way of principle, and extensive extracts from the 1906 edition are
embodied into the later one, a close comparison of the two versions
would be an interesting exercise in tracing the growth of Nigeria's
political progress and of Lugard's administrative concepts.[58] The
reissue after ten years of further trial was, it has been suggested,[59]
'the finest possible confirmation of the validity' of Lugard's indirect
rule system. Such a comparative analysis is outside the scope of this
introduction, but one comment may be made here. The outstanding
item lacking in the 1906 edition and given such prominence in the
1918 one is the institution of the Native Treasury, evolved after
Lugard's departure from the North and destined to become the

sine qua non of the whole Native Administration structure. On the other hand, a prominent omission is the earlier memorandum on 'Fulani Rule'.[60] Another significant addition is the stress on the Political Officer's responsibility for development—an advance from his primarily law-and-order function of 1906 and a move toward his Native Authority training role, demanded by Cameron in 1934 and re-emphasized in the post-1947 administrative policy of social development.

By way of summary, a look at the two tables of contents is instructive:

Despite their unparalleled value, the *Political Memoranda* are obviously too long to quote in full.[61] I have been guided in my selection by what I consider to have been the four pillars of any worthwhile Native Administration: taxation and finance (Native Treasury), justice (Native Courts), the chief and his council (Native Authority), and administrative supervision (the responsibilities of the Resident and the District Officer). Social and economic development have, regrettable as it may seem, been later considerations, but because of its wide interest I have included extracts from a fifth Memorandum, that on Education. Though all are worthy of study, it is perhaps Memoranda nos. IX and I, on 'Native Administration' and the 'Duties of Political Officers', that are the most important in our context.

Lugard's instructions to his staff on indirect rule as set out in his *Political Memoranda* may—and they make an interesting comparison with Cameron's subsequent credo[62]—be summarized thus:[63]

1. *De facto* rulers were to be recognized and upheld as a reality.[64]
2. Residents were to rule through chiefs and to educate them in their duties as rulers.
3. Chiefs thus recognized were the delegates of the Governor, who reserved to himself the rights of taxation, laws, armed forces, and some land processes.[65]
4. Independent pagan tribes were not to be included under Moslem rulers unless they agreed to this and the Governor gave his personal sanction.[66]
5. Residents should 'maintain and develop all that is best in the indigenous methods and institutions. . . . We must utilize the existing machinery and endeavour only to improve it', but always 'ruling' through the chiefs and not simply 'governing' by advice and consent.[67]
6. Native authorities should collect and disburse their own revenues.[68]

At every turn in these *Political Memoranda* the reader is conscious of Lugard's prodigious and comprehensive concern with detail. It is not hard to guess at the truth: here was a perfectionist incapable of easy delegation. For instance, half of the memorandum dealing with the duties of the political staff is devoted to minute instructions about the preparation of the annual report from Residents: its format ('the report will be written on foolscap paper, on one side of the page only, and a third margin will be left. . . . The pages will be numbered, and fastened together at the extreme left-hand corner only. . . . It will be on fairly strong paper and sent unfolded'), its maps, the spelling of the place names, its contents (seven pages are devoted to listing the required headings), and its reception ('the Governor's notes on these reports must necessarily be so terse that they may sometimes possibly read as though they conveyed dispraise [sic] when no such intention existed. . . . Residents will bear in mind that the pressure of work necessitates brevity in these replies and that the report is only one of many with which the Governor has to deal'). Another forty-page memorandum, including specimen forms, deals solely with the books, returns and office records to be maintained by the Political Department.

The memorandum on education would excite admiration from any of the expert commissions that are today such a common feature of developing nations, with its introductory historical survey, wealth of statistics, educational philosophy and curricular details. Nor was this the incarnation of a dreaming amateur. Miss Perham has shown how seriously Lugard took his plan to establish a university in Hong Kong, while in her chapter on his enlightened opposition to Sir Hanns Vischer's educationist policies—policies so attractively in keeping with the 'preservation' rationale of indirect rule and the desire to safeguard native institutions rather than risking their demise by attempting to revitalize them—Lugard's careful thinking is well revealed.[69] It is perhaps ironical that Lugard should sometimes be blamed for the North's educational handicaps, whereas in reality it was he who was the liberal—though cautious over the missionary role—opposed by indirect rule's right wing team of Temple and Vischer.

In what light did Lugard consider his own child, the *Political Memoranda?* He has this to say, and as it is virtually his only comment, I have quoted it *in extenso*:

It is especially important that the decisions of the Governor should be fully recorded in writing, and not merely by an initial of acquiescence or a verbal order. This involves heavy office work, but it is work which cannot be neglected if misunderstandings are to be avoided and continuity preserved. The very detailed instructions regarding the duties of each newly-created department which were issued when the administration of Northern Nigeria was first inaugurated, served a very useful purpose in maintaining continuity of policy, till superseded on amalgamation by briefer general orders.

In the sphere of administration there are obviously many subjects— education, taxation, slavery and labour, native courts, land tenure, etc.— in which uniformity and continuity of policy is impossible in so large a country, unless explicit instructions are issued for guidance. By a perusal of the periodical reports of Residents, the Governor could inform himself of the difficulties which presented themselves in the varying circumstances of each province, and think out the best way in which they could be met, and could note where misunderstandings or mistakes had been made. By these means a series of Memoranda were compiled, and constantly revised as new problems came to light, and as progress rendered the earlier instructions obsolete. They formed the reference book and authority of the Resident and his staff.

In a country so vast, which included communities in all stages of development, and differing from each other profoundly in their customs and
traditions, it was the aim of these Memoranda to preserve this continuity
and uniformity of principle and policy. Newcomers, by studying them,
could make themselves fully acquainted with the nature of the task before
them, the problems to be dealt with, and the attitude of Government
towards each of those problems. Senior officers were spared the labour
and loss of time involved in frequent iteration, when noting any mis-
understanding or ignorance in the reports of their subordinates, by simply
inviting attention to the pertinent paragraph of the Memorandum.
Subversive policies cannot gradually creep in, and any change must be
deliberately inaugurated by the formal cancellation of the particular
instructions in the Memorandum. Though the preparation of the Memoranda involves considerable labour, they result in an eventual saving in
the time both of the Governor and of the senior officers. They are the
embodiment of the experience of the most capable officers co-ordinated
by the head of the Government, who has access to the reports and is
familiar with circumstances of all. When any point of particular difficulty
presents itself where opinions are in conflict, and the information insufficient to form a clear judgement on the principles involved, the
Governor may perhaps cause a precis to be circulated before a final
decision is reached. The little volume of *Political Memoranda* has been of
much use in Nigeria. It deals solely with the actual problems of practical
administration.

The Statute Book, the Regulations and Orders made under the laws,
the General Orders, and the Governor's Memoranda on administrative
subjects, contain between them in a readily accessible and compact form
the whole structural policy of the Administration, and constitute the
'Laws and Usages' of the country. Had such a quartette existed, revised
decennially since the earliest origin of our Indian Empire and of our
Crown colonies, they would have formed valuable material for the history
of the Empire. In Africa we are laying foundations. The superstructure
may vary in its details, some of which may perhaps be ill-designed, but
the stability of the edifice is unaffected. You may pull down and re-erect
cupolas, but you cannot alter the design of the foundations without first
destroying all that has been erected upon them.[70]

One of Lugard's ablest lieutenants, Sir Charles Orr, has emphasized the part played by these memoranda, in which the High
Commissioner was able to place on record and communicate his
views on the countless administrative problems revealed as
the country was opened up, in ensuring a continuity of governmental policy—and on Lugard's departure in 1906 there were no
less than four officers administering the Government of Northern
Nigeria within the space of just over three years.[71] One officer
confided in his Resident, 'Reading *Political Memoranda* is like
reading the Bible, the more you read it the more you find there is
in it', while another referred to them as 'the well-tempered base of

his *Dual Mandate*'.[72] In the history of local administration in Northern Nigeria, it is surely not without significance that Malam Abubakar Tafawa Balewa—as the Prime Minister then was—should have based his watershed speech of 1950, which opened up a new era of native administration in the North at a time when even to question indirect rule was a bold act,[73] upon Lugard's *Political Memoranda* and called for a return to their original spirit: 'Lord Lugard, whom we shall always respect, . . . surely never intended that the expedient of the hour should remain the unchanging authority of all time'.[74]

1922: LUGARD'S POLITICAL TESTIMONY

His great work done in Nigeria—with whose creation as a geographical and political entity he had been associated[75] in a leadership role for nearly a quarter of a century—Lugard retired in 1919. Two years later he finished *The Dual Mandate in British Tropical Africa*, following hard on the heels of the publication of his two other monumental contributions to administrative theory, the revised *Political Memoranda* and the *Amalgamation Report*.[76] The timing was perfect. On to his enormous reputation for his work in Nigeria was now built the current talk of League of Nations mandates, whose principal of trusteeship of the native races dovetailed so neatly with the elements of preservation and protection inherent in the philosophy of indirect rule. It was, indeed, in the very year of its publication (1922) that Lugard accepted an invitation to become the British member on the Permanent Mandates Commission of the League of Nations.

The title Lugard chose for his book emphasizes the mutual responsibility and advantage to be gained from what he envisaged as the ideal colonial partnership, economic development and protective tutelage—perhaps a refinement, purged of its cynicism, of the motto of 'philanthropy and 5 per cent' borne by an earlier trading generation on the Coast. Lugard's Foreword is characteristic of his modesty and certainty: no fanfare or apologia, simply half a page of acknowledgements and a one paragraph definition of his objective in setting down his 'notes on administration in British Tropical Africa':

In the first place I have hoped to put before those who are interested in the development of that part of the British beyond the seas . . . an outline of the system under which those responsibilities have originated and are being discharged, and some idea of the nature of problems confronting the administrator. In the second place, in discussing these problems I have ventured to make some few suggestions, as the result of experience,

in the hope that they may be found worthy of consideration by the men
'on the spot' . . .[77]

Even the bitterest of critics of indirect rule, himself a District Officer
in Nigeria, had no hesitation in describing *The Dual Mandate* as
'a book that for its effect on the minds of those interested in colonial
policy can be compared only with such a work as Durham's Report
on Canada a century earlier or Burke's speeches on the Warren
Hastings trial. . . . There is nothing else quite like it in all the literature of British imperialism'.[78]

The reviews of 1922 were uniformly laudatory and are informative
in many ways. So, too, is the perceptive comment of Lugard's
definitive biographer:

Into this book Lugard, quite unconsciously, put the whole man, character,
experience and ideas. From the mass of material in the book two main
ideas seem to stand out. Firstly—and this was not then so obvious to the
public, that empire was no monolithic layer of mastery, whether beneficent
or oppressive, but had to be broken down into a dozen or so branches
of administration. These, the products of European experience and
concepts, had to be intricately adjusted to their points of contact with the
hundreds of the separate tribes of Africa. Lugard explained, of course,
the part which he believed his indirect principle could play in at once
softening and activating the contact. The second main theme, which gave
its title to the book, was the mutuality of the colonial relationship, expressed
in an unemotional calculation of the economic advantages for both sides
and in the apprenticeship to civilization given to Africans.[79]

The main criticism voiced today in discussions on native administration is that in neither his *Political Memoranda* nor his *Dual
Mandate* did Lugard ever follow through the theory of indirect rule
to its logical end. Though this is not the place to develop the arguments, it is appropriate to ask, as students of imperial administration
have done since the ethics of indirect rule first came under open fire
in the '30s, whether in fact it ever had any goal, clear-cut and
acceptable, or whether the vagueness of its conclusion was not
conveniently left shrouded in the mists of 'indefinite time ahead'.[80]
Inevitably, the result was that the means threatened to become the
end—a danger that was averted by Cameron in the very nick of
time.

The fact that the excerpts made here have been reduced in no way
suggests any diminished importance of this fundamental source for
an understanding of the philosophy of indirect rule. My original
intention was to reproduce the key chapters on 'Methods of Ruling
Native Races', 'Some General Principles of Administration', 'The
Machinery of Administration', and 'Taxation'. This was in keeping
with my purpose set out above, for *The Dual Mandate* is no exception

to the scarcity of these prime sources, even in the university libraries of Africa. However, it has been announced that a fifth edition of the *Dual Mandate* is to appear soon, and this welcome news has led me to abbreviate the passages selected for this book.[81]

The concept of a 'dual mandate', now a political byword, was Lugard's own. As he saw it:

Let it be admitted at the outset that European brains, capital and energy have not been, and never will be, expended in developing the resources of Africa, from motives of pure philanthropy; that Europe is in Africa for the mutual benefit of her own industrial classes, and the native races in their progress to a higher plane; that the benefit can be made reciprocal, and that it is the aim and desire of civilised administration to fulfil this dual mandate.[82]

One of the finest tributes to Lugard's classic political testimony of empire is to be found in a notice of its publication appearing in *The National Review*, where the reviewer claimed that its unique merit was 'that it had not been written; it has been lived'.[83]

1922: THE CLIFFORD MINUTE

There are two important statements of Nigerian policy that are referred to as the Clifford Minute. One is concerned with the principles on which the system of provincial administration was based, with particular reference to the relationship between administrative and departmental officers. This directive was published by the Governor, Sir Hugh Clifford, in the *Nigerian Gazette*,[84] and was the subject of a further statement by one of his successors, Sir Donald Cameron, when he disagreed with the principle laid down by Clifford that 'a District Officer in charge of a Division occupies within the area under his administrative charge a position as nearly analagous to that of a Resident in his province as the relative dignity and importance of the two offices render possible'.[85] In view of the frictional misunderstandings that had arisen between administrative and departmental officers, Cameron had this explanatory note expunged from the original directive. This Clifford Minute is thus of greater relevance to an examination of the position of the District Officer than of the principles of native administration.[86]

The second Clifford Minute, however, is germane to our study. Sir Hugh Clifford assumed office from Lugard in 1919, though without his predecessor's personal title of Governor-General. Early in 1922 he undertook a long and close tour of the Northern Provinces, visiting every Native Administration in Kontagora, Sokoto, Katsina, Kano and Zaria provinces—in short, the classical emirates, the birthplace of indirect rule and the cradle of native administration.

He was far from pleased with what he saw. From the memorandum he composed and signed before leaving Kaduna, it is evident to even the least sensitive reader that Clifford had been disappointed in much of the tenor of the native administration and in the attitude of some of its senior as well as junior administrative officers. He requested that a copy of his Minute, in which he recorded some of his shock along with his wishes for an overhaul of those aspects of native administration that were out of tune with the times, should be issued to every officer in the Political and Education Departments on the strength of the Northern Provinces.

This was an exceptional, and unmistakably firm, directive from His Excellency; the tone and contents of the Minute are no less so.

After warning the administration against resting on its laurels, however deservedly won—'there must be no yielding to the temptation to judge that the success so far achieved calls for no betterment' —he called upon them to steer a middle course between Scylla and Charybdis:

. . . too frequent and too personal or direct interference with native administrative methods being, in its own way, scarcely less mischievous in the results it is apt to produce than is the converse policy of blind confidence in the integrity and trustworthiness of officials, and the reluctance to intervene, the slackness of supervision, and the consequent toleration of, or failure to detect, abuses that commonly result therefrom.[87]

Clifford found, within the practice of indirect rule as it had by then developed, a lack of what he called chivalry—'treating them [the Native Administration officials] with a measure of dignity and courtesy which usually inspires their own behaviour, and scrupulously avoiding violent gestures, loudness of speech, or even the unnecessary raising of speaking voice'.[88] He was also strongly critical of the lack of manners and good breeding displayed by some Political Officers in their dealings with a Moslem population. Finally, His Excellency felt constrained to record that during his several visits to the North he had not found himself 'particularly impressed by the knowledge of the vernacular possessed by the generality of the officers belonging to the Political Service', and called for a greater effort by Administrative Officers in learning local languages, on pain of withheld promotion.[89]

What, in summary, Clifford was calling for was the need for those intimately involved in the day to day exercises of native administration to learn

two elementary but essential facts—*viz.*, the great importance of cultivating good manners in their dealings with Muhammadans of all classes; and the impossibility of achieving this without first undertaking a careful and sympathetic study of native ideas, standards of courtesy, prejudices and predilections.[90]

This was a severe condemnation of those responsible for the execution of native administration, the more so as it was the Northern administration that had exported its principles of indirect rule to the South and had established for itself an enviable reputation as the exponent of a successful system of local administration. Skilfully, His Excellency turned away the possible protests from these senior officials:

I would repeat that this minute, though addressed to Your Honour, is primarily intended for the guidance and instruction of the junior members of the Political Service of the Northern Provinces; and I should like to add that, before it assumed its final form, it had the incalculable advantage of being subjected to your expert comments, advice and criticism, and may now be taken as embodying views and opinions that are held no less strongly by Your Honour than they are by me.[91]

The whole Minute is valuable for its insight into the working of indirect rule—as opposed to the policies behind the system of native administration—and, together with the Secretariat directives that follow, fills in some of the background to the attacks subsequently launched first by some officers of the Nigerian Service,[92] next by academics and politicians in Britain, then by the Nigerian nationalists from Lagos and the South, and finally by the educated members of the Northern Native Authorities themselves.

1928: TWO SECRETARIAT DIRECTIVES

The Lieutenant-Governor of the Northern Provinces from 1925–30 was H. R. (later Sir Richmond) Palmer. Appointed as Assistant Resident in 1904, he was instrumental in devising the Beit-el-Mal—based, as we have seen, on his own private experiment with the Emir of Katsina[93]—and even, with strong support from Temple in Zungeru, in developing this Native Treasury system against the inclination of Lugard himself. For eight years, from 1917 until his translation to Kaduna, Palmer ruled—and the word is advisedly chosen—the remote and unique province of Bornu,[94] the highly able scholar-administrator invested with all the unquestioning respect that in those days attached to the incumbent of the Residency. Palmer was both an architect and an archdeacon of indirect rule.

During Palmer's tenure of office in Kaduna he issued a circular to all Residents headed 'The Training of Junior Officers in the Methods of "Indirect" Administration'. In this he expressed his gubernatorial displeasure at the lack of understanding shown by

C

junior administrative officers, especially in the smaller emirates, of the 'correct procedure to be followed in dealing with Native Authority officials, and indeed an inadequate knowledge of the working of the Native Authority machinery in the chain of administration from the peasant through the Village and District Head to the Emir'. In particular, he frowned upon 'the amateur or experimenting Administrative Officers content to work by the light of nature and to deal with each problem as it arises without taking advantage of the accumulated body of precedents and experience' acquired by their seniors. The notes now issued by Palmer were held to be weighty enough to be read as a supplement to Lugard's *Political Memoranda*, and it was His Honour's intention—though the project was never put into practice—that they would be incorporated into any future revision of *Political Memoranda*.

Among the Residents who reacted promptly to this *ex cathedra* pronouncement on how to improve the understanding and practice of the tenets of indirect rule among their District Officers was the Resident of the new province of Adamawa.[95] Palmer was so impressed by the memorandum this Resident had been prompted to issue to his staff that he ordered it to be circulated to all the Northern Residents. To it Palmer added a minute of his own, with the request that both documents should be handed to every Administrative Officer in the North—not forgetting those on leave.

Both these directives are important for an understanding of several features of the make-up of the school of indirect rule.[96] They throw light on the basic principles of native administration, both in its original flexible form and in its subsequent hard-setting of spirit; they illustrate what Cohen, from the outside, has called the 'fossilization' of indirect rule, and what Crocker, from the inside, called 'an elaborate facade . . . much ado about nothing—cardboard and plaster patched up by the careerists'.[97] They reveal something of the conflict of conscience between the old guard of the Administration and the post-war officers, some of whom were the first products of the new post-graduate Tropical African Service training courses at Oxford and Cambridge; and they must, unhappily, raise a doubt about the calibre of some of those at the top of, and the consequent morale of the rest of, an administrative service in which a Resident could declare as his policy towards his staff—and, what is more, receive the public endorsement of his Lieutenant-Governor —that, 'as regards qualifications for promotion and passing efficiency bars I put first the question whether an officer is imbued with the true spirit of indirect rule'.[98]

Finally, these two Secretariat circulars are among the very few policy-directives ever issued to the District Officer to explain the philosophy and outline the details of his job. The absence of any codified manual of administrative practice was much criticized in the 1950s by the first intake of Nigerian cadres into the Administrative Service, and its replacement by loyalty, tradition and experience[99] is such a feature of the British attitude towards public service that the issue of a document of actual guidance deserves comment. Ephemeral circulars apart, the handbooks on administrative policy given to British District Officers can, unlike those of their counterparts in similar situations, be counted on two hands over the span of sixty years of native administration. *Political Memoranda* were deliberately written for the edification of Administrative Officers; copies of Clifford's *Minute* and Cameron's *Memorandum*, originating from their inspectorial tour of the provinces, were printed and issued to every Political Officer; then, apart from the two Secretariat directives discussed here, no major guidance on policy was given to any District Officer until the Northern Government issued its *Duties of an Administrative Officer* (1952) and the Western Government its *Handbook for Officers Joining the Western Region Public Service* (1959). True, a large and useful corpus of procedural and legislative guidance accumulated through the years. These include such documents as the periodical issues of *Financial Instructions, Financial Directions, General Orders* or *Government Standing Orders of Northern Nigeria* (1910), *The Criminal Law Manual* (1924), *The Northern Provinces Office Guide* (1932), *Outlines of General Office Routine and Correspondence* (1952), *A Guide to the Penal Code* (1959), *Guide to Procedure* (1957), *Administrative Directions to Provincial Commissioners and Provincial Secretaries* (1962), and *Administrative Service: Checklist for Visits* (1962). In some instances these were locally supplemented by *Provincial Guides to Procedure;* and, later, by an excellent series of Native Administration guides like *Financial Memoranda, The N.A. Office Guide* (1959), and *Records in Native Courts* (1963); but chapters that might make up the District Officer's Bible, if I may use the analogy, were remarkably few over the half century of native administration in Nigeria.[100]

1934: CAMERON'S POLICY OF INDIRECT ADMINISTRATION

Sir Donald Cameron's *Principles of Native Administration and Their Application* provides, along with Lord Lugard's *Political Memoranda* and the Secretary of State's *Despatch on Local Government* (1947), a watershed in the history of the development of native administration principles.[101] The three documents may be said to embody the respective schools of indirect rule, indirect administration, and local government. From each derived effective and significant legislation touching the whole of Nigeria: the 1916 Native Authority Ordinance, supported by the Native Revenue and Native Courts Ordinances of 1914; the 1933 Native Authority Ordinance; and the Local Government Laws of 1950 (Eastern), 1953 (Western) and 1954 (Northern).

Cameron's *Memorandum* superseded all previous directions on native administration in Nigeria, with, however, the caveat that 'any approved practice founded on previous Memoranda (or otherwise) concerning the details of administration and not opposed to the spirit of this Memorandum may be preserved'.[102]

Cameron was appointed Governor of Nigeria in 1931. But he was no stranger to the country, for he had worked under Lugard as his Chief Secretary in Lagos[103]. Nor was he any stranger to native administration, despite his lack of provincial experience in Nigeria,[104] for the whole framework of native administration in Tanganyika was his handiwork during his governorship there in the formative years immediately after Great Britain had been awarded the League of Nations mandate over German East Africa. Under Cameron's predecessor, Sir Graeme Thomson (1925-31), the political staff—and in particular the senior Residents of the Northern emirates—had tended to set both their chiefs and themselves up into something approaching sovereign states, independent of Kaduna and unmindful of Lagos. This challenge to authority met quite the wrong person in the new Governor.[105]

While in Tanganyika, Cameron had in 1930 issued a directive *The Principles of Native Administration and their Application*, being the first of a series of N.A. Memoranda for Tanganyika Territory.[106] On his arrival in Nigeria a year later, the Lieutenant-Governor of the Northern Provinces had suggested to Cameron that he should reissue it, pending the preparation of a revised version more strictly applicable to Nigeria. It was this edition that Cameron published in 1934, under the same title, as a statement of policy formally endorsed by the Secretary of State for the Colonies. Though in this work we are concerned only with Nigerian materials, political scientists will wish to note the fruitful field for a close comparative study of the two documents and of the reflexion of their philosophy found in Cameron's autobiography.[107] Throughout, Cameron's dominant theme is that of the mandated powers' tutelary duties of guardianship—'the primary factor on which everything else should be based in Tanganyika in considering the political life of the country'—and their 'sacred trust' towards 'peoples not yet able to stand by themselves under the strenuous conditions of the modern world'.[108]

Here is a continuation of Temple's fear of the disintegration of native society under the impact of the modern world; here is the extension of Lugard's ethic of mutual benefit, trusted and trusting; here is the successor to the foundation principle of indirect rule, that the objective of native administration should be not only to utilize the existing machinery but also to improve its performance standards; here is a more reasonable follow-up to the threat by the Resident Adamawa to his District Officers that there would be no promotion for non-indirect rulers—'I desire it to be understood that so long as an officer is loyally doing his best to interpret the Memorandum in the spirit in which it has been written, he may count on support from headquarters . . . no officer should have any hesitation in asking for the further elucidation of any matters contained herein of which he is not satisfied that he has acquired perfect comprehension'[109]; and here, too, is a parallel to the 1922 Minute, for both directives were issued after a thorough tour of the homeland of indirect rule[110] and both condemned the dangers of what Cameron chose to call 'drifting into the habit of mind that a feudal monarchy . . . is the be-all and end-all of indirect administration'.[111]

This is perhaps the right place to comment on the development of indirect rule since its inception by Lugard, for it was Cameron who, to put it bluntly, shook the indirect rulers out of their dangerous state of self-satisfaction 'sanctified by its own success'. If, as we have seen, Lugard was disturbed by the way the senior officials had misinterpreted indirect rule on his return to Nigeria in 1912, few students doubt that he would have been dismayed by the solidification of his philosophy had he revisited Nigeria in the 1930s, to find his administrative staff more royal than the king. This was no less true of Tanganyika[112] than of Nigeria[113]. Cameron, who is highly critical of the Nigerian Administration in his *My Tanganyikan Service and Some Nigeria*,[114] earns the credit of having sought to exterminate the worst of these excesses and to bring indirect rule back into its proper perspective. This he achieved by, *inter alia*, his professionalization of services like audit and judiciary,[115] which had hitherto been the closed shop of the Political Department; by reducing the over-independent Lieutenant-Governors to Chief Commissioners; and by his forthright *Memorandum* in which he restated the principles of native administration.

And yet, if Cameron's memorandum is not a departure from Lugard's views, it was anything but a mere reaffirmation of Lugard's indirect rule. It advocated indirect rule with a difference, a new look, modified and revivified;[116] and this difference was at once marked by a subtle yet significant change in nomenclature. Henceforth the philosophy of native administration was to be known not as 'indirect rule' but 'indirect administration'. These terms were at once a continuation of and a break with the past.

What were the differences? In Cameron's mind, the cardinal principle of his policy was that 'the allegiance of a people to a tribal head, freely given and without external cause, is the essence of true indirect rule'.[117] In this process he distinguished three stages: the investigation, of an intense anthropological nature,[118] to discover who held authority; the voluntary and contemporary acceptance by the people of that authority; and finally Government's legal recognition of the authority. Its fundamental objective he saw as the need 'to adapt for the purposes of local government the tribal institutions[119] which the native peoples have evolved for themselves, so that the latter may develop in a constitutional manner from their own past, guided and restrained by the tradition and sanctions which they have inherited, moulded and modified . . . on the advice of British Officers'.[120] The major points in Cameron's re-interpretation of Lugard's indirect rule[121] may be summarized thus:

1. He altered the emphasis from 'support' to 'improvement' of Native Administrations.

2. He refused to countenance the growth of Native Administration into *soi-disant* states, insisting on the sovereignty of Government and on the Native Administrations' status as no more than an integral part of the total local administrative machinery: 'The Native Administrations are not independent rulers; they are merely the delegates of the Governor, whose representative is the Resident'.[122]

3. He underlined the importance of 'pagan' areas, hitherto regarded by senior officials as 'second-class' provinces.[123]

4. He urged that educated elements should be represented on Native Administration councils.[124]

5. He advocated a formalized conciliar rather than an apparent one-man rule.[125]

6. He required Administrative Officers to think less of their own competence in running a Division and to take a more active part in the deliberate administrative education of the chiefs: 'The ideal of highest efficiency . . . must be subordinate to the main policy of encouraging and training the Native Administrations to undertake the functions of administration'.

1939: THE BOURDILLON MINUTE

We have already seen how, although Lugard made no reference to any system of Native Treasuries in his original *Memoranda*, their development and institutionalization became the foundation-stone of indirect rule and native administration. The existence of a recognized system of taxation, from which can grow a viable budgetary procedure, has been the blessing of the Northern emirates, while its absence has been the curse of the Native Administrations of the South-Eastern provinces and the cause of the early riotous troubles of Egbaland and the Yoruba provinces. The Native Treasury system, whereby a Hausa emirate like Kano collects over £1m. tax in a matter of weeks, till this day arouses the admiring envy of the financially perplexed councils of Iboland.

Right from the acceptance of the Native Treasury principle, largely at the behest of such senior Northern administrators as Temple and Palmer, the corollary question has inevitably been the division of revenue and responsibilities between the Native Administrations and Government. Lugard treated of this in his long memorandum on taxation[126] and in his revised version of *Political Memoranda*; Cameron, too, discussed the formation of the Native Treasury; but not until the governorship of Sir Bernard Bourdillon, by which time (1935) Nigeria was just about pulling itself out of the economic doldrums of the 1930s and was preparing to implement some of the fine policies enunciated by Cameron but postponed because of the slump, was a serious appraisal undertaken of the principles of a just appointment of revenue and responsibilities between the Native Administrations and the central government.

Bourdillon's memorandum on this subject is therefore a direct contribution to an appreciation of one of the pillars of sound native administration, namely a healthy and effective local government financial system: a local authority that is merely consultative, deliberative or bankrupt can rarely command any respect and seldom be worth the trouble taken to sustain it. It is, in the words of one of Nigeria's greatest financial experts, ' a document of great importance, as it represents the first authoritative attempt to relate the division of financial resources to the division of executive responsibilities'.[127] But the memorandum means more than this. With the expansion of Native Administration developmental responsibilities as agents of the central government in keeping with Cameron's insistence that Government had a duty not only to support but to catalyse Native Administrations, the time had come to review the extent to which these Native Administrations could properly be expected to perform those services on an agency basis. Hence Bourdillon's classic criteria of 'competence', 'consent' and 'cash'.

Finally, this memorandum provides a notable starting point to a number of important documents on Native Treasury work in Nigeria, prominent among them being Sir Sidney Phillipson's report on the *Administrative and Financial Procedure under the New Constitution: Financial Relations between the Government of Nigeria and the Native Administrations* (1946) along with its Nigeria White Paper, *Apportionment of Duties between the Government of Nigeria*

*and the Native Administrations: Statement of Policy (1947); Grants
to Native Authorities and Townships in the Northern Region* (1953);
the forthcoming Sowerby report on local government (1965); and
the various directives on grants-in-aid and local education finance,
leading in some areas to a review of the whole concept of local
council relationships with the Regional government.[128]

1947: THE LOCAL GOVERNMENT DESPATCH

The year 1947 not only ushered in the post-war period of colonial
policy, with all its then unforeseen developments of rapid independence; it also wrote the official *finis* to both Lugard's indirect rule
and its restatement in Cameron's indirect administration by introducing the British concept of local government.[129] At last it was
admitted by the outside what had been recognized by the inside
for a decade or more, namely that indirect rule and democratic
self-government were mutually exclusive.[130] The instrument for this
conversion—and if the word suggests a certain amount of force,
it is apt—was nothing less than an official despatch from the
Secretary of State addressed to all Governors; and in the Government Houses of the day such counsel was tantamount to a mandate.

Though not quite within our terms of reference here, it is important to view this directive from Whitehall against the sentiments,
both academic and political, of contemporary England towards its
imperial charge. The late 'thirties had seen a serious intellectual
searching of the soul about the validity of the much-vaunted policy
of indirect rule, culminating in Lord Hailey's unarguable rejection
of its principles because of its vagueness of ultimate objective and
its unacceptability by local educated men and women. The year
1946 saw a Labour Government returned to power in Britain, and
under the vigorous leadership of Arthur Creech Jones as Secretary
of State it was to be expected that his sincere Fabianism should
be reflected in his colonial policy.[131]

In brief, his despatch called on colonial governments to introduce
without delay a system of grass-roots government at the local level,
not only as an instrument in maximizing the efficiency of the substantial grants that the United Kingdom was pouring into those
territories under its Colonial Development and Welfare funds to
underpin the various Ten Years Development Plans, but also as a
positive step in potential advance towards the preparation of a
colony for national self-government. 'I believe', the Secretary of
State declared, 'that the key to success lies in the development of an
efficient, democratic system of government'.[132]

He went on to emphasize these key words, not because they

introduced any new conception into the British policies of African administration, but because they formed the heart of the matter:

Local because the system of government must be close to the common people and their problems; efficient because it must be capable of managing the local services in a way which will help to raise the standard of living; and democratic because it must not only find a place for the growing class of educated men but at the same time command the respect and support of the mass of the people.[133]

So great was the importance which the Secretary of State attached to the contents of his despatch that the Colonial Office went to the unusual length of having copies printed, despite its restricted classification, for confidential distribution to every Administrative Officer.

This despatch set the ball rolling in a number of directions important to our study of the principles of native administration. Once local government was safely launched into the colonial orbit, its impetus had to be sustained from the firing site. The first step was to call a conference of all African Governors. This was followed by a Conference of unofficial Legislative Council members. Next came the establishment of a clearing house on African problems, in the shape of the African Studies Branch of the Colonial Office. Fourthly came the inauguration of a top-calibre forum dedicated to problems of African government, the *Journal of African Administration*[134] (1949). Fifthly came the first of a continuing series of high-level conferences held at the University of Cambridge, where for the past sixteen years senior government officials, academics and Ministers from Africa, the United Kingdom, the United States of America, and Europe have been able to discuss common problems of African local administration.[135] Finally came an overhaul of the curricula of the Devonshire courses for Colonial Service probationers at the universities and the incorporation of local government, including a practical council or borough attachment, into the syllabus.[136]

As a supplement to this despatch, we have in our text quoted passages from a complementary speech by Mr. Creech Jones. Attention is particularly invited to his assessment of the contribution of the past policies of indirect rule and indirect administration to the new policy: 'It is the result of a natural organic growth which has quickened its pace as it developed and which owes much to the many far-sighted administrators who guided it through the various stages of native administration to present conceptions'.

Together these two extracts form the third milestone in our historical documents illustrating the principles of native administration in Nigeria: its definition as indirect rule, its revision as indirect administration, and its reorientation as local government.[137] A fourth variant, that of the politicization of the provincial administration superstructure, is already in operation.[138] Whether we are now on the threshold of a fifth dimension, that of the political party assuming the control and drive of local administration as a direct executive arm of the centre, remains to be seen.[139]

Ahmadu Bello University,   A. H. M. KIRK-GREENE
Northern Nigeria.

NOTES

1. Because of the confusion that sometimes exists between 'Native Administration' and 'Native Authority'—a confusion exacerbated by the fact that the abbreviation so commonly used, N.A., is applicable to either—it is necessary to explain the definitions adopted in this book. I have, following Sir Sidney Phillipson (*Administrative and Financial Procedure under the New Constitution: Financial Relations . . .*, 1946, para. 48), confined my use of 'Native Authority' to the offices of native authority constituted under the Native Authority Law, 1954, and accepted 'Native Administration' as referring to those 'administrative and/or financial units with a definite identity and with functions essential to the working of the whole system' (Phillipson). Without upper case letters, 'native administration' refers simply to the general process of administering all areas in Africa outside those administered directly by the Townships Ordinance. Lord Hailey sets up a similar criterion when he talks of 'the Native Treasury becoming a recognized and indeed fundamental feature in native administration. . . . The existence of a Native Treasury became the proof that a "native authority" had been recognized as a "native administration" ' (*An African Survey*, 1938, pp. 421–2). Cf. D. A. Low and R. C. Pratt, *Buganda and British Overrule*, 1960: 'The tendency for the term "native administration" to replace "native authority" marks the transition from a local authority preoccupied with law and order and tax collection to one striving to perform a whole range of modern local services' (p. 203). By extension, I come to agree with L. Gray Cowan, who equates the Native Administration system with the general structure of indirect rule in West Africa, and who defines it as 'the practical application of indirect rule' (*Local Government in West Africa*, 1958, pp. 14–23).

2. For a stimulating analysis of the difference in approach to 'native administration' and 'indirect rule', see Michael Crowder, "Indirect Rule—French and British Style", *Africa*, vol. XXXIV, July 1964, pp. 195–205. This is a reply to Gouverneur Deschamps' Lugard Memorial Lecture, "Et maintenant, Lord Lugard?", published in *Africa*, XXXIII, December, 1963, in which he sought to equate French native administrative policy with Lugard's indirect rule: "*la seule différence est que nous n'avons pas tenté, comme vous, Lord Lugard, de moderniser ces états anciens, ni de créer des embryons d'états là où il n'en existait point*". Mr Crowder's riposte reinforces the traditional view that the two policies were very different, especially as regards their respective attitudes to chiefs. Also relevant is the on-the-spot report made on the two metropolitan powers' educational policies in Africa, carried out by W. B. Mumford and published under the title of *Africans Learn to be French*, 1935.

3. The term is borrowed from the excellent study of the Colonial Service by

Robert Heussler, *Yesterday's Rulers*, 1963. The idea is echoed by T. Russell Pasha: 'Time passes, memories are short, records are destroyed, and many of the present generation are unaware of the constructive work done in those days' (*Egyptian Service*, 1949, p. ix).

4. M. M. Mahood, in her *Joyce Cary's Africa*, 1964, questions the value of an administrative system which assumed that the whites would always be on top, and shows (pp. 65 ff.) that even some of the pre-Tropical African Service officers, including Joyce Cary, had their doubts whether indirect rule in the long run could enable colonial peoples to develop along their own lines.

5. Nobody has yet done for the Colonial Service what Philip Woodruff has done so superbly in his two volumes of *The Men Who Ruled India*, but a recent issue of *Commonwealth Challenge*, 'Legacy of Imperialism' (April 1964), provides an attractive anthology and updates H. Evans, *Men in the Tropics*, 1949.

6. Cf. Lucy P. Mair, *Native Policies in Africa*, 1936: 'For an understanding of the Indirect Rule policy in all its implications no area is more instructive than Nigeria, its original home.' (p. 118.)

7. Tanganyika remodelled its local administration on indirect rule in the 1920s; Northern Rhodesia 1927; and the High Commission Territories in the 1930s and 1940s. In East and Central Africa indirect rule carried the undertone of being held as a protective instrument for the African against settler's 'exploitation' and as the best alternative to white settler rule. Such an element was absent in the West African experience of native administration policies.

8. See Percival Spear, *The Nabobs*, 1963, p. xiii.

9. In his advocacy of indirect rule, Lyautey cited Montesquieu: 'Alexander resisted those who wished him to treat the Greeks as masters and the Persians as slaves. He left the vanquished races not only their manners, but also their civil law, and often even the kings and governors whom he had found'—André Gide, *Lyautey*, 1936, p. 90. It was Sir Donald Cameron who suggested that Exodus xviii, 17–21, contains the elements of indirect rule: *My Tanganyikan Service and Some Nigeria*, 1939, p. 80.

10. Royal Niger Company Regulation No. IX, July 1886, 'Warrants for District Agents'. For a summary of the Regulations, see A. H. M. Kirk-Greene, 'Expansion on the Benue 1830–1900', *Journal of the Historical Society of Nigeria*, Vol. 1, No. 3, December 1958, pp. 228–230.

11. Seymour Vandeleur, *Campaigning on the Upper Nile and Niger*, 1898, introduction by Sir George Goldie. For an evaluation of this essay, see J. E. Flint, *Sir George Goldie*, 1960, pp. 258–263.

12. Flint, *op. cit.*, p. 94. Dorothy Wellesley, in her *Sir George Goldie*, 1934, quotes Lord Scarbrough as stating that 'The policy of ruling through Native Chiefs was his [i.e. Goldie's]' (p. 156). Support for this is found in an article by Major Leonard Darwin based on a shorthand transcription of an interview he had with Goldie in March 1899 and published in *Journal of the African Society*, April, 1933. Here Goldie is quoted as saying: '. . . In such regions the only true policy is to adopt the local Native governments already existing, and to be content with controlling their excesses and with maintaining peace amongst themselves'.

13. 'With regard to internal control in Uganda, in my opinion the object to be aimed at in the administration of this country is to rule through its own executive government. The people are singularly intelligent, and have a wonderful appreciation of justice and of legal procedure, and our aim should be to educate and develop this sense of justice. I think myself that, by careful selection, even now the various provinces could be ruled by chiefs, who would rapidly conform to European methods'. F. D. Lugard, *The Rise of our East African Empire*, 1893, Vol. II, pp. 649–51.

14. *Annual Report for Northern Nigeria, 1902,* No. 409, paras. 62, 67 and 20. Of the last-named ceremony, at Zaria, the Nigeria Military Museum possesses an old photograph of the swearing-in of the Emir. The actual Sokoto ceremony is recounted in detail in paras. 59–60.

15. Sir Eric Ashby, the leading authority on problems of higher education in contemporary Africa, has no doubts on the matter: 'The chiefs and hereditary rulers, protected by the device of indirect rule, saw in education (and even in incipient African nationalism) a threat to their power'—*African Universities and Western Tradition,* 1964, p. 15. Miss S. F. Graham's study of the pioneer work of Sir Hanns Vischer in founding the Department of Education in Northern Nigeria, shortly to be published by Ibadan University Press, has much of interest to say in this connexion, in particular with regard to her defence of the charges of 'indirect rule conservatism' levelled against Vischer by Miss Perham in her biography of Lord Lugard.

16. Political Memorandum No. IX, para. 6.

17. This statement, originally published in 1957, was reiterated in 1961.

18. Though one might have expected the South to have rued the amalgamation because of the extension of Northern concepts of native administration brought in its train, it was the North which, in 1953, regretted it first in the historic, two-sentence speech made by the Premier in the House of Representatives: 'The mistake of 1914 has come to light and I should like to go no further'. See Sir Ahmadu Bello, *My Life,* 1962, p. 133.

19. The categorisation is that of M. Fortes and E. E. Evans-Pritchard in their *African Political Systems,* 1940, Introduction, p. 5.

20. Lord Hailey, *An African Survey,* 1938, p. 416.

21. Anthropologists may find it interesting to speculate on how two of the ultra-'segmented' societies in Nigeria, the Ibo and Tiv, have over the past two decades developed strong 'state' tendencies.

22. Miss Perham, in her biography of Lugard, calls one of her chapters 'Indirect Rule and Western Obscurity', but Dr. Peter Lloyd, in a masterly review of *Lugard: The Years of Authority* appearing in *Ibadan,* No. 10, November 1960, takes the view that Lugard could have found out the true political structure of the Yoruba kingdoms had he wished.

23. *Amalgamation Report,* 1919, Cmd. 468, para. 15.

24. The difference in administrative nomenclature is significant. Lugard explained it thus:—'The term "Resident" implies duties rather of a political or advisory nature, while the term "Commissioner" connotes functions of a more directly administrative character.'—Political Memorandum No. 1, para. 4.

25. *Amalgamation Report,* para. 16.

26. ibid., para. 26. One is, of course, reminded of Sir Donald Cameron's dictum about the folly of seeking to 'make, as it were, a crown or a king at the top and then try to find something underneath on which it might—perhaps—appropriately be placed'. N. U. Akpan comments that 'the commonest mistake committed by the early apostles of the Indirect Rule system was the frequently over-hasty assumption that hardly any indigenous authorities worthy of reckoning with existed wherever they failed to see such institutions as the emirates of Northern Nigeria'—*Epitaph to Indirect Rule,* 1956, p. 33.

27. ibid., para. 27.

28. The Southern Provinces were divided into Western and Eastern Provinces in 1939.

29. H. R. Palmer.

30. The Aba Riots Commission of Enquiry noted how in the Yoruba states 'the conditions bore a certain resemblance to those prevailing in the Fulani states prior to the British occupation'—*Report of the Aba Commission of Inquiry,*

1930, para. 4, p. 2. The resemblance may have been clearer to those who were looking for it.

31. *Report of a Tour in the Southern Provinces*, unpublished MS., 1914. Perham comments that 'this was exactly what Lugard wanted from his investigator' (op. cit., p. 444), while Lloyd (op. cit.) echoes the same judgement: 'he reported to his master the conclusions he wished to hear'.

32. Discussions on the introduction of taxation into the Eastern Provinces, first mooted by Lugard in 1914, were revived in 1924, but the Bill was not passed until 1927; and even then a whole year was allowed for propaganda before the tax came into force in April 1928. There is a useful account of the introduction of native administration into the Eastern and Western Provinces in Hailey, *Native Administration in the British African Territories*, 1951, Vol. III, pp. 108–13 and 156–60.

33. The scheme for a poll tax was put forward by the Lieutenant-Governor of the Eastern Provinces in 1924, but His Excellency the Governor preferred to take no action on such a major policy matter and left it for his successor! The Lieutenant-Governor was not satisfied with the Ordinance proposed by Lagos and drafted a different one, pointing out that in his opinion the provisions of the Native Revenue Ordinance, which was 'framed to meet conditions in a predominantly Mohammedan country organised on feudal lines', were inapplicable to the Colony and the Eastern Provinces.

34. In 1947 there were 217 Native Authorities in the East and 300 Subordinate N.As, and 86 N.As and 280 subordinate ones in the West, compared to 119 and 113 respectively in the Northern Provinces. The clustering of Native Authorities in the south and their wider distribution in the north is well depicted in the map in K. M. Buchanan and J. C. Pugh, *Land and People in Nigeria*, 1955, p. 89.

35. In marked contrast to the East, where the term 'Native Administration' was vigorously rejected in 1949 as being offensive (*Report of the Select Committee to Review the Existing System of Local Government in the Eastern Provinces*, 1948, and the *Memorandum* thereon, dated 16 July 1949), the North has respected the term 'N.A.' and has even incorporated it into the Hausa language as *'ene*.

36. This also applied to the 'southern' parts of the North. The rationale of this extension is well expressed in the following extract from the *Annual Report of Nigeria*, 1914: 'A system so advanced and so elaborated as indirect rule could not, of course, be at once adopted in the areas occupied by the primitive pagan tribes who inhabited fully a half of the Northern Provinces, but the general outlines of this scheme of administration were made equally applicable to all, and it devolved on the political staff by constant effort to endeavour to raise these to the same level as that of the Hausa and Bornu states, but without encouraging them to adopt the Mohammedan religion'.

37. For inside views of the imposition of indirect rule on 'segmented' societies, valuable material is to hand in N. U. Akpan, *Epitaph to Indirect Rule*, 1956; *Akiga's Story*, edited by Rupert East, 1939; and in the novel by Chinua Achebe, *Things Fall Apart*, 1958. Chinua Achebe's latest novel, *Arrow of God* (1964), contains a masterly parody of a Secretariat circular impressing on 'all Political Officers working among tribes who lack Natural Rulers the vital necessity of developing without any further delay an effective system of "indirect rule" based on native institutions' (p. 67). Its rather pompous tone makes an interesting comparison with that of the actual circulars quoted in this book at p. 187.

38. Perham suggests that the reason that Temple was never awarded the governorship he deserved was the reprimand he received from the Colonial Office over his handling of an affray in 1913 in which a mining prospector was killed (*Lugard*, 1960, p. 477).

39. See Perham, ibid., Chapters XIX and XXIV, *passim,* especially pp. 474–78.

40. Though acknowledging the initiative of Palmer and Temple in their development, Lugard criticized the choice of title *Beiyut el Mal*: Political Memorandum No. IX, para. 49. The first printed N. T. Estimates (1911–12) showed a total revenue of £170,752 against an expenditure of £173,762.

41. The sketches accompanying the text in his *Native Races and Their Rulers* are fine evidence of his artistic ability.

42. Perham, op. cit., pp. 388–89.

43. See James S. Coleman, *Nigeria: Background to Nationalism,* 1958, Chapters 10 and 11, especially pp. 253–54.

44. From Preface to Temple, op. cit.

45. ibid., p. 78.

46. A. V. Murray, author of *The School in the Bush,* defined Temple's philosophy as 'a closed circle within which the political officer was the father of his people and ruled them wisely for their own good but according to his own ideas'—'Education under Indirect Rule', *Journal of the Royal African Society,* July, 1935, pp. 227–68. Of the sincerity of these 'preservationists', however misguided, there is no doubt: 'The authors of indirect rule believe that if the traditional group life of the native disappears without a new group life being put in its place, the continent of Africa will disintegrate', commented R. Buell, *The Native Problem in Africa,* 1928, Chapter 41. Of the 'disintegrating' dangers that indirect rule was so anxious to avoid two quotations—both, interestingly enough, from articles dealing with Temple's attitude—are worth quoting. One is the oft-cited comment from a review of an article by Temple in *West Africa,* 2 November, 1918: 'Every school, every book, newspaper, bicycle, motor-car, railway, every article of commerce exposed for sale, every sight of a steamer, every exercise in the use of English language is a sapping of the foundations. They are new wine. The old bottles will not serve for them'. The other is from A. Victor Murray, *The School in the Bush,* 1929, p. 285, and echoes the very same sentiments: 'Every "factory" that is opened in Kano, every motor-car that squeezes through the Nassarawa gate, every Hausa who leaves his native city to seek his fortune in other countries or to learn the white man's language and ways in Southern Nigeria, is an influence that is modifying every day the situation which the political officers of the North have to meet.' This is from a chapter devoted to an attack on Temple's dogmatic resistance to educational liberalism in the Northern Provinces.

47. Victor Murray, op. cit., p. 275, links the *volte-face* of the Administration on their attitude towards the site of the Church Missionary Society within the walls of Zaria City (for the full story see A. H. M. Kirk-Greene, ' . . . An Abiding Memorial', *Nigeria Magazine,* No. 74, 1963) with the emirate holiness of indirect rule: ' . . . by being true to the letter of "indirect rule" they have missed the spirit of it'.

48. Sir Andrew Cohen, *British Policy in Changing Africa,* 1959, Chapter I, nevertheless gives an admirable summary of the setting, philosophy and achievements of indirect rule.

49. The chief's dual role, with his responsibility towards the central government and his duty towards his people, has still to be examined in detail, though an interesting preliminary analysis is to be found in Lloyd A. Fallers, *Bantu Bureaucracy,* 1956, Chapter VII, 1951 and in the focus of K. A. Busia, *The Position of the Chief in the Modern Political System of Ashanti.* See also the chapter by Southwold in *The King's Men,* ed. L. A. Fallers, 1964, and the theme of *East African Chiefs,* ed. A. I. Richards and L. A. Fallers, 1962. Much has, of course, been written about the role of chiefs in African society, and given their traditional importance much more can be expected from studies of their function

in a transitional society. Of their part in indirect rule, three lesser-known sources may be worth quoting. One is Perham's definition, given in her Reith Lectures 1961: 'They took the strain of indirect rule, breaking down, like human transformers, the powerful current from above and distributing it in voltages that their people could take' (*The Colonial Reckoning*, Chapter 5). The other is taken from a short story by Robert Browne that appeared in *Insight* (Lagos: U.K. Information Services), No. II, March 1963:—'If you talk about the political aspect, well, there's the Chief. Under this wonderful invention of yours of indirect rule, he's going to do it: not you, not Government, but the Chief in Council. So *you* tell the Chief to make the rules. . . . Your conscience is clear. You are not forcing the people. The Chief and his Counsellors know what's good for the people—because you have told them. *They* are forcing the people, not *you*.' A recent novel by W. Fowler, *Harama* (1963), is also valuable for the analysis it affords of the conflict in the mind of both chiefs and senior administrative officers in the transitional period of political advancement in West Africa. At one stage a new Africa *élites arrivées* advises that 'the old benevolence is offensive' (p. 119), a succinct summary of one aspect of such conflict. The moral struggle and the *crise de conscience* are carried a stage further in T. M. Aluko's novel *One Man, One Matchet*, 1964, in which for the first time we see the psychological difficulties and personal problems that confront the new generation of District Officers—the African administrators.

50. Quoted in Perham, *Lugard*, 1960, p. 476.

51. Those who impatiently tend to 'look upon this whole period as if it were almost in the Dark Ages' (Cohen, op. cit., p. 28) would do well to recall the warning given by Sir Charles Orr in his review of W. R. Crocker, *Nigeria: A Critique of British Colonial Administration*:—'A fly travelling on the bonnet of a motor car might paint a lively picture of the eccentricities of the car and its driver, but it requires some knowledge of the mechanism inside the bonnet to render an account of the journey really informative.' *Journal of the Royal African Society*, July 1936, pp. 343–46.

52. Leonard Woolf, *Growing*, 1960, p. 230.

53. Some of the extracts, I fear, reveal a lamentably ponderous style (e.g., pp. 50, and 63).

54. Perham, *Native Administration in Nigeria*, 1937, p. 69.

55. Perham, *Lugard*, 1960, p. 156. Unconsciously, perhaps, this echoes W. R. Crocker's praise of Lugard's *Dual Mandate*:—'There is nothing else quite like it in all the literature of British imperialism' (op. cit., p. 214).

56. Earlier, when he was High Commissioner of Northern Nigeria, the Colonial Office had rejected his scheme for a similar 'Continuous Administration'.

57. From the Preface to *Political Memoranda*, 1919 edition.

58. Plans are in hand to republish *Political Memoranda*, and in this I would hope to treat both editions comparatively.

59. Perham, *Native Administration in Nigeria*, 1937, p. 69.

60. This should be read in conjunction with *Annual Report of Nigeria*, 1902, paragraphs 25–36.

61. The 1906 edition had 319 pages, the 1918 one 455. The former was marked as a Confidential document; the latter forbade any material to be circulated to the press—Lugard's *bête noire* (see Perham, *Lugard*, 1960, p. 597 ff. for his feelings towards the 'scurrilous local yellow press', as he termed the Lagos newspapers). The copy of the 1906 edition lent to me by the kind permission of the Librarian of the Royal Commonwealth Society, is inscribed: 'E. J. Lugard from F.D.L. A memento of our work together 1905–07'. Interestingly enough, the pages are uncut!

62. And perhaps, though I have not been able to consult this work here in Zaria, with the French Administrative Service's *Manuel à l'usage des Administrateurs et du Personnel des Affaires Indigenes de la Colonie du Sénégal et des Colonies relevant du Gouvernement de l'Afrique Occidentale Française*, compiled by E. Roux in 1911.

63. I am grateful to J. G. Davies for permission to use this material from our unpublished MS *The History of Local Government in Northern Nigeria.*

64. One is reminded of Bishop Tugwell's accusation that 'Indirect rule is direct rule by indirect means', quoted by Lugard in his *Dual Mandate*, p. 223. The relationship between the chief and his people was, of course, a 'direct' one; only that between the chief and Government, as represented by the Administrative Officer, was 'indirect'.

65. Cf. Speech at Sokoto, 1903.

66. A good example of how this was ignored is found in the old Yola Province, where in 1912 all the pagan tribes were experimentally placed under Fulani *kalifaen* or 'guardians'. This was quickly abandoned. See A. H. M. Kirk-Greene, *Adamawa Past and Present*, 1958, p. 150. Cameron, in a footnote to his Memorandum on Native Administration, 1934, quoted a similar policy for the non-Moslem peoples of southern Dikwa on the appointment of a new Shehu.

67. Cf. Resident's Proclamation, 1900, and Enforcement of Native Authority Proclamation, 1907.

68. This is, of course, a post-1906 concept.

69. *Lugard*, 1960, Chapters XVII and XXV.

70. *Dual Mandate*, pp. 103–105.

71. C. W. J. Orr, *The Making of Northern Nigeria*, 1911, p. 142.

72. Quoted in Perham, op. cit., p. 524; see also H. R. Palmer, *Journal of the Royal African Society*, 1934, p. 47.

73. 'A courageous speech . . .': Sir Ahmadu Bello, *My Life*, 1962, p. 74.

74. Northern House of Assembly Debates, 4th Session, 19 August 1950, p. 92.

75. I have always been fascinated by the happy coincidence that Lugard, the father of Nigeria, should have married Flora Shaw, the creator of the name 'Nigeria'. See A. H. M. Kirk-Greene, 'The Name "Nigeria" ', *The Times Colonial Supplement*, April–June, 1959.

76. Though this Report was finished in 1913, it was not published till 1919.

77. From the Foreword. See also p. 7.

78. W. R. Crocker, *Nigeria: A Critique of British Colonial Administration*, 1936, p. 214. He is, however, critical of its effect on the Nigerian Service.

79. Perham, op. cit., p. 643.

80. See Cohen, op. cit., pp. 26–28: Perham, *The Colonial Reckoning*, 1963, p. 86.

81. Previous editions were published in 1922, 1923, 1924 and 1929. In 1928 Blackwood published a 66-page pamphlet, *Representative Forms of Government and 'Indirect Rule' in British Africa*, as an excerpt from *Dual Mandate*, advertised as 'being an extract from the Textbook Edition of "The Dual Mandate" (in preparation)'.

82. Lugard, *Dual Mandate*, p. 617. Cf. Goldie in his Foreword to Vandeleur, op. cit.; 'While, however, this consideration should satisfy the consciences of persons interested in the welfare of the oppressed millions of Africa, the material importance of opening up the Sudan cannot be overlooked by any European State which subsists largely on its manufacturing and shipping interests.'

83. *The National Review*, November 1922, quoted in Perham, op. cit., p. 644.

84. 21 November, 1920. It was republished, with slight amendments, in the *Nigeria Gazette* of 2 March, 1926.

85. Appendix to Memorandum on Native Administration, 1934.

86. In this connexion it is interesting to note Lord Milverton's address to the Nigerian Legislative Council made on 10 December, 1945:—'It seems to me that the administration is too loosely knit and that a lack of general co-ordination has deprived Government efforts of some of the effective force which comes from joint effort. There has been a growing tendency towards departmentalism and the emergence of insulated departmental autocracies. The present Government intends to control the policy of all departments and to insist that at each level of the Administration the Administrative Officer in charge, whether it be the Chief Commissioner or the Resident or the District Officer, must be regarded as the captains of a team which works together for the benefit of the people and the progress of the country, and as such must be in a position to co-ordinate effort without, of course, in any way interfering with the technical achievement of an accepted purpose.'

87. Paragraph 5.

88. Paragraph 7.

89. Paragraph 23.

90. Paragraph 9.

91. Paragraph 24.

92. Cameron's judgement on Clifford was that ' . . . his task was to open the windows and the doors in the public service of Nigeria . . . admitting light and air where, here and there, some mildew, some dry rot was to be discerned'—*My Tanganyika Service and Some Nigeria*, 1939, p. 153.

93. Perham, *Native Administration in Nigeria*, 1937, pp. 70–72.

94. Administrative lore in Northern Nigeria has it that, among the many pecularities of Bornu in the 1920s, permission was required—though not always given—from the Resident before anybody might visit the Province!

95. Formed out of the old Yola and Muri Provinces after the vast 1926 provincial reorganisation.

96. 'Indirect rule passed through three stages, first of a useful administrative device, then that of a political doctrine, and finally that of a religious dogma'— D. A. Low and R. C. Pratt, *Buganda and British Overrule*, 1960, p. 176, note. A. N. Cook, *British Enterprise in Nigeria*, 1943, puts it another way: 'The circulars and orders emanating . . . were loud in their praise of indirect rule but not very enlightening to joining officers who, it was felt, could never quite understand the mysteries they were expected to administer'—p. 268.

97. Crocker, op. cit., p. 222. See also an earlier attack by another ex-District Officer from Nigeria, J. F. J. Fitzpatrick, 'Nigeria's Curse—Native Administration', *National Review*, December 1924.

98. Cameron, in his autobiography (p. 147) spoke of Northern Nigeria as a place where 'advancement in the ranks of the Administrative Service was in a measure reserved for those who were prepared to worship unquestionably at that shrine of indirect rule'. Crocker testified to the same spirit: 'No more damning remark could be made in the annual secret report on an officer than that he was "direct" and not sufficiently imbued with the spirit of indirect rule'— op. cit., p. 217.

99. Cf. Rupert Wilkinson, *The Prefects*, 1963, p. 102: ' . . . The "District Commissioner's" office depended for responsible government on a gentlemanly tradition of unwritten restraint. In a remote district far from higher authority, in a position of great power not simply as an administrator but also as a judge, the D.C. had every opportunity to be lazy, corrupt and unjust. In fact, he was nearly always honest, humane and hard-working'. Sir Alfred Milner used to talk of 'the indefiniteness of British authority'—*England in Egypt*, 1899, p. 31.

100. 'In practice a system of this kind of indirect rule can never be reduced

D

to rule-of-thumb methods. It demands from the advisers to the native authorities training, knowledge of the psychology and history of the people, and a constant skill and attention to determine when to intervene and when to leave well alone, when to hasten the development of more advanced methods and when to advise a slowing down of progress too rapid to be assimilated'—Margery Perham and L. Curtis, *The Protectorates of South Africa*, 1935, p. 259.

101. W. M. Macmillan has called Cameron 'the prophet of the second and expansive phase of native administration'—*Africa Emergent*, 1938, Chapter XII.

102. Paragraph 67.

103. Such links were even more pronounced in the Northern Provinces, where in their whole administrative history down to the appointment of an indigenous Governor in 1962 only two of Lugard's successors were not drawn from the Nigerian Administrative Service: Sir Gawain Bell (1957–62) and Sir Theodore Adams (1937–43). It is therefore especially interesting to note the reactions of the first 'outsider' Chief Commissioner to the home of indirect rule. Sir Theodore Adams prefaced his *Annual Report to the Northern Provinces*, 1937, with these comments:—

'As this is the first report written by an officer who has not had previous experience in Nigeria I propose to vary it slightly from former reports, by giving shortly my reactions on experiencing in practice a political system of which I had only known previously from reports. To the newcomer the Emirate system with British advice and control appears very similar in its working to the system of administration in Malaya—though in many matters of detail there are differences. The ruler in council is here and makes regulations but not enactments; he has his own budget approved by the Governor; his own organisations for education, public works, medicine and so on; but there is still no clear distinction between his functions as a Native Authority and those of the Central Government. The Engineer may be pressed to complete one public work financed in the Central Government estimates while the Native Authority wishes him to get on with another work of the same nature financed from the Native Administration Estimates;—one could cover many pages of instances of the fact that we have outgrown the original basis of the allocation of functions and revenue, and have now to decide either to allocate functions or to slip by slow degrees yet very surely into centralisation, which will have far worse results than in the much smaller and less numerous Malay States. During the last part of the year tentative proposals have been made, on which consideration continues, for the acceptance of principles and the consequent allocation of functions, which alone can preserve a vigorous Indirect Rule capable of adjusting itself to new conditions and to the generations which education will make so very different from those of even the present day. [i.e. the Bourdillon Minute].

Notwithstanding the emphasis placed in the past on the status of the Emirs as 'Governors', as 'integral authorities' side by side with the British officials, there has persevered the native installation of the Emirs, which—unless it is regarded cynically as a meaningless ceremony acquiesced in so as to avoid trouble—does confer on the Emirs a status quite different from that of any administrative officer. It is a recognition of the fact that the Emirs are looked on as Rulers by their peoples. It is unnecessary to go into detail but I can find no one who can accept the definition of the Emirs as 'Wakils of the Governor' as a full and correct definition of their status—though in certain respects it is a correct definition in that it is the Governor who, as representative of the suzerain, declares what executive and administrative powers the Emir shall possess as a Native Authority and what the Central Government retains from time to time. This is a necessary control with which I have been familiar in the past. The Native Administrations are officiating with an efficiency which increases with experience, and are live bodies which will before long develop greater critical capacity.'

104. Dr. P. Lloyd, in his review of *Lugard: The Years of Authority in Ibadan*, November, 1960, wonders whether the fact that Lugard never saw any ultimate goal to his indirect rule policy might be attributed to the fact that he had never been a District Officer in the field.

105. It was Cameron who reduced the status of the Lieutenant-Governors by restyling them Chief Commissioners.

106. In the East African context this has useful parallels in the Ugandan memoranda prepared by Sir Philip Mitchell (1939) and Sir Charles Dundas (1941). Dundas, in addition to his *Native Administration in Uganda* memorandum, made an important speech on native administration to the Lukiko in 1944: this is reproduced in part in David Apter, *The Political Kingdom in Uganda*, 1961, p. 211, note. In Tanganyika, Cameron published a preliminary explanation of his principles (Circular No. 50 of 1925) contained in the draft 1926 Native Authority Ordinance. This was reproduced in *Annual Report for Tanganyika*, 1925, pp. 6–10.

107. *My Tanganyika Service and Some Nigeria*, 1939. See also his 'Native Administration in Nigeria and Tanganyika', *Journal of the Royal African Society*, supplement dated 30 November, 1937. This, together with Perham's 'A Restatement of Indirect Rule', *Africa*, July 1934, pp. 321–34, are two of those fugitive materials that deserve wider circulation and reading.

108. Introduction to the Tanganyikan Memorandum on Native Administration, paragraph 2. This echoes the sentiments behind Article 22 of the League of Nations Mandate Covenant.

109. Memorandum, paragraph 67.

110. The next official publication of the impressions by the Governor on his tour of the country was not until that of Sir John Macpherson in 1949.

111. Speech to Legislative Council, 6 March 1933. This address should be read alongside Cameron's Memorandum.

112. In Tanganyika Cameron's successors were unable to maintain the vitality of the system: 'they emphasized adherence to the idea of traditional authority sometimes to the point of ridiculousness'—Margaret Bates, in Gwendolen Carter, *African One-Party States*, 1962, p. 410.

113. 'Indirect rule became a formula as hieratic and as dead of creative development as an outworn theology'—Crocker, op. cit., p. 215. Sir Philip Mitchell, who favoured the idea of indirect rule but would have forbidden the use of tho name, describes a similar phenomenon in Tanganyika where there grew up 'a cult whose devotees were in some danger of becoming a sort of orgiastic order of monks—if there can be such a thing.'—*African Afterthoughts*, 1954, p. 127. Awolowo talks of 'a tradition of original sin . . . it was not part of the plan, as it unfolded itself, to train the people in the art of government'—*Path to Nigerian Freedom*, 1947, pp. 58–59. This distrust, however, he cancels on the next page: 'It is to the immortal glory of Lord Lugard that his device of indirect administration, which was a child of necessity, a crucial experiment, now provides the most effective medium of giving the people the necessary training, provided (and this is a big proviso) this device is judiciously, honestly and courageously applied.'

114. E.g., pp. 14–15 and p. 76.

115. The Provincial Court of the Resident was now abolished and Native Treasuries were henceforth susceptible to audit by the Audit Department.

116. Perham devotes a whole chapter of *Native Administration in Nigeria*, 1937, to a discussion of the liberalizing effect of Cameron's Governorship, and

attributes to it (p. 333) such novelties as the *first* visit by the Emir of Kano to Lagos and the Sultan of Sokoto to England in 1934.

117. Paragraph 14.

118. The influence of anthropology upon British colonial practice, though well recognized, has still to be totally assessed—it is certainly a long way from the naive judgement that anthropology became an imperial tool! 'Those who deplore the new theory of administration are apt to regard anthropology as the evil genius'—Margery Perham, 'A Restatement of Indirect Rule', *Africa*, July 1934, pp. 321–34. See also Audrey I. Richards, 'Anthropology on the Scrapheap?', *Journal of African Administration*, Vol. XIII, January 1961. The heyday of this partnership was the '30s; its doyen was Malinowski, who towards the end of his academic career became absorbed with the interplay of the two phenomena. He believed that 'anthropologists have a moral obligation to communicate research knowledge and advice to missionaries', as he put it in his *Dynamics of Culture Change*, 1948. (See also the symposium edited by Malinowski, *Methods of Study of Culture Contact in Africa*, 1938). Nigeria was in the midstream of this intensive anthropological research, and in the decade *c.* 1925–1935 literally hundreds of investigations were undertaken. This was also the period when Nigeria carried on its civil service cadre a professional anthropologist. Lucy Mair, who dedicated her *Native Policies in Africa*, 1936, to Malinowski, stated that 'the study of human culture along the lines first traced by Professor B. Malinowski in the functional theory of anthropology throws an entirely new light on the problems of colonial policy' (p. 4). A generation later, but with less accuracy, Professor W. E. Abraham noted how 'The British, with a sensitive, if prominent, nose for subtle changes, devised indirect rule through local chiefs, and so instead of wasting energy fighting deep-rooted traditional forces, used them. They had their sensible anthropologists to thank for this. Lugard [*sic*] made use of a social-anthropological discovery'—*The Mind of Africa*, 1962, p. 156. In a discussion on a paper read to the Royal African Society by A. V. Murray in 1935 (subsequently published in the Society's *Journal*, July 1935, pp. 227–68, under the title of 'Education under Indirect Rule'), Dr. Mair summed up the anthropologists' interest: 'The reason why students of anthropology believe in the system of indirect rule is not that it aims at preserving native societies in their original form. To us the problem is to enable the changes which modify conditions required of African society to be made without unnecessary dislocation of its structure, and this we believe can be done by preserving and adapting those institutions which are still working and are capable of adaptation, rather than adding to the process of disintegration by destroying those which have not been and need not be destroyed' (p. 267). As late as 1940, when M. Fortes and E. E. Evans-Pritchard published their *African Political Systems*, the credo continued: 'The policy of Indirect Rule is now generally accepted in British Africa. We would suggest that it can only prove advantageous in the long run if the principles of African political systems, such as this book deal with, are understood' (p. 1).

119. The trouble with tribal institutions is that 'they remained tribal and there was no provision or consideration of intertribal affairs'—Margaret L. Bates in *African One-Party States*, ed. Gwendolen Carter, 1962, p. 407.

120. Paragraph 1.

121. How consciously, one may wonder, did both Lugard and Cameron echo, in their advocacy of the indirect method in imperial administration, the thoughts of Edmund Burke expressed at Warren Hastings' trial a century earlier: 'If we undertake to govern the inhabitants of such a country, we must govern them upon their own principles and maxims, and not upon ours. We must not think to force them into the narrow circle of our ideas; we must extend ours to take in

their system of opinions and rites. . . .'—*The Collected Works of the Right Honourable Edmund Burke*, 1822, Vol. XII, p. 65, quoted in Ashby, op. cit., p. 2.

122. The seal to the dependent status of the Native Authorities, repeated from time to time under colonial rule, was finally put in the post-independence era by section 9 of the Provincial Administration Law, 1962, which states that 'The Premier may, through a Provincial Commissioner or, where the office of such Provincial Commissioner is for any reason vacant, through the Provincial Secretary, direct a native authority to carry out any of the functions vested in it by any written law or by native law and custom, and the native authority shall comply with such direction'.

123. The dichotomy was formalised, in the event, by Lugard's official designation of certain provinces as First-Class and others as Second Class with regard to the status of Residents appointed to them. (Annual *Report for Nigeria*, 1904, paragraph 5 and Political Memorandum IX, paragraph 78). The stigma, so unjustifiably attached, remained, and as late as 1950 stations like Yola, Makurdi and Lokoja were affectionately known among the Administration as 'punishment postings'.

124. This pious hope was finally exploded by the Gibbons report *African Local Government Reform in Kenya, Uganda and Eastern Nigeria*, 1949, where the true picture was vividly painted: 'A man has only one life, and it is idle to expect an educated African gentleman, eager to work for the self-government of Nigeria, to fritter away his efforts in argument with yokels round the parish pump. The Native Authority Councils continue to consist, therefore, for the most part of worthy but unlettered men with a parochial horizon and people who, though literate, have enjoyed little enlargement of either education or experience' (paragraph 93). Nor, by and large, were these educated elements welcomed with any enthusiasm by the traditional councils of the emirates.

125. I have advisedly used the word 'apparent', for although Sole Native Authorities were abolished in 1952, I incline to the opinion that the traditional emirate councils were never quite so autocratic as they may have seemed to the committee-conscious European eye. The Premier of the North, Sir Ahmadu Bello, has recorded his view that 'the old emirates were originally much more democratic than they were when the British left them' (*My Life*, p. 229), and for once he is supported by his political rival, Chief Obafemi Awolowo, who writes that 'they were all clothed with powers and prestige far in excess of what they ever wielded or enjoyed before the advent of the British conquest' (*Path to Nigerian Freedom*, p. 59). Cf. Abubakar Tafawa Balewa's speech to the Northern House of Assembly, 19 August 1950.

126. Attachment to *Annual Report for Nigeria*, 1905–06. See also C. W. Orr, *The Making of Northern Nigeria*, 1911, p. 150 ff. It is largely because of the similarity between Lugard's chapters (XII and XIII) in his *Dual Mandate* and Political Memorandum No. V that in this book the former source has not been given more fully.

127. Sir Sidney Phillipson, *Administrative and Financial Procedure under the New Constitution . . .*, 1947, paragraph 60.

128. This list excludes, by definition, important policy statements on the solely financial procedures of the Central Government, such as those by Phillipson and Hicks (1951), Raisman (1958) and Archer (1961).

129. 'No longer [post-war] a slogan or an end in itself, Native Administration gets the place and function proper to it as a beginning of African local government'—W. A. Macmillan, *Africa Emergent*, 1948 ed., p. 268. Cf. the knell sounded in Dr. Ronald Robinson's Introduction to Cambridge Summer Conference *Local Government in Africa*, 1961.

130. 'The principles of indirect rule, if not in competition with the ideal of

self-government by representative institutions, are at all events so alien to it as to suggest that native institutions must be materially modified if they are to fit into any scheme involving an elected parliament'—such was Hailey's warning in 1938 (*An African Survey*, p. 1640). The pre-war system of indirect rule 'was not primarily concerned with nation-building', as Carl Rosberg and Aaron Segal point out in *An East African Federation*, May 1963, p. 45. This selection of documents is not concerned with the grounds for the attacks on indirect rule, nor has it sought to explain its cause or anatomy: this has been well done by other scholars. But for a general lead-in see Hailey, op. cit., and the lesser-known source of Z. K. Matthews 'An African View of Indirect Rule in Africa', *Journal of the Royal African Society*, October 1937, pp. 433–37.

131. Cf. *Fabian Colonial Essays*, ed. Rita Hinden, 1945; Rita Hinden, *Local Government and the Colonies*, 1950; J. S. Furnivall, *Colonial Policy and Practice*, 1948; A. Creech Jones, *New Fabian Colonial Essays*, 1959.

132. 'Democratic' was subsequently changed to 'representative'.

133. Paragraph 1.

134. In 1962 it was renamed the *Journal of Local Administration Overseas*.

135. The published reports of these annual conferences make valuable reading.

136. The move to include this subject in the course came as a result of the recommendations of the Devonshire Committee in 1945, and received warm support from senior serving officers consulted in the field by the members of the 'Nuffield Visit' to Nigeria in 1945–46 by the Oxford–Cambridge–London delegation.

137. Cf. R. E. Robinson, 'Why "Indirect Rule" has been replaced by "Local Government" ', *Journal of African Administration*, Vol. II, July 1950.

138. See, for example, C. A. G. Wallis, 'Local Administration in the Sudan', *Journal of African Administration*, Vol. XIII, July 1961; W. J. Warrell-Bowring, 'The Reorganisation of the Administration in Tanganyika', ibid., October 1963; and A. H. M. Kirk-Greene, 'A Redefinition of Provincial Administration: The Northern Nigerian Approach', ibid., January 1965.

139. Cf. B. Keith Lucas, 'The Dilemma of Local Government in Africa', *Essays in Imperial Government*, 1963, pp. 193–208.

1903: THE SPEECH AT SOKOTO[1]

The extracts are taken from the speech reproduced in NORTHERN NIGERIA: ANNUAL REPORT, 1902, NO. 409, APPENDIX III, *as given in the collector's piece* ANNUAL REPORTS: NORTHERN NIGERIA 1900–11, *London, pp. 163–5. Although the Kano-Sokoto campaign took place in 1903, Lugard decided to include its account in his Report for 1902 so as to make for a complete narrative. A full description of the campaign is given in paragraphs 37–63 of the Report.*

Sokoto fell to the British troops on 15 March, a fact commemorated by the Premier of Northern Nigeria. Alhaji Sir Ahmadu Bello, Sardauna of Sokoto, by his deliberate choice of 15 March as the day for the North's self-government in 1959. Lugard addressed the Sokoto councillors on 20 March in an effort to persuade them to select a new Sarkin Musulmi to replace the fugitive Attahiru. On the following day he made his second address to the Waziri and elders of Sokoto, after they had put forward the name of the new Sultan, and it is from this speech of 21 March that the following excerpt is made. It was translated by Lugard's messenger, Kiari, and was carefully checked by Major A. Burdon, Hausa Scholar of Cambridge University and the first Resident of Sokoto Province.

. . . The old treaties are dead, you have killed them. Now these are the words which I, the High Commissioner, have to say for the future. The Fulani in old times under Dan Fodio conquered this country. They took the right to rule over it, to levy taxes, to depose kings and to create kings. They in turn have by defeat lost their rule which has come into the hands of the British. All these things which I have said the Fulani by conquest took the right to do now pass to the British. Every Sultan and Emir and the principal officers of state will be appointed by the High Commissioner throughout all this country. The High Commissioner will be guided by the usual laws of succession and the wishes of the people and chiefs, but will set them aside if he desires for good cause to do so. The Emirs and Chiefs who are appointed will rule over the people as of old time and take such taxes as are approved by the High Commissioner, but they will obey the laws of the Governor and will act in accordance with the advice of the Resident. Buying and selling slaves and enslaving people are forbidden. It is forbidden to import firearms (except flint-locks), and there are other minor matters which the Resident will explain. The Alkalis and the Emirs will hold the law courts as of old but bribes are forbidden, and mutilation and confinement of men in inhuman prisons are not lawful. The powers for each Court

[1] For a commentary on each of these ten passages, the reader is invited to refer to the corresponding section of the Introduction.

will be contained in a warrant appointing it. Sentences of death will not be carried out without the consent of the Resident.

The Government will, in future, hold the rights in land which the Fulani took by conquest from the people, and if Government requires land it will take it for any purpose. The Government hold the right of taxation, and will tell the Emirs and Chiefs what taxes they may levy, and what part of them must be paid to Government. The Government will have the right to all minerals, but the people may dig for iron and work in it subject to the approval of the High Commissioner, and may take salt and other minerals subject to any excise imposed by law. Traders will not be taxed by Chiefs but only Government. The coinage of the British will be accepted as legal tender, and a rate of exchange for cowries fixed, in consultation with Chiefs, and they will enforce it.

When an Emirate, or an office of state, becomes vacant, it will only be filled with the consent of the High Commissioner, and the person chosen by the council of Chiefs and approved by the High Commissioner will hold his place only on condition that he obeys the laws of the Protectorate and the conditions of his appointment. Government will in no way interfere with the Mohammedan religion. All men are free to worship God as they please. Mosques and prayer places will be treated with respect by us. Every person, including slaves, has the right to appeal to the Resident, who will, however, endeavour to uphold the power of the native courts to deal with native cases according to the law and custom of the country. If slaves are ill-treated they will be set free as your Koran orders, otherwise Government does not desire to interfere with existing domestic relations. But slaves set free must be willing to work and not remain idle or become thieves. The Resident may give permits to trustworthy men to bear firearms. . . .

It is the earnest desire of the King of England that this country shall prosper and grow rich in peace and in contentment, that the population shall increase, and the ruined towns which abound everywhere shall be built up, and that war and trouble shall cease. Henceforth no Emir or Chief shall levy war or fight, but his case will be settled by law, and if force is necessary Government will employ it. . . .

In conclusion, I hope that you will find our rule sympathetic and that the country will prosper and be contented. You need have no fear regarding British rule, it is our wish to learn your customs and fashions, just as you must learn ours. I have little fear but that we shall agree, for you have always heard that British rule is just and fair, and people under our King are satisfied. You must not fear to tell the Resident everything and he will help and advise you.

1914: THE AMALGAMATION REPORT

The extracts are taken from the REPORT BY SIR F. D. LUGARD ON THE AMALGAMATION OF NORTHERN AND SOUTHERN NIGERIA, AND ADMINISTRA- TION, 1912–19, *Cmd. 468, London, 1920, paragraphs 16–32. Though not published until 1920, it was on the recommendations of this report, compiled by Lugard on his return to Nigeria in 1912, that the amalgamation of the two Protectorates was effected on 1 January, 1914, by means of the Nigeria Protectorate Order in Council of 22 November and Royal Letters Patent dated 29 November, 1913.*

24. The system of Native Administration in the separate Government of Northern Nigeria had been based on a recognition of the authority of the Native Chiefs. The policy of the Government was that these Chiefs should govern their people, not as independent but as dependent Rulers. The orders of Government are not conveyed to the people through them, but emanate from them in accordance where necessary with instructions received through the Resident. While they themselves are controlled by Government in matters of policy and of importance, their people are controlled in accordance with that policy by themselves. A Political Officer would consider it as irregular to issue direct orders to an individual native, or even to a village head, as a General commanding a division would to a private soldier, except through his commanding officers. The courts administer native law, and are presided over by Native Judges[1]. . . . Their punishments do not conform to the Criminal Code, but, on the other hand, native law must not be in opposition to the Ordi- nances of Government, which are operative everywhere, and the courts, as I shall presently describe, are under the close supervision of the District Staff. Their rules of evidence and their procedure are not based on British standards, but their sentences, if manifestly faulty, are subject to revision. Their prisoners are confined in their own native gaols, which are under the supervision of the British Staff. The taxes are raised in the name of the native ruler and by his agents, but he surrenders the fixed proportion to Government, and the expenditure of the portion assigned to the Native Administration, from which fixed salaries to all native officials are paid, is subject to the advice of the Resident, and the ultimate control of the Governor. The attitude of the Resident is that of a watchful adviser not of an

[1] There were 417 Native Courts in Northern Nigeria, with a total revenue in 1917 of £28,500. Of these, six were classified as 'fully organized': Sokoto, Kano, Katsina, Gwandu, Zaria and Bornu. A further 22 were 'partially organized', while the remainder were labelled as 'unorganized'.

interfering ruler, but he is ever jealous of the rights of the peasantry, and of any injustice towards them.

This system is clearly only adapted in its fullest application to communities under the centralized rule of a paramount Chief, with some administrative machinery at his disposal, and finds its best exposition in the Moslem communities of the North. Nevertheless, its underlying principles are applied, to the varying extent to which it is possible in each case to apply them, even to the most primitive communities in the North. The first step is to endeavour to find a man of influence as chief, and to group under him as many villages or districts as possible, to teach him to delegate powers, and to take an interest in his 'Native Treasury', to support his authority, and to inculcate a sense of responsibility.[1]

27.—The system may thus be said to have worked with good results in the North, and I desired to introduce its principles in the South. It is, however, obvious that it depends essentially on the principle of direct taxation, which provided the means whereby the Native Administration can pay salaries to the paramount Chief and all other officials, and so put an end to the unlimited exactions on which they had previously lived, and reduce their number to those actually required for the service of the Native Administration. . . .

28.—Towards the close of 1916 the financial position, owing to the War, had become very serious, and I was accorded permission to introduce direct taxation in Yorubaland, Egba, and Benin on my own responsibility, and subject to the proviso that both chiefs and people voluntarily agreed to it, and that no more was asked of the people than they were already paying by tribute and other levies to their chiefs. The favourable moment of transition to the new regime had already passed. . . .

During 1918 taxation was successfully introduced in Yoruba; the people appeared thoroughly convinced of the advantages of consolidating the demands made upon them in a single payment, and there was something almost approaching enthusiasm in the way the money poured in[2]. . . . The inauguration of Native Administrations was then a comparatively easy matter. The division of the province into districts, each under a Headman, the assessment of salaries to them and to the Chief's Council, the preparation of Estimates of the Revenue and Expenditure were all completed by the end of the year. . . .

29.—The disintegration of Yorubaland was arrested, and the supreme authority of the Alafin recognized by all, to the immense benefit of the country. . . . A strong Native Government is in process

[1] By 1917 there were 50 Native Treasuries in the Northern Provinces. Out of their total revenue of £441,000, that of Kano was £69,000.

[2] Receipts for 1918 totalled £72,000.

of being built up under its own rulers, which will be able to resist the sinister influence of more or less educated aliens which was rapidly destroying it. The Native Courts are reported to be a 'huge success'.

30.—The difficult task still remains of extending these principles to the remainder of the Southern Provinces when the Secretary of State consents to this course, which is strongly urged by the most responsible officers. The Native Revenue Ordinance, hitherto applicable to the Northern Provinces only, has recently been applied to the whole of the Southern Provinces. This step had been deferred (as in the Northern Provinces) until actual experience should show the form of legislation required. The Lieut.-Governor expresses the view that before many years the tax should yield a Revenue of a million sterling, thus fully replacing the indirect tax accruing from duties on spirits . . . .

1918: TEMPLE'S POLITICAL TESTIMONY

The extracts are taken from C. L. Temple, NATIVE RACES AND THEIR RULERS, *Cape Town,* 1918, pp. 29–30; 49–50; 53–79. *The two chapters are entitled 'Direct versus Indirect Rule, with Specific Reference to Nigerian Practice' and 'Indirect Rule and What it Means: a Plea for a Settled Policy in Nigeria'.*

There are three different systems any of which may be adopted by the dominating European race for the control of a native race. One of these may be termed Direct Rule and another Indirect Rule. To the third it is hard to attach a brief designation, it is a kind of half-way house between the other two.

By Direct Rule I mean that form of administration which places the Government of the country entirely in the hands of European officials, minor posts only, such as clerkships, being filled by natives, while the policing of the country is entrusted to European officers, with coloured subordinates in Government employ wearing Government uniforms. This system necessarily entails either the abolition of Emirs and Chiefs, or their retention as figure heads only; the abolition of native Courts of Justice or such curtailment of their powers as to render them of little effect. In short it means replacing the Native Leader by the European Official, with his native staff. The underlying policy of this system is the establishment of European institutions and modes of life and thought among the native as possible.

By Indirect Rule I mean a system of administration which leaves in existence the administrative machinery which had been created by the native themselves; which recognizes the existence of Emirs, Chiefs and Native Councils, Native Courts of Justice, Muhammadan Courts, Pagan Courts, Native Police controlled by a native executive, as real living forces, and not as curious and interesting pageantry: by which European influence is brought to bear on the native indirectly, through his chiefs, and not directly through European officers—political, police, etc., and by which the European keeps himself a good deal in the background, and leaves the mass of native individuals to understand that the orders which come to them emanate from their own chief rather than from the all-pervading white man. The underlying policy of this system is to assist the native to develop that civilization which he can himself evolve.

The third system is a mixture whereby the white man, realizing that he has not the force necessary to enable him to deprive the native governing classes of all their power, at least whittles it down to a great extent; still retaining in a certain measure native forms, and etiquette, but in point of fact depriving the native to an ever-growing degree of any real control in the Government of the country. The underlying policy of this system is identical with that underlying Direct Rule. . . .

I have described Indirect Rule as the government of natives through their own institutions, possibly modified to some extent in order to avoid practice which rightly or wrongly we consider repugnant to reason and humanity. This sounds rational enough in theory and it may be asked: 'Whoever would question the feasibility of so obvious a proposal?'. In practice, however, the matter is not quite so simple as might be thought. To put this policy into real effect means first of all that you must shut your eyes, up to a certain point, to a great many practices which, though not absolutely repugnant to humanity, are nevertheless reprehensible to our ideas, and especially to those ideas which inform the mind of the British official. You must have patience with the liar though he lie seventy times seven; you must at times have patience with the peculator of public funds (a hard pill this to swallow); you must very generally have patience not only with the honest fool but with the slacker too. . . . You have to make up your mind that men are not all equal before the Law and cannot be so treated. An important chief must not be made to work among a gang of felons from the common herd, even though his crimes be far blacker than theirs. This is difficult to do in practice. . . .

Nevertheless, it is hard to get some officials to realize that it is right to punish by imprisonment a policeman who, when travelling, every evening demands, and is given by the villagers, free of charge, a fowl for his supper; whereas it may be crass folly so to punish a native chief travelling with perhaps a number of followers, who does exactly the same thing on an infinitely greater scale.

If it is difficult for the officer in immediate administrative charge to shut his eyes to, and even authorize, practices which stir the very depths of his nature to holy indignation, it is ten times more difficult for the higher powers, subject as they are to criticism of well-meaning but possibly ignorant persons at home to risk incurring the odium which may be acquired by allowing, and even more by authorizing, European officers under their control thus to countenance practices which to the public opinion of this country are abhorrent. Nevertheless I desire to say, with all the emphasis at my command, that unless men are found with shoulders broad enough to carry such responsibilities, the British nation will inadvertently fail to discharge in a proper manner those duties towards the native races which it has itself undertaken.

Granted patience, careful study, real administrative ability, qualities which are all at the disposal of the nation, thanks to Providence, in a remarkable degree, there is no reason whatsoever why the native should not be led up the steep slope of civilization gradually without reducing him to a state of collapse on the journey. The process must necessarily be slower in some districts than in others, but I believe that there is one, and only one, road, however long it may be, by which we can truly assist the development of the native under our care. That path follows the natural evolution of the native race. We must lead him along that path, and not persuade or compel him to leave it and follow our path. We must teach him to be a good citizen of his own section first and he may then become a good citizen of the Empire.

By implanting in his mind a contempt for his own institutions, by persuading him or compelling him to adopt our modes of life, we divorce him from his own natural entourage and he becomes 'alienated'. And what have we to give him in exchange? We give him stiff fronted shirts and starched collars and clothes well cut according to our own ideas, but which certainly offend his aesthetic sense as much as they do our own, and which reduce the natural vitality of his constitution. We may even give him, in very limited numbers, the keys of learning, of art, of science. But what are all these things compared to fellowship, companionship, the society of equals, pride of race, patriotism? Of all these great essentials we deprive him when we persuade him to leave the fellowship of his kind, the frame in which Providence has set him, and to enter within the pale of our society where he must be as a stranger at the feast. If our responsibility is great in so doing, when we balance the good we can do him with such disadvantages, and the scale turns against us to an immeasurable extent, how great does our responsibility become when we consider the active harm which contact with our civilization may cause him, nay, as example after example in the past has shown, will certainly cause him. The temptations to the vices of civilization to which we subject him! Nature has protected him against such dangers in his own society; but we step in and throw him like a crab without a shell amongst a horde of ravening sharks. . . .

But it may be said, 'There is no idea of creating independent Native States. The proposal is to rule the native by means of an European Executive with native subordinates. This Executive is, gradually in some cases, to take the place of native institutions. As individual natives become educated on European lines of thought, it will be open to them to enter the Government service. Thus in due course you will have selected natives taking a share in the government of natives.' I admit that this sounds well, and but for certain facts might be the best course to pursue.

A very important point to be kept in mind is the influence of the House of Commons over the administration of the native subject races. There is a very great measure of centralization in the government of every one of the dependent native races. All attempts to decentralize, and they have been and are frequently being made, are rendered unavailing, or restricted, by the fact that all action taken in any but the Self-Governing Colonies must be susceptible of explanation by the Government of the day to public opinion generally at home, as expressed by the House of Commons. Where the native is ruled directly the responsibility for every action taken is clearly traceable right through from the district officer or Resident who took such action through the senior officers of the Government of the Colony up to the Secretary of State for the Colonies with whom the ultimate responsibility lies. This fact renders centralization unavoidable; every one of these officials must be in a position to show that he has not been remiss, and further to convince persons quite unacquainted with native affairs of this. The result is what a great authority—I think I am right in saying Lord Morley—has described as 'a striving after over-efficiency'. Every officer right down the service becomes over-anxious in case one of his juniors should commit, not a mistake, for such anxiety is right and proper, but what may be by any means construed as a mistake by a possibly hostile and misinformed critic. So we have a continual tendency to centralization. A Resident makes a mistake; we promptly set up a system by which neither he nor any other Resident shall ever be in a position to make such a mistake again; quite forgetting the adage that he who never committed a mistake never committed a wise act. So gradually all power becomes more and more centralized until the man who alone is in the best position to act wisely, because he is in closest touch with the native, that is to say the Resident or District Commissioner, is deprived of all opportunity to make mistakes, which is tantamount to saying that he is deprived of all opportunity of exerting any useful initiative. To a certain extent this disadvantage is a concomitant of foreign rule over native races whatever system be adopted, but misinformed ignorant criticism has far more power thus to damage a 'Directly' than an 'Indirectly' ruled native community. Public opinion, guided by a natural and very sound instinct, is more likely to think that action strange to European ideas may nevertheless be justifiable if it be performed by a native authority rather than by an alien authority. Direct Rule therefore, has a tendency to centralize authority and to render it difficult to introduce measures beneficial to the natives but strange to European ideas. Indirect Rule has an exactly contrary tendency.

To turn to another point. It is true that educated natives may be safely entrusted to fill subordinate government posts and even fairly responsible posts. The experiment has been tried, and has, to a certain extent, been successful. But there are, in my opinion, fundamental objections to the adoption of the principle. In the first place it is quite possible, nay probable, that in the process of education the native will have lost touch with native ideas and native ideals. It may very well happen that he is just as much an alien to the native communities as is the European. In that case the best to be hoped for is that he will do his work not less well than does the European on the average. Moreover, a very important point, such an educated native could only be employed in the community which bore him. I can just conceive an educated native of Kano being employed as a police officer, or assistant-district-officer in Kano Emirate, but to so employ an educated native of Lagos in Sokoto would be a blunder of inconceivable magnitude.

The number of posts which could be filled by educated natives must always remain few and must be posts which do not carry high responsibility. I will not strain the reader's capacity by asking him to imagine a native Governor of a Colony or Protectorate, but let him imagine for a moment a proposal to create an educated native of Kano Colonial Secretary of Nigeria! The proposal does not come within the bounds of practical politics. It is true that educated natives can be admitted to administrative and deliberative councils and assemblies, but, especially in the case of the Crown Colonies and Protectorates, would it be possible ever to grant them a controlling voice in such assemblies or councils? (when, that is to say, any real power of control is vested in such institutions). Why, it is not possible, in practice, to admit even unofficial Europeans in a majority into such Councils in most cases.

Under Direct Rule therefore the native, even the educated native, can never take any but a very small share in the Government. Under Indirect Rule the native can and does fill not only positions of great responsibility but the highest positions, positions which place him in the social scale on an equality with the King's representative himself. . . .[1]

In my experience the native cannot be ruled by the white man but he can be ruled by another native acting under the guidance of the white man. The white man can 'boss about' the native, there is no doubt about that, but he being in the minority and the native in the majority, the control thus exerted is very superficial. The native very

[1] The passage in ellipsis deals with questions of hygiene.

soon learns that with the exercise of a little ingenuity he can hood-wink the white man. Moreover, the native's nervous constitution is the more robust and the white man in the act of 'bossing' undergoes a process of battering highly prejudicial to his mental and bodily strength. . . .

In my opinion, people who, when considering a native question, are not able to divorce their minds from premises and deductions which are applicable to their own countrymen only, are not tempera-mentally suited to deal with native affairs. I can only say that European institutions introduced into native communities, unless they happen, as may perchance occur, indeed very often do occur, to coincide with native institutions (in which case they are redundant) are unsuited to native needs because they are not effectual in most cases; and because, though capable of modification, such modifica-tion is not necessarily in any way suited to the needs of the natives.

It may be argued by many persons well qualified by their experience of natives and native affairs to give an opinion on the subject, that although such reasoning may be valid in respect to certain native communities, as for instance the Filane Emirates in the Northern Provinces of Nigeria or the Yoruba pagan Chieftainates of the Southern Provinces, which had advanced some way along the road of civilization before they came into contact with the European, yet it is invalid when applied to the even greater sections of the native community which are more backward. 'It is all very well,' they say, 'for you to talk about native institutions. You have your Emirs with their subordinate Chiefs, with their law courts administering well-established native laws and customs, their system of collecting a public revenue by well-recognized forms of taxation, their organiza-tions for war-like purposes which they can employ also for the execution of rudimentary works of public utility. You have in short all the machinery of Government already created and at your disposal. All you have to do is to see that this machinery is used in the proper manner. Your work is to control only, not to create. How is it possible to draw any parallel between such states and the cannibal tribes of the Bauchi hills, or the intractable and primitive denizens of the forest? They have no "native institutions" as you call them. Here we have to create—not only control. Is it not reasonable in such cases to introduce at once the institutions and customs which have been proved to be of value in our own country?'

In the first place I do not admit, as I have said before, that any tribe which we find in being can have survived the struggle for existence through past centuries without an organization. In my experience it is rather the difficulties thrown by the natives themselves

E

in the way of the questioners than the absence of an organization which has led European enquirers to suppose that any native section has no organization. I submit that the very existence of certain abuses which must fill us with horror, such as the selection of victims for human sacrifice, or to feed the crocodile, or for sale as slaves, proves in the most incontrovertible manner that amongst the most savage and rudimentary peoples organizations did exist and were moreover remarkably effective. The individual in his thousands could not naturally have regarded with liking such institutions as those mentioned, seeing that he himself might be the next victim, he could only have tolerated them either because his body was restrained by some material force, or his ideas by some powerful mental control. Now such material force or mental control must surely and infallibly indicate the existence of some form of the machinery of government, that is to say, some form of machinery by which those whom we have described as marching at the head of the column of a nation as leaders succeed in imposing their wills upon the rest. It is a problem for patient study and administrative ability to solve what exactly that organization is in the first place, next to use it for the purposes of developing the character and material state of the race.

Even if a tribe can be found which has no organization, a purely hypothetical proposition in my humble opinion, then I submit that it would be far better that a European officer with the necessary qualities set to work and study the nature and the needs of that tribe, and gain a dominating influence over the minds of the more robust, physically and mentally, of its members, and that he should then, with their help, evolve an organization suited to their requirements; better this, than that a European officer, backed with material force, possibly with the necessary ability but without the necessary knowledge, be directed to introduce a series of rules and customs, the result of generations of study but especially adapted for the needs of a race in a totally different stage of civilization, probably with radically different racial characteristics. It is generally far better, I submit, to leave the tribes alone than to adopt the latter course. If it be unavoidable to coerce them materially, in order to protect their neighbours, let them at least remain uncoerced in respect to their ethics, and unmolested in their intercourse as between individuals of the same tribe.

I can perhaps best illustrate the preceding remarks by describing the work of a Resident. The duties of a Resident, a term used to designate the senior officers of the Political or Administrative branch in Nigeria, placed in charge of a native unit with directions to put into effect the principles of Indirect Rule are, it may well be supposed, of a highly responsible description, they give indeed opportunities for the exertion of any degree of administrative capacity, tact, and industry. . . .

I would state in the first place that the Resident, as administrator, is held responsible that the wheels of Government work smoothly within his jurisdiction, which is tantamount to saying that should anything go wrong in the district he will he held accountable. Should native unrest appear for any cause; should the work of the Technical Departments, such as the Public Works, Forestry, Agriculture, Mining, Postal, or any other department, be hampered in any way, such as by lack of labour, hostile attitude of the natives, scarcity of food, etc., the person who is first called upon for an explanation is the Resident. He may aptly be termed the maid-of-all-work of the Government. It rests chiefly with the Residents whether the Government is a success or the contrary, as all Government orders are conveyed to the natives by the Political Officers. I use the term all orders literally, as including orders which are given by means of Laws as well as those which take a possibly more ephemeral form and are called 'executive' orders. It is the Political Officers, and they only, who are in a position to see that these orders are carried out. I say that the success of the Government rests chiefly with them because it would not be correct to say that it rests only with them. The work of the Political department may be rendered abortive, either by a wrong orientation of the general policy laid down by the Government or by over centralization, that is to say, the curtailment of the executive power of the Residents, rendering necessary a reference of too many questions to Headquarters. Such references operate adversely in two ways, first they entail great delays in the execution of orders, secondly, they lower that moral prestige of the Resident among the natives on which he must chiefly depend as his main asset to enable him to carry out his duties successfully. Given a fairly free hand however, and a rightly directed main policy, a Resident can properly be held responsible for practically all administrative matters within the area under his jurisdiction. Moreover, beyond affording him the help that a free hand and a sound policy give Headquarters can do little to assist him, though much may be done to thwart him.

I will first briefly describe the work of a Resident placed in charge of one of the more advanced groups, such as a Filane Emirate or one of the more organized Yoruba Chieftainates. In these there exists all the machinery of a small Government. There is the Emir or Chief, in theory, his group of Councillors (the diwan of India), his District Heads who represent him, each one of whom is in administrative control of a section of natives, these in turn have under them official termed Village-Heads who are in charge of small sections; the native

Courts of Law where native law and custom are administered and where sometimes, by arrangement with the Emirs, laws and proclamations enacted by the Government are also enforced; the native administration police ('dogarai' as they are called in the Northern Provinces) who work under the orders of the Emir or District Heads as the case may be; the native administration Public Works, which keeps roads in repair, constructs rough roads, builds mud buildings, and other such elementary works; in addition sometimes native hospitals, leper camps, etc., are maintained by and at the cost of the native administration. The collection of the State revenue is in the hands of the District and Village Heads. It is exacted in the name of the Emir, one half being paid into the Government Treasury (the common fund of the Protectorate) and one half into what is generally termed in the Northern Provinces the Beit el Mal or Native Treasury. The latter is used to meet the expenses of the Native Administration which I am describing, such as the salaries of the Emir, District and Village Heads, Native Justiciary, cost of labour and material for public works, etc. Over all this machinery, over all appointments of the District Heads, Judges, etc., over expenditure, the Emir has control. The Resident, of course, has great 'influence' over the Emir, he tenders the advice of the Government and that advice must be taken. Further, as President of the Provincial Court the Resident wields great judicial powers for the repression of crime, and settlement of disputes, outside those of the Native Administration. In this capacity he also controls the Native Courts, being empowered to transfer any cause from those Courts to his own as he may think necessary. . . .

It will be seen that the influence of the Resident placed in such a position is immense and that the power he wields for good, or harm, is immense. It may even be said to be too great and that his actions should be closely controlled by Headquarters. I admit that it is a great responsibility to place in the hands of an individual and that reference to Headquarters should be insisted upon so far as is feasible, but I hold strongly that reference to Headquarters is useful only if it be strictly limited to those questions on which persons at Headquarters are in a position to arrive at valid decisions. On all other questions the decision, for better or for worse, should be left to the Resident. In a vast number of matters, and important matters, the Resident only is in a position to give a right judgement. If he cannot do so and continually blunders then he must be replaced by another more qualified. Reference *pro forma* to Headquarters is in my humble opinion wholly mischievous in almost every case. As stated above, loss of time, an important point when large territories are under consideration, is the least evil which may result. More important is the loss of prestige on the part of the Resident in the eyes of the Emir; and even more important still is the loss of prestige on the part of the Emir in the eyes of the people. As I shall proceed to explain it is essential for the success of Indirect Rule that the European control be kept in the background and the prestige of the Native Administration be maintained. If the Emir and the Resident are together called upon to obtain sanction from a higher power before they can perform the least administrative act, or spend the smallest sum of public money, what prestige can the Emir enjoy in the eyes of the natives generally?

The office of an Emir or great native Chief before we occupied the country conferred great dignity and power on the holder, so long as he could keep order among his subordinate Chiefs. His position was one of some delicacy however, as it was often necessary for him to restrain those very Chiefs from acts of oppression on whose support he depended to enable him to control the populace, and to defend him from any usurper who might appear or from outside invasion. This state of dependency did much to restrain the Emir himself from tyrannous action and introduced to a certain extent the wholesome constraint of public opinion which safeguards a people from the oppression of its rulers. . . .

In many ways the native communities of the larger Emirates were advancing, and slowly but surely evolving a civilization of their own. Since the occupation of these territories we have in the Northern Provinces of Nigeria in a great measure supported the Emirs and Chiefs and to a limited extent in the Southern Provinces also. In my opinion we should continue to do so and to an ever increasing extent.

The position of an Emir has, since the occupation, changed in one all-important feature. He is no longer subject to the influence of the public opinion of others of his kind, nor has he to trim his sails and to modify his actions accordingly. He is securely seated on his throne operating from afar and quite outside all local influence. It is this foreign power only that he need propitiate in order to enable him to preserve his possessions and office. This is by no means a good thing for him or for his people and, unless the disadvantage can be made good in other directions, must operate as a drag on the moral advancement of the Chief and his subjects. The Resident in charge of the Province takes the place of the influence of public opinion as a controlling force over the Emir's actions to keep him on the right track.

The carrying out of all these duties satisfactorily gives great scope for administrative capacity on the part of the Resident. His main object, one which he must ever bear in mind, is to create a situation resembling as far as possible that which existed, or might be imagined to have existed, were a thoroughly able, well-meaning, liberal-minded Emir ruling over a unit untouched by foreign influence. He must as far as possible keep his authority in the background and concealed, if not from the Emir and his immediate entourage, at all events from the people generally. At the same time he must be on the alert to stamp out and if possible forestall the growth of the thousand and one measures by which oppression and malpractices can be exercised. When abuses arise he must put an end to them, not by outward and visible acts of his own, generally speaking, but by causing the Emir to move in the right direction. To do this he must be well and fully informed as to all that is going on among the people, that is to say he must be in touch with the people; he must get his knowledge at first hand; it follows that he must be readily accessible to the common folk. At the same time he has to be on his guard lest by so doing he should encourage the people to despise their own Courts and thus impair the authority and prestige of the Emir. Should he fall into this error he will, as a first result, place the Emir in a difficult position, lessen his power over his people, and engender hostility in his breast towards the European administration; and as a second result find himself spending hour after hour, day after day, settling the ownership of a goat, a fowl, or a native robe worth five shillings.

It may readily be supposed that this keeping in touch with the people without impairing the authority of the Emir and consequently of the whole native administration, is no easy task, and one on which any amount of administrative tact and ability can be exerted. It is generally the case that the Resident has to deal with an Emir or Chief possessed of an extremely sensitive character, not by any means always inclined to play a fair game, or averse to doing a little extortion for his personal advantage; with a group of powerful subordinate Chiefs, each of whom is playing for his own hand, greedy of power, as jealous and sensitive as the Emir himself, and all too prone to take advantage of any opportunity given them to play off the Resident against the Emir and to commit acts of oppression if they see their way to debarring the Resident from contact with the common people; and last, but not least, with a populace prone to vacillate between two extremes, either to bring frivolous complaints against their Chiefs or to submit without complaint to surprising exactions. It will be evident also that the Resident must keep himself in the background, resist the temptation to become a popular hero with the people (a comparatively easy thing to do), to fill the position of a big native chief, to wear, figuratively speaking, the turban of the Emir, a temptation to which human nature renders him susceptible.

But, on the other hand he must be a living force, regarded with confidence by the people as their protector in the last resort, and with respect by the Emir and his Chiefs, who must feel that they cannot throw dust in his eyes, but that at the same time they can rely on him to support them in the exercise of their legitimate authority.

Of all the qualifications necessary to a Resident, I think the first to be an inborn sympathy and liking for the native and his affairs. This may be said to be rather a trait in character, or an instinct, than a qualification. Next after this by far the most important qualification, more important far than special industry or special facility in acquiring native languages for example, is a sense of proportion. To recognize where a reform is urgently required and must be effected at any cost, or where it may be postponed, or where it may be counted on to effect itself without outside influence, and, perhaps most important of all, to be able to recognize the fact that certain reforms would be beneficial could they be effected but that it is not possible to effect them at all; to be able to arrive at a right decision on such points as these is what is chiefly required of a Resident. He must be able to decide rightly whether a native chief's first offence should be punished, or whether patience should be exerted until he has offended ten, nay twenty times—either course may be the right one, it depends entirely on circumstances. He must be able to judge not only when and how, but where his weight should be applied. It is of no avail for instance for him to waste his time forming the character of a native of mean nature and meagre capacity, who will never in any case carry other natives with him, but he must conserve his force for moulding characters naturally apt and qualified to exert a widespread influence.

Such being the principal work which the Resident is called upon to perform under the system of Indirect Rule, it will be seen that he can receive little help from outside sources, excepting in so far as he receives general instructions as to the policy adopted by the Government. Clear and distinct instructions as to the general trend of policy, he should, I think, receive and, I need hardly add, carry out strictly. But outside interference with the mode of carrying out that policy, and as to what action should be taken in a special case, can rarely, if ever, be of assistance to him. It is necessary to insist on this point, even at the cost of repetition. So subtle are often the bases on which he arrives at a decision that he may sometimes find considerable difficulty in making a good case on paper for some action he may have taken, even though he feels, and subsequent events may prove, that action to have been perfectly correct. In my humble opinion he should not be called upon for such justifications. The general well-being, or not, of the native group should be the justification or condemnation of his conduct of affairs. . . .

To turn to the case of a Resident in charge of a unit less advanced than are most of the Filane Emirates. Here it may be thought that the Resident should mount a higher pedestal, and bulk larger in the eyes of the people. This is true in the case of very primitive peoples when the 'prestige of the white man' must first be established, but when that preliminary stage is passed it is even more important for the Resident to conceal from the people that it is his hand that guides the ship than in the case of a Filane Emirate. In the primitive groups it is unavoidable that he interfere more with the tribal institutions than is the case in the more advanced sections. Their habits are more at variance with humanity and reason. So the Resident finds it necessary to interfere, and all such interference weakens the hold of the Chief or Elders of the tribe as the case may be. It is, therefore, doubly important for him, once the preliminary stage is past, to avoid the temptation of posing as a great native chief. The true measure of his success will be the respect and regard with which the populace hold their own Chiefs and Elders, and not him, combined with general good relations between the private individuals which compose the clan, and the general prosperity of the unit. This is a hard lesson to instil into the mind of many a political officer. The desire to bulk large in the eyes of a native population is a very natural temptation to fall into, and indeed it is a very laudable ambition, but where the policy of Government is to rule indirectly the political officer must be satisfied with the knowledge, locked securely in his own breast, that he is very important to the native population although they are not aware of it.

What I have written applies to every political officer in charge of a unit, not necessarily to the Resident of a Province only. . . .

Under the system of Indirect Rule, the European officer, by his influence in guiding and controlling the native leaders, if his work be properly performed, can wield an enormous power for good in the destinies of the section of which he is in charge. The power thus exerted is infinitely greater in scope than any power or influence which it can be hoped that he will exert under the contrary system of Direct Rule. If the conditions were entirely altered, and, as I have said before, we could divide the natives up into groups the size of a company of soldiers and place a political officer in charge of each, and if the climate of Equatorial Africa were completely different and European officers could stay out for many years at a stretch without being compelled to break the continuity of their service every twelve or eighteen months; if, in short, the premises were all quite different, then there might be something to say in favour of Direct Rule. But we have to take things as they are.

I assume as a postulate the influence exerted by a European official over the natives of whom he is in charge to be the most important administrative asset. The opening up of new markets and the spreading of commerce, the provision of means of transport, railways, ships, etc., all these are matters of the highest importance from the point of view of the administrator, but I submit that they are, when we are gauging our duties and responsibilities as a whole, a secondary consideration. It is our first duty, I take it, to ensure that our rule operates as an elevating and not a degrading force on the characters of those subject races, the direction of whose affairs we have assumed. We may take the son of a Kano farmer and make him a highly skilled mechanic, or even turn him into a barrister (a vocation for which the native mind alas! is only too suited), we may enable him thus to earn what for him may be termed fabulous wealth, yet, if we have in the process damaged the mental and moral side of his character we shall have failed to discharge our first responsibility towards the man himself, and towards the community to which he belongs. It had been, I hold, far better for all concerned to have left him in a state of comparative simplicity, to bring up a family and to carry on elementary but all important work.

Granted this postulate and regarding as all important the influence of the European character over the native character, I submit that it can be more effectually exerted through Indirect Rule, as stated above, than through Direct Rule. Indeed, I do not admit that such influence can be exerted to any appreciable extent under a system of Direct Rule, in the peculiar conditions of climate and the relative numerical proportions of white man to native imposed thereby. Take a well-organized native group such as the Emirate of Kano for example, where two million persons are ruled indirectly through the native Emir and his attendant sequence of native institutions, and say that you decide that you really cannot put up any longer with with their inefficiency. I grant that there are weak points, only too many. The native judges do take bribes at time and sometimes have to be punished for so doing; but did judges never take bribes in our own country? Not the Emir, for he is by now far too shrewd and knows very well which side his bread is buttered, but some of his Chiefs are spending rather larger sums on their retinues when they visit the Durbars and in the entertainment of their brother Chiefs, than we think they could possibly afford to do were their gains strictly limited to the official salaries paid by the Emir, all of which are set forth in printed estimates annually. We have reason to suppose, nay, to know, that even in this, the most advanced of the Filane Emirates, a certain amount of peculation of public funds, before they reach the Treasury, takes place, that certain native officials who to outward appearances leave nothing to be desired in respect to ability and zeal have still, concealed under their robes, a sticky patch on their palms to which public funds, bribes and other illegitimate gains are liable to attach themselves. But we know also that these phenomena have not always been confined to natives of Africa. We know that the palms are far less sticky than they were a few years ago; we confidently hope that in course of time these phenomena will become as rare as they are in our own country. But say, for purposes of argument, that we decide that we cannot put up with this any longer. 'Away with all this corruption. Decentralize the Emirate; divide it up into districts, as many as your political staff will allow, put clean-minded, clean-living young Englishmen in charge of each district, then you will have a pure administration, then the European character coming into contact at many more points with the individual natives will really have an opportunity of modifying it.' A charming picture, but is it in accordance with facts? I contend that it is nothing of the sort. In the first place your staff of young Englishmen will be strictly limited by questions of finance. It is true that the funds of the native administrations thus abolished will be available and that the European staff could be increased accordingly, but this increase will not so alter the numerical proportion of white to black as to become a governing factor in the situation, or indeed a factor which can be taken into account at all. For the purpose of this argument it makes no difference whatever if you have one European for 200,000, for 100,000 or for 20,000 natives for that matter. A European officer cannot exert a personal influence on the characters of more than one hundred to two hundred natives. If the natives so affected should be, as they are in the existing state of affairs where the Native Administration is retained in full swing, in positions to influence in their turn other natives, then a political officer's influence is magnified by a natural process a thousandfold. If, on the contrary, they are not so placed, then whatever influence the political officer may have over the few with whom he can come into close contact becomes a mere drop in the bucket and is lost in the mass.

Moreover, the native very soon detects this and comes to regard the white man as a person of really very little importance, as in point of fact placed in such circumstances, he is. Hence, you find the phenomenon, very well recognized to exist, that whereas in communities governed by native institutions the white man, *qua* white man, is regarded with great respect, in those districts where the native administrations have been swept away he is regarded as a person of no very great significance.

But even more important than the loss of any material influence of the European over the native mind is the fact that once the native institutions are overthrown; once the Native Chief or Emir, with his picturesque surroundings, his gaily caparisoned, or even gaudily dressed cortege, so dear to the native eye, and which appeals so strongly to his reason and judgement as to what is right and proper, disappear, and are replaced by the, to him, uninspiring formalities and repulsively cold and precise methods of direct European rule— once the dignified circumlocution, which in his eyes it is meet and proper should accompany all important transactions, gives place to the brief and dried formulas of British official practice, and above all once the truth dawns upon him that it lies well within his power, if he do but exert a little of the ingenuity with which nature has gifted him, to throw dust in the eyes of this once mysterious but really quite insignificant and impotent stranger sitting aloft on a pinnacle above him; to bribe, league with, intrigue with, such of his interpreters, political agents and police as are dishonest; to concoct successfully false accusations, to intimidate and even to poison such as are honest, and to misbehave generally under the white man's rule, in a way that he would never have dared to do under his own institutions, then indeed does a dry-rot set in—discipline goes to the wall *vis-à-vis* the higher powers. As a natural corollary, the discipline of the children *vis-à-vis* their parents, the bed-rock of all African well-being, disappears also. This disappearance of the power of the head of the household over its members is a well-established, well-recognized incontrovertible fact deplored by Africans even more than by Europeans, in all those districts where the native administrations have been swept away.

Having stated the reasons which in my opinion render Indirect Rule the only means by which we can properly discharge the immense burden and moral obligation towards native races which we have, of our own accord and without any compulsion, assumed, I would only add a plea that the highest authorities should in respect to each group come to some decision as to the general lines on which that group should be governed and instruct the political officers accordingly. Personally, I think that by following the principles of Direct Rule we land the Natives, and ourselves, into a *cul-de-sac* from which it will be hard to escape. But at all events we march more or less in order. Where there is no policy we land in the same *impasse*, but in a state of great disorder, which it will be even more difficult to rectify. . . .

Two administrative difficulties may be cited in adopting the policy of Indirect Rule in every case. It may be said: 'I agree with a good many of the arguments that you have adduced in connection with Indirect Rule, but there are two obstacles which will render the adoption in many cases impossible.

'First, how are you going to introduce the many modern improvements necessary to ensure economic prosperity into districts so governed? It would be all very well if you could keep your native units detached from the rest of the world, under glass covers as it were, but to do so would seriously handicap their material prosperity. Railways, for instance, how are they to be constructed? Roads too? The native staff at the disposal of the Emir is incapable of effecting such improvements unless educated in Europe and thus denationalized, as you call it. Moreover, there are certain duties which, even were they so educated, they could not perform and for which a European staff is necessary. How are you going to get over this difficulty? Do you propose that the Native Administrations should be permitted by the protecting Government to employ, promote, and dismiss Europeans? Surely this would be inexpedient. Next, what do you propose to do with those areas which have been already for many years under Direct Rule, and where the native institutions have been already eradicated, and where it would be difficult if not impossible to resuscitate them?'

These two obstacles I freely admit are difficult to surmount. Before discussing them I would insist upon the fact that in no country has the art of Government reached such a stage of perfection as to merit the name of an exact science. All Governments have to admit the necessity of the toleration of inconsistencies in practice, of the adoption of principles apparently contrary, and the existence side by side of theories which if carried to their logical conclusions in practice would be in exact opposition to each other. I adhere to the statement in another paragraph that ultimately the Native Administrations could be entrusted with all affairs connected with the internal administration of their territories, including the construction of large public works and the employment of Europeans where necessary. The national spirit once it has grown robust under the fostering care of a paternal Government would be strong enough to permit of natives receiving European technical education without destroying the influence of their own homes. That would be in the more or less remote future, however. Meanwhile, the wheels of progress cannot be stopped and I freely admit that it is a difficult matter to meet the problem in such a manner as to solve the requirements of modern civilization and the imperative necessity of preserving the hold of native institutions over the minds of the natives. To a certain extent at the present stage of the development of the native institutions it is sometimes necessary to employ the methods of Direct Rule in ruling those natives who are in the employ of the

Government and, to a certain extent also, those in the employ of non-official Europeans, so that it may be at times unavoidable that small areas should be administered under Direct Rule, which are dove-tailed into the mass governed by the methods of Indirect Rule. This constitutes a difficulty. The solution of this difficulty is to create native authorities to deal with some matters even in directly ruled districts. A certain duality of control will thus occur and this is regrettable, but perhaps unavoidable for a time. The difficulties in respect to small directly ruled areas existing alongside of large indirectly ruled areas need not, however, be so great as they sometimes are. To avoid them it is only necessary that the administrative officers in charge of the directly ruled enclaves should work with the officers in charge of the indirectly ruled areas, and especially that the officers in charge of the technical departments which employ large quantities of native labour should work with, not against, the policy of Indirect Rule. . . .

How often have I after passing in review the work of some of our native clerks in government service, or transacting business with denationalized natives of the non-official classes, thought to how great an extent the man's energies and talents, character and ability were being wasted. How infinitely greater would be the services which he would render the community, how infinitely greater would be his own contentment were he filling the post of leader of native thought and development for which nature had intended him.

To turn to the question of the employment of Europeans by the Native Administrations, I agree that it is highly inexpedient at the present moment that they should be so employed. It is of no use to make any bones about it—the 'prestige of the white man', to use that hackneyed phrase, must be maintained. If the native is not imbued with a thorough respect for the white man he rapidly flies to the other extreme; further, he loses respect for the native institutions, and chaos results. This obstacle is not by any means insurmountable, however. There is no reason why the Native Administrations should not be lent European officers by the Government for the execution of public works, for instance; their costs being defrayed in bulk by the Native Administrations. Such European officers would work either as Heads of their own Departments or they would be under the general control of the Head of the corresponding Government Department. Such an arrangement would be easy of management so long as, and it is again very necessary to insist on this point, the officers of the Government generally speaking (not only administrative officers but those in the technical departments also) loyally support the Government policy of Indirect Rule. That is to say, loyally assist and support the Native Administrations. It should, again, be unnecessary to labour this point, nevertheless, it is an undoubted fact that, especially when the Government adopts a wobbling policy, there is a tendency for the officers of the technical departments whose work does not bring them into close contact with native affairs, except to a minor degree and in respect to their own employees, to regard the native institutions with a great measure of contempt. The conditions which they consider necessary to prove the existence of a sound policy and an efficient administration are that labour, skilled and unskilled, and also food, should be plentiful and cheap. Those two conditions satisfied, they are, with rare exceptions, willing to put up with or close their eyes to, any amount of moral and physical degeneration among the natives generally; at least, that is my experience.

There is yet a further question which may very reasonably be asked. The enquirer may say 'I admit that a strong case is made out for "Ruling Indirectly", but I still have some doubts in my mind as to the validity of your arguments and the practicability of what you propose. You said in the beginning of this discussion that we must look to the future, even the obscure future. I now ask you to do this. What is to be the upshot? You have said that we cannot check the development of the native population, that we can only guide—hindering or assisting it. What do you forecast as to the future of the natives if "Ruled Indirectly"?' To this I would reply that by means of Indirect Rule you can so allow natural conditions to exert their influence in a manner modified to meet the requirements of the native group that in due course of time it will become robust enough to stand by itself. 'Then you actually mean to propose,' the horrified enquirer may be imagined to say, 'that we should withdraw or prepare to withdraw from the control of the magnificent Empire which we have inherited? In short, you are a "Little Englander" '.

If by this expression is meant a person who would limit the scope of British ideals and would urge that the nation should voluntarily sacrifice the commanding position which it holds, and which enables it to extend and spread the influence of those ideals, I repudiate the charge. But I freely confess that I do not believe that a process which has been repeated so often in history that it would appear to be a natural law will not in course of time affect our rule as it has affected the rule of the empires of the past unless we take steps to avert such a disaster. I mean that I do not believe that one race can remain subject to another for an indefinite length of time. I hold strongly that fusion, extermination, or the reclamation of liberty of action must, sooner or later, be the destiny of the subject race. At the same time, I do not see why in due course, if proper use is made of native institutions, whose races which are now subject should not take their places in the ranks of that group of allied nations, as they may I think rightly be called, which forms the British Empire. In this manner only, I strongly hold, can complications of the most serious description, gravely threatening to the well being, and even to the existence, of the Empire be avoided in the future; only in this manner can we discharge our moral obligations to the natives, a consideration to which we are bound to give precedence over all others, and next preserve our own best interests. I see no reason whatsoever, to take the more organized Filane Emirates and Yoruba Chieftainates as examples, why some of the more advanced communities should not enjoy many of the advantages of self-government today, and why powers equal to those wielded in respect to the management of internal and domestic affairs by the Self-Governing Colonies could not, if the policy of Indirect Rule should be consistently and intelligently applied, be granted to such units within one or two generations. In the case of those groups which are less advanced today the process will take longer, but that is all the difference.

1918 (1906): LUGARD'S POLITICAL MEMORANDA

The extracts are taken from four of the thirteen memoranda that comprise Lugard's REVISION OF INSTRUCTIONS TO POLITICAL OFFICERS ON SUBJECTS CHIEFLY POLITICAL AND ADMINISTRATIVE, London, 1919, commonly known as POLITICAL MEMORANDA, 1918 [sic].[1] The actual memoranda quoted are:—

I.   Duties of Political Officers and Miscellaneous Subjects, pp. 9–40.
IV. Education, pp. 123–164.
V.   Taxation, pp. 105–216.
IX. Native Administration, pp. 296–339.

MEMO. NO. IX
NATIVE ADMINISTRATION

PART I. NATIVE RULERS AND THE SUZERAIN POWER

'INDIRECT RULE' IN NORTHERN NIGERIA

1. The cardinal principle upon which the Administration of Northern Nigeria was based was what has been commonly called 'Indirect Rule', viz., rule through the Native Chiefs, who are regarded as an integral part of the machinery of Government, with well defined powers and functions recognized by Government and by law, and not dependent on the caprice of an Executive Officer.

OPPOSING THEORIES IN 1903–1904

2. There were many—perhaps a majority—who, when this policy was first inaugurated, were opposed to it, and thought, not without reason, that it was hopeless to expect to develop good rulers out of the existing Moslem Emirs, who had been accustomed all their lives to wield unlimited and despotic power, the exercise of which —owing to the decay of religious restraints—had degenerated into tyranny and gross oppression of the lower classes.

While some few were inclined to the view that the Fulani rule should not only be maintained, but should be extended over hitherto independent Pagan tribes, others thought it should be superseded by re-establishing the pre-existing non-alien rulers (Habe) under direct British administration. 'Both views (I wrote) have found strong

[1] I have retained, in these extracts, all Lugard's oddities of style, punctuation, capitalization, etc. Even in the oath of appointment, he had no time for such trimmings as the deliberate avoidance of a split infinitive!

supporters. The arguments for the former are that the Fulani are a ruling caste, far more able than the indigenous peoples; that their organization is singularly complete and effective, and adapted to the requirements of the country; that, shorn of evils which are not necessarily inherent in it, such as slave-raiding and slave-trading, bribery in the administration of justice, and punishment by mutilation, etc., it would be not merely the best rule obtainable, but a model for our guidance, and hence that it would be advantageous to support it in every way, to restore to Fulani rule Pagan tribes who have revolted, and even to extend it over outlying Pagan tribes.

'The other view is that the Pagan tribes, who have a passionate love of liberty, and will fight (and have fought) almost to extermination in defence of it, are entitled to their independence under British rule, and that it would be an act of injustice on the part of Government to place them under the heel of the Fulani by the aid of our maxim guns; that the Fulani are an effete race no longer able to fight and to maintain their control; that their love of slavery is ingrained in them, and bribery and extortion can never be eradicated; that however much by deceit and *munafiki* they may bend to the pressure of force and pretend to carry out British ideas, they do, and always will, resent the curtailment of their despotic rule, and loathe us in their hearts; that it is impossible for us to prevent the secret oppression which they will always continue to inflict on their Pagan vassals; that, since they are Mohammedans, our support of their rule is tantamount to an enormous aid to the spread of the Mohammedan religion, subject as it is to waves of fanaticism, and to co-operation with the great forces of Islam outside this Protectorate, and susceptible to the influences which those forces may exert in the direction of rebellion; that safety in so vast a country, controlled by a handful of British, lies in the maxim *Divide et Impera*; and, finally, that the Pagan is a better man than the *soi-disant* Mohammedan, less treacherous and less deceitful, and capable of progress on his own lines.'

POLICY LAID DOWN FOR NORTHERN NIGERIA

3. It was necessary that a definite and clear policy should be laid down at the head of the Government. . . . The policy thus inaugurated may be briefly stated as follows:—

(a) *Support of Chiefs*

The *de facto* rulers who after the British conquest of Northern Nigeria had been reinstated or appointed to the various Emirates, and all other *de facto* Chiefs who had been recognized by Government, were to be supported in every way and their authority upheld.

F

Already it had been laid down that it was the duty of a Resident to rule through the Chiefs, to endeavour to educate them in the duties of rulers, to seek their co-operation and to maintain their prestige.

(b) *Independent Pagans to remain free*

It was laid down, however, that no independent or revolted Pagan tribes were to be included in the jurisdiction of a Moslem ruler without the express sanction of the Governor.

(c) *Limitation of powers of Native rulers*

The Native Chiefs thus recognized were not to be regarded as independent rulers. They were the delegates of the Governor whose representative was the Resident. The Central Government reserved to itself the sole right to raise and control armed forces, to impose taxation of any kind, to make laws and to dispose of such lands as are, under Native law and custom, vested in the paramount power. These limitations were specifically set out in the letter of appointment under which each Chief of the higher grades held his office.

ANTICIPATIONS AND RESULTS

4. Subject to these limitations it was the declared policy of the Government to restore to the Chiefs the prestige and authority which they had lost by the British conquest, or forfeited by their own previous maladministration. I was not myself very hopeful of far-reaching reform among the men who had for a lifetime been used to other methods, and who would necessarily chafe under the restraints imposed by British rule and the curtailment of their despotic power. 'It is from the rising generation that we must hope to produce the elements of real progress and enlightenment.' It stands to the immense credit of the Administrative Staff in the North, as well as to the qualities of the Moslem rulers themselves, that so much progress has been achieved in so short a space of time.

JUSTIFICATION OF POLICY

5. I justified the adoption of this policy—as against those who regarded it with misgiving—by three arguments in particular:

(a) That the Political Staff available for the administration of so vast a country, inhabited by many millions, must always be inadequate for complete British administration in the proper sense of the word, and that it was, therefore, imperative to utilize and improve the existing machinery.

(b) By the example of the loyalty and progress made in the Protected States of India under the sympathetic guidance and control of Residents—though it will be noted that the status of the Chiefs in Nigeria differs fundamentally from the Independent Native States in India.

(c) By the obvious folly of 'attempting any drastic reform which would cause a dislocation of methods which, however faulty, have the sanction of traditional usage, and are acquiesced in by the people, until we had an increased knowledge both of Moslem methods of rule and of Native law and custom.'

The policy to which I have referred is now well understood in the Northern Provinces, but I propose in this Memo. to recapitulate its principles, both for the instruction of newly-appointed Officers, and in view of its extension to the Southern Provinces.

POSITION AND AUTHORITY OF CHIEFS TO BE UPHELD

6. 'The prestige and influence of the Chiefs (I wrote) can be best upheld by letting the peasantry see that the Government itself treats them as an integral part of the machinery of the administration. That there are not two sets of rulers—British and Native—working either separately or in co-operation, but a single Government in which the Native Chiefs have well-defined duties and an acknowledged status equally with the British officials. Their duties should never conflict, and should overlap as little as possible; they should be complementary to each other, and the Chief himself must understand that he has no right to his place and power unless he renders his proper services to the State. . . . It is obviously desirable that Government should be called upon as rarely as possible to intervene between the Chiefs and people, for if a Native Chief has lost prestige and influence to such a degree that he has to appeal to Government to enforce his order, he becomes not merely useless but a source of weakness to the Administration.' This does not of course mean that any community may by appealing to Government throw off its allegiance to its Chief, or that mere unpopularity, which may be due to the exercise of very necessary discipline, forms any grounds for the deposition of a Chief.

STATUTORY POWERS OF NATIVE AUTHORITY

7. The position and authority of 'recognized Chiefs' has been safeguarded by several enactments. The Native Courts Ordinance enforces Native law and custom, confers on Native Tribunals powers of arrest, and imposes upon them the duty of maintaining order. They may make Rules with the concurrence of the Head Chief, and the approval of the Governor, with the object of adding to Native customary law, so as to enable the Courts to take cognizance of offences against particular Ordinances which are not offences

against Native law, and otherwise to maintain good order, and to promote the welfare of the Natives. In the more advanced communities it establishes a Judicial Council of which the paramount Chief is President, and which may be vested with large executive powers by the Governor. Among less advanced tribes the local Chief sits with others as Head of the Native Court of his district.

The Land and Native Rights Ordinance vests the control over all Native lands in the Governor, and he alone can authorize the use and occupation of Native lands by persons who are not Natives of the Northern Provinces. The occupation of Native lands by Natives of the Northern Provinces is, however, in practice controlled through the Chiefs who, acting as delegates of the Governor, are guided by the Native law and custom governing the occupation and use of land.

Under the Native Revenue Ordinance, the Chief is recognized as the authority to whom the taxes or tribute are due, and is directed to pay a portion into General Revenue and the remainder into the Native Treasury, and the position and powers of the District and Village Headmen through whom they are collected are set out.

But the Ordinance which most directly secures the position of the Chiefs is the Native Authority Ordinance. A Chief appointed under this Ordinance to be the Native Authority is constituted the guardian of public order in the area to which he is appointed, and is vested with powers over all Natives residing in that area. The provisions of this Ordinance are dealt with in detail in the next paragraph.

These laws constitute the charter of the 'Native Administration' by giving a legal status to the Chiefs and vesting in them powers enforceable in the Courts, of which they cannot be deprived by arbitrary action.

NECESSITY FOR DELEGATION OF POWERS BY CHIEFS

9. Naturally one of the greatest difficulties in re-organizing Native rule has been to convince the Head Chief of the necessity of delegating authority to District Headmen, and the creation of these district authorities was viewed at first with much misgiving and dislike by the Emirs. They have, I think, now learnt to recognize that their authority has in no way been decreased, and that effective Administration is impossible without delegation. This cardinal fact should be constantly impressed upon them, for it is natural that a capable ruler, keenly interested in his work, should exhibit a tendency to keep too much in his own hands. It is perhaps superfluous to add that delegation must be exercised with discrimination, for if extended powers are conferred upon an office because the particular holder happens to be an exceptionally able man, it will inevitably happen that his less able successor will fail—perhaps with disastrous results.

ALIENS, CONVERTS AND OTHERS

10. It may perhaps be well to add here, that any Native alien from another part of Nigeria, or elsewhere, who by permission has taken up his residence in a Native community, must accept the authority of the Chiefs, and the jurisdiction of the Native Court. If he is not usually amenable to such Courts he has the option of residing in the nearest Township.

Natives who have become converts to Christianity, or Natives in a Pagan community who have become Moslems, are not thereby in any way released from the authority of the Chiefs and Native Courts, and any tendency to exclusiveness should be discouraged, nor can any Society—secret or otherwise—confer any exemption or immunity upon its members.

EXECUTIVE PUNISHMENTS BY CHIEFS

11. A Chief is not now authorized to impose fines or imprisonment at will, and collective fines inflicted on a community must be dealt with as laid down in the Collective Punishment Ordinance. It must be impressed upon the Chiefs that every serious case must be taken before a Court. Fines must never be imposed except by a Court, by which they are paid into the Treasury. By upholding the authority of the Chiefs, down to the Village Head, there is no doubt that crime is reduced. District Officers when on tour should take particular pains to see that these principles are carried out.

RECOGNIZED CHIEFS AND NATIVE AUTHORITIES

12. A 'Native Authority' is defined as any Chief or other Native so appointed by the Governor, and a 'Recognized Chief' is one whose status has been formally recognized by Government.

It is necessary that the status of a Chief[1] . . . should be created and defined by some specific act. All Chiefs of the 1st and 2nd grades must be gazetted with the approval of the Governor. By Government Notice all chiefs of these grades are appointed 'Native Authorities' for the areas over which they are recognized as Chiefs, and power is delegated to them to appoint subordinate Chiefs as Native Authorities (of course with the approval of the Resident) within those areas.

Where there is no Chief of the 1st or 2nd Class, 'recognition' and appointment as a Native Authority must be conferred by the Resident. There is no need for the names to be Gazetted, but the lists will be recorded in the Secretariat and the Provincial Office, in case it should be necessary to prove in a Court of Law that his actions were warranted by his status as a Chief.

[1] The title was defined in the Interpretation Ordinance.

It will be noted that a 'Native Tribunal' may be constituted as a 'Native Authority'. This will only be done in the case of such primitive tribes as have not yet emerged from the family or patriarchal stage, and among whom there is no individual at all capable of exercising the authority of a Chief. The Native Authority is the Executive Power, as distinct from the Native Courts (the Judicial Power), and it is only in the most backward communities that the two should be combined.

INDEPENDENCE OF FREE TRIBES PRESERVED

13. The second head of the system described in para. 3 referred to the maintenance of the independence of those tribes who had maintained their liberty against the Moslem conquerors. It is no part of the policy of this Protectorate to place these tribes forcibly under Moslem rule (which in practice means their conversion to the Moslem faith) even though that rule may be more advanced and intelligent than anything they are as yet capable of evolving for themselves. 'Good government is no equivalent for self-government,' and though the more direct British administration, which is temporarily necessary among these primitive tribes, is not self-government, its aim is to develop among them the same measure of self-government as is accorded to the Moslem States, to foster their own institutions and to refrain from turning them into Moslems by imposing Moslem rule upon them—or even by the more insidious process of appointing Mohammedans as their Chiefs, or as Judges for their Courts, or teachers for their schools, while nominally allowing them independence. My successor, Sir P. Girouard, wavered in this view, and while leaning towards the principle of placing Moslem Chiefs over these tribes, concludes with the words 'whether it would be politic or not is another matter'.

VERDICT OF EMIR OF YOLA

14. A very striking illustration of the way in which the policy laid down in my Memo. appealed to the Native mind (and incidentally of the breadth of view of the Fulani rulers) is afforded by a letter written by the Emir of Yola after a tour in 1913 among the Pagan tribes in that Province, who had been placed under Moslem rule. Pagans (he wrote) should be governed by a Pagan, even when included in an Emirate, if they are a district of their own. 'The nominal Moslem District Head should constantly tour among them, and visit them at all times except at tax-time, when he should only go if the Pagan Chief could not collect by himself. If you put a Fulani to live all the time amongst them and build a Fulani town, they think you are trying to make them Fulani and Mohammedans,

and they resent this.' To this the Waziri added 'as the British govern us through ourselves, so we must govern the Pagans, through their own Chiefs. If we think we can deal direct with the Pagan peasantry we are deceived. We should know nothing of what was really going on, and so should do no good.' The Resident reported that the Emir and his Council had added that as soon as a Fulani District Headman got over his fear of the Pagans his hereditary instinct to treat them as slaves asserted itself, with the result that he would either be murdered or tried for oppression.

This testimony is the more remarkable since it would seem that in that Province the Government policy with regard to Pagans had not been followed and the views expressed were apparently therefore opposed to the policy of the Resident. Independent Pagan tribes had been placed under the Fulani rule with five consecutive cases of failure. The views of the Emir and his Waziri show a very striking appreciation of the policy of Government.

PRESSURE OF POPULATION

15. Cases may arise where the pressure of population in a district under Moslem rule has become very great, while adjacent lands belonging to a Pagan tribe are lying waste. In these circumstances, it may be justifiable to include a portion of such lands in the Emirate, with the prior approval of the Governor. The Pagan community will be informed, and any representations they may have to make will be submitted.

LIMITATION OF POWERS OF NATIVE RULERS

16. The third head in paragraph 3 deals with the status of the Native Administrations ruled over by paramount Chiefs *vis-à-vis* the Suzerain or Protecting Power. 'I have observed (writes Sir P. Girouard) a tendency in some directions to impress Emirs with the idea that they are sovereign rulers over independent States. I must strongly insist that such action is most unwise, and might prove disastrous. I have impressed upon Emirs that they are my Wakils in their emirates, but they must be guided by the word of the Resident, who speaks for me. . . . If we are to have Native Administration, the use of the Fulani and Kanembu would appear to be inevitable, not as ruling Sovereigns or Princes, but as Governors, which is all they are entitled to claim by their own faith.' He goes on to claim for the British Raj the right to determine boundaries of emirates, and 'to be trustee for the people in all matters affecting general interest, and particularly land'. The title of 'Emir'—or 'Amir'—indicates that these Head Chiefs, though servants of the Government, amenable to all the laws of Nigeria, and liable to removal in case of treason

or other sufficient cause, are the trusted Governors of their 'Emirates', and the Government will deal with all Chiefs and peoples subordinate to them solely through their agency.

I lay great stress on the position of the Emir as a 'Wakil' or Governor under the Suzerain power, for it is the basis, as my successor rightly perceived, of the whole structure of the Native Administration in Nigeria. Nor is there any need for me here to discuss the position of Native rulers in that very elastic and nebulous thing called a 'British Protectorate'. Suffice it to say that whatever may be the evolution of the future, there can be no question but that British guidance and control will be required for many years—possibly generations—to come.

(a) *Control of armed forces*

17. The main points on which I laid emphasis were very briefly the following:—

Let us set aside, as being beyond question, the absolute loyalty of the leading Native rulers—it remains to consider whether in a moment of religious or secular excitement, they themselves would be able to control the excitable material of which African forces are made up. Above all there has not yet been created, and will not be for many years, among Native rulers, that appreciation and application of military discipline, which alone renders the existence of armed forces a safeguard and not a menace to the civil population.

My successor differed, he said, from my policy only in the question of the value of Native Police. There is, however, no difference between us. *Dogarai* (or *Iranse* or *Olopa*) are not armed forces.[1] I welcome them as an invaluable aid to the Native Administration.

(b) *Levying taxes, &c.*

18. The Central Government has the responsibility of adjusting the burden of taxation, direct or indirect, between the Non-Native and Native, and between the Natives of the North and South. Moreover, this is a right universally admitted to be an attribute of independence. . . .

(c) *Power of Legislation*

19. The power of Legislation is retained by the Suzerain. The power to make Rules within certain defined limits is delegated to Native Authorities and to Native Courts (including, of course, Judicial Councils). Native Administrations are expressly authorized to make Rules under certain Ordinances. . . .

---

[1] These are the predecessors of today's *'yan doka* and Local Authority police forces.

(d) *Disposal of Lands*

20. Under the 'Lands and Native Rights Ordinance', the powers of disposing of lands is vested in the Governor as Trustee for the Natives, so far as the Northern Provinces are concerned. ...

(e) *General guidance of British Resident*

21. Apart from these four main limitations, there are others which are expressed or inferred in the ordinances. Thus the disposal of the annual revenue of the Native Administration, the appointment and dismissal of important Chiefs and Officers of the Native Administration, and indeed all the important executive acts of a Native ruler, though emanating from himself, are subject to the guidance and advice of the Resident. The Native Ruler's initiative and suggestions for reform or progress should always be encouraged, and all orders to subordinates should go through him. He is, in fact, as Sir P. Girouard expressed it, the Wakil or Governor guided by the Resident who speaks for the Suzerain power. In order to exercise this guidance Administrative Officers will not reside permanently elsewhere than at the capital Native town. They should endeavour to keep in close touch with Native opinion and feeling, and report fully.

POINTS OF DIFFERENCE IN THE SOUTHERN PROVINCES

22. In the foregoing paragraphs my point of view has been concentrated on the Northern Provinces, but the principles laid down apply with equal force to the Southern Provinces. There is the difference, that among the few communities in the South which have reached the stage at which the authority of a single paramount Chief is recognized, he is of the same race as the people over whom he rules, and is not, as in the Moslem States in the North, usually the scion of a conquering dynasty. There is also the difference—which is sometimes regarded as more important than it really is—that British rule over some of these communities was not established by direct conquest but by treaty. In the case of Benin—the most advanced in social organization—this exception does not apply, as it was conquered by force of arms in 1896.

The Oyo Province has accepted British Suzerainty, and its loyal and enlightened ruler, the Alafin, is anxious to accept the same status as the paramount Emirs of the North. The recent uprising of a portion of the Ibadan Bale-ship against the authority alike of the Alafin and of the British Raj, which was suppressed by force, has deprived the subordinate district of Ibadan of any claim to independence of the Alafin, which, however, it never possessed.

Egba-land alone possessed by treaty a so-called independence, [though the Commissioner sat as President of the 'Mixed Court', and the Supreme Court alone had jurisdiction in murder cases] but the local Government had to appeal from time to time to the Governor for the aid of armed force to maintain its control. After a recent collapse of this kind the treaty of independence was by mutual consent cancelled and the Alake became *de jure* what he had always been *de facto*—a protected Chief on the same plane, and subject to the same limitations, as the other great Native rulers of Nigeria.

For all practical purposes therefore the Southern Provinces may now be regarded as in an identical position towards the Suzerain power as the Northern Provinces, and the foregoing paragraphs apply *mutatis mutandis*.

Land in Southern Provinces

In one important particular, however, the attitude of the Central Government differs in the South from that in the North, viz., in the matter of the disposal of lands. The Land and Native Rights Ordinance of the North is replaced in the South by the Native Lands Acquisition Ordinance, under which a Native ruler with the consent of the community, may dispose of lands to aliens and receive rents therefor, with the prior consent of the Governor.

TRIBAL AND VILLAGE ORGANIZATION OF PRIMITIVE COMMUNITIES

23. I have alluded to the Ogboni Chiefs at Abeokuta, and to the Village Elders whom I compared with the Indian 'panchayet', but there is little accessible and reliable information regarding the social organization of the tribe and the village among the primitive races of the Southern Provinces, and those allied to them in the South of the Northern Provinces. There are, no doubt, many valuable accounts by Officers who have studied this subject (one or two of which I have seen), but they have become buried in Secretariat archives. Nor have Missionaries (who in the past have with few exceptions been the only Europeans who could speak the Native languages) contributed much to our knowledge. They are naturally more concerned with the religious beliefs than with the purely secular and social organization. I propose to inaugurate a record of Minutes by experienced Officers on this all-important matter, with a view to co-ordinating and comparing the evidence submitted, and arriving at some really reliable data regarding each tribe of importance.[1]

[1] The outcome was the valuable production of the various Gazetteers of each Province (1920–28) and O. Temple's *Notes on the Tribes, Provinces, Emirates, and States of the Northern Provinces of Nigeria*, 1919.

It is believed that in most of these tribes and clans, the youths are circumsized [sic] in batches every three or four years, and form a group or grade (Egbe), and to each grade special duties and functions are assigned. The selection of the elders—called 'Ubo' or 'Uto' or by other titles—is said to be attended with much ceremonial, and among tribes which are loosely organized, and own allegiance to no Paramount Chief, these titles—which I believe are often graded into different classes—confer great influence in the community.

It is reported that in some districts the custom of buying titles prevails, and considerable sums are paid, not only by young men who have not yet qualified by age and acknowledged ability, for the position of Elders—but even by Aliens. Among the Kukurukus and kindred tribes the 'Ubo' are distinguished by Red Hats.

NATIVE 'SOCIETIES'

24. Some District Officers have held the view that the titles alike of 'Ogboni' and of 'Ubo' designated the grade of 'Elders'. Others have affirmed that both, with other similar designations were the names of Secret and dangerous Societies.

It is obvious that if the policy which is outlined in this Memo. is to be applied with sympathy and success—especially to tribes who do not as yet recognize a paramount Chief—it is essential that these tribal organizations and social customs should not only be fully understood, but should be utilized as a framework on which to build. It is very desirable also that the objects for which the many Native 'Societies'—which exercise great influence on the Native mind—exist, should be fully investigated, since they also may become valuable factors in a system of Native Administration adapted to these tribes.

Some few societies existed no doubt for purposes of Fetish worship combined with human sacrifices, enslaving and other crimes—and for these complete suppression is the only course which can be adopted. But there are many others whose origin and main purpose supplies a want—probably by exercising discipline and control, and by promoting cohesion. In such cases it is better policy to purge them of their undesirable characteristics and accretions and to utilize them, than to attempt ineffectually to suppress them. In some cases it may be that a class or grade of tribal organization has been mistaken for a Society, as possibly in the case of the Ubo and Ogboni. In other cases it may be that what was originally a class or grade, has in fact developed into a Society, and has adopted customs or pursued objects incompatible with law and order. Or it may be that the crimes committed by its Members are in no way due to the dictates of the so-called Society, or again that a title in one tribe has gained such prestige that it has been adopted and debased by another.

25. The subject is large enough and important enough to form the subject of a separate Memo., and my purpose in these paras. is limited to impressing on all Political Officers the vital necessity of a knowledge of the social organization of tribes who lack a paramount Chief, if they hope to gain their confidence, and to develop an effective system of 'indirect rule', based on their own institutions, and acceptable to them.

CHIEFS OF THE 1ST AND 2ND GRADES

26. The formal recognition of the position of a 1st or 2nd grade Chief is notified by the presentation of a 'Staff of Office', and in the case of the former by a Letter of Appointment on a parchment scroll. These appointments are notified in the Gazette.

The Staff is surmounted in the case of a 1st class Chief by a silver, and in the case of a 2nd class by a brass headpiece. Only those Chiefs who own allegiance to no other and are described as 'paramount' or principal Chiefs, or as 'independent Headmen' are included in these grades.

The higher rank is accorded to the Sultan of Sokoto, the Shehu of Bornu, the Emirs of Kano, Gando, Bauchi, Zaria, Katsena, Yola, Bida, Ilorin, Kontagora and Argungu in the Northern Provinces,[1] and to the Alafin of Oyo, the Oba of Benin, the Alake of Egbaland, the Awujale of Jebu-Ode, and the Oni of Ife in the Southern Provinces. The second grade has been conferred upon the Emirs of Nassarawa, Muri, Lapai, Agaie, Shonga, Lafiagi, Pateji, Hadeija, Katagum, Gummel, Daura, Kazaure, Gombe, Wushishi, Birnin Gwari and Messau in the Northern Provinces, and upon the Oshemowe of Ondo, Chief Dore Numa, the Bale of Ibadan, and others in the Southern Provinces. The staves of office, letters of appointment and the Native insignia of office (if any) of the 1st grade will be presented to them personally when possible by the Governor—of the 2nd grade by the Lieutenant-Governor—at a parade of the troops, and in the presence of the Resident and of their assembled people. They will, on installation, take an oath of allegiance on the Koran, or in such other method as may be most binding upon them[2]. . . .

Chiefs of these grades will be appointed on a period of probation before receiving the insignia of office. Chiefs of the 1st grade may fly the Union Jack at their residences (*fadawa*).

[1] In 1964 there were 16 First Class Chiefs and 33 Second Class in the North.
[2] Here followed the oath of allegiance in translation.

THE THIRD GRADE &C.

27. The more important District Headman and Pagan Chiefs occupy the third grade, and the less influential the fourth and fifth, according as the Resident may recommend. Those who are subordinate to a Chief of the first and second grade, will have their staves presented to them by the paramount Chief, in the presence of the Resident and their people—if independent of any superior Chief the Resident will present the staff. No formal oath will be required of them. A Chief of the third grade may carry a short baton; lower grades will not carry any symbol of office. Staves of office are only given to Chiefs who occupy a position as executive rulers of communities and not to office holders, however important the office they hold.

NATIVE ETIQUETTE

28. Official etiquette and ceremonial are matters of great importance to African Chiefs, and are strictly enforced among themselves. No doubt the people narrowly observe the conduct of British Officials in these matters, and the prestige of a Chief may consequently suffer, and a feeling of soreness and humiliation be engendered, by a thoughtless and quite unintentional act. The assumption, moreover, of privileges by petty Chiefs, or office holders, which they would not have dared to assume in old days, tends to lower the dignity of the rulers whose sole right such privileges used to be. Residents should therefore be careful to study Native etiquette, and to prohibit the assumption of privileges or dress by those not entitled to them by Native custom.

In the Northern Provinces, as a general rule, when a Resident interviews a Chief of the first grade, he will offer him a carpet or mat to sit upon unless, as is usually the case, he brings his own. The Resident should rise to meet him and should dismiss him with similar courtesy. In the Southern Provinces, Chiefs of the first grade have been accustomed to be offered a chair.

On ordinary occasions of business the Resident will receive the Chief at the Residency, and he should take occasion to go himself to the Chief's residence from time to time to discuss official matters. In either case notice should if possible be given to him the day before, and a suitable hour fixed. On public occasions, a small guard may be mounted, and a special marquee or *rumfa* may be erected.

A Government audience room should as of old be maintained inside the city, with a small retiring room attached. Here the Lieutenant-Governor or the Resident can on occasion receive the Emir, or any Native notables or merchants. A space of 15 yards

round should be enclosed by a 15-inch dwarf wall, and kept scrupulously clean, within which only authorized persons may enter. A
small guard house and sentry box will be provided in one corner
for the escort. The Union Jack will be flown. The Resident should
never sleep in the building. The existence of such a building within
the city walls has its value as a symbol apart from its purely practical
uses.

Chiefs of the second grade should be given a small carpet or mat,
and of lower grades a Native mat. In the Southern Provinces there
has been a somewhat indiscriminate use of chairs without distinction
of grade. This should not be suddenly altered so as to cause offence,
but when possible a reed platform, raised a foot or so off the ground,
should be substituted, so as to preserve the privilege of the chair to
the Paramount Chief. Whenever a Resident visits a Native Chief he
should take a chair with him, and at least one soldier or police
Orderly. Office Holders or *Sarakuna* in the Northern Provinces
should not be given mats—in the Southern Provinces the traditional
Native custom should be enforced. A Government Official should
never sit on the ground in the presence of a Native Chief, and while
himself taking off his hat in the house of a Chief, he should insist on
a corresponding observance from Chiefs who visit him. A Mohammedan should not remove his head-dress for it is disrespectful for
him to be uncovered in the presence of a superior—he should
remove his shoes before entering a room. Whatever local customs of
ceremonial or courtesy exist among non-Moslem communities
should be ascertained and enforced.

ETIQUETTE FOR THE GOVERNOR

29. These rules will be emphasized in the presence of the Governor
as the representative of His Majesty. He will only shake hands with
Chiefs of the first grade. Principal Chiefs in the Moslem States must
meet the Governor when he visits their capital at the customary
distance from the City, and escort him to the Residency. They should
be accompanied by their Headmen, Office Holders, and a suitable
escort of horsemen. In Kano and Zaria, when the Governor arrives
by Railway, the train will stop at a pre-arranged place to receive the
salute of the Emir. The Chief will call upon the Governor, who may
before leaving return the call of a first class Chief. The Governor will
at his discretion summon the Chief to any audience or private interview. All British Officers invited to such an audience will provide
themselves with seats and attend in uniform. These rules apply also
to Lieutenant-Governors, with such modifications as they may
consider suitable. Formal functions, such as the installation of a
Chief, will usually take place in the open air, and the Resident will

make all arrangements in anticipation, so that the Chiefs may know what to do and feel at their ease.

NATIVE CEREMONIAL TOWARDS EUROPEANS

30. On the other hand Residents will be careful to exact from Native Chiefs all proper respect and courtesy; the proffer of a contemptible present, manifestly disproportionate to the rank and wealth of the donor, the despatch of a low grade or dirty messenger, intentional delay in keeping an appointment, or in receiving an Officer when the time has been previously fixed, and such-like acts are in the eyes of the Natives grave insults, which are noted by the people. A Resident should at once call for an explanation, and take care that the Chief has no further opportunity of repeating such discourtesy. He will at the same time report the incident to the Lieutenant-Governor.

SPECIAL PRIVILEGES OF CERTAIN CHIEFS

31. Residents will use their discretion as to which Chiefs may be allowed to use the *Kakaki* (Chief's trumpets). In the Northern Provinces in former times there was a strict rule as to who might bear a sword. In the Southern Provinces the question of wearing a crown is equally important. Throughout Nigeria the right to certain Native titles, and to corresponding dress or insignia is jealously regarded. These customs should be maintained and Chiefs should be encouraged to punish transgressors.

OFFENCES BY CHIEFS

32. Important Chiefs, viz., those of the first three grades, and persons holding high rank in a Native Administration, will never be kept under detention in the common prison or elsewhere, unless such extreme measures are necessitated by a very serious political crisis. In such a case the Chief should, if possible, be immediately sent under strong guard to Headquarters, for even in a time of crisis the importance of sending a seditious or rebellious Chief out of the Province, may probably be greater than the disadvantage of detaching the soldiers necessary for his escort. Non-compliance with reasonable requests, or dilatoriness in fulfilling promises, should first form the subject of protest, and if this is unheeded, of report to the Lieutenant-Governor. More serious crimes, such as embezzlement of the tribute, secret extortion, offences against the Slavery Law, refusal or neglect to carry out the awards of the Native Court or interference with it, should be at once reported to the Lieutenant-Governor for instructions as to the course to be taken. If it is necessary to bring the Chief to trial (as in a case of murder, or of one

of the serious offences mentioned, when previous warning has already been given), he will probably be tried by the Provincial or Supreme Court at Headquarters; otherwise, if the offence is very serious, he may be deposed. The deposition of a Chief with its break in the continuity of succession which the Natives so greatly prize, is a step which should only be resorted to when no other course is possible.

Minor Chiefs (such as village heads) and minor officials who commit any such serious offences may be arrested, if thought advisable by the Resident, and tried at his discretion in the Provincial Court or by the Judicial Council; or the case may be reported to the Lieutenant-Governor, with a view to trial at a distance by a British Court, or to the removal of the Chief and his replacement by a better man. Minor causes of complaint, such as negligence to carry out orders, etc., can, in the case of such Chiefs, best be dealt with by the Judicial Council of the Principal Chief (if there is one), and, if repeated, by deprivation of office, reduction of salary (if any), or otherwise by fine. Small fines (viz., a deduction from salary) may be imposed by the Resident on Minor Chiefs 'executively', where warnings have produced no effect, if there is no Head Chief through whom they can be dealt with. The reason why Chiefs may thus be dealt with extra-judicially for minor offences is in order to save them from the humiliation, and consequent loss of influence, incurred by a public trial, but if the offence is one amenable to law, and not mere obstructive negligence or incapacity, they will invariably be offered the option of trial, before fine or removal from office. Offences arising out of old custom and habit, such as accepting unauthorized taxes, or inflicting fines without informing the Resident, will be dealt with leniently at first. Wilful neglect to carry out the duties imposed upon him renders a Native Authority liable to fine. Unauthorized assumption of powers may be punished by imprisonment for six months under the authority of the Governor. Removal of a Chief from his town or province, could hitherto only be effected by conviction under the Criminal Code, but 'The Deposed Chief's Removal' Ordinance now renders possible the deportation of a deposed Chief, if by Native Law and Custom it is improper for him to remain with his former Jurisdiction.

TITLES OF CHIEFS

33. Chiefs will be described by their proper Native titles, and not as 'Kings' or 'Princes', etc. In the Moslem States, the proper title is Sarki, but the Sokoto Chief is known as 'Sarkin Muslimin', and by courtesy as 'Sultan', and the Bornu Chiefs as 'The Shehu'. The Chiefs of the other principal Moslem States are usually termed

Emirs (or Amirs), viz., Governors (or Wakils) and this term may be used in official documents addressed to them.

Fancy titles conferred by Emirs upon themselves in past days such as 'Sarkin Sudan', etc., should be suppressed, and I should also like to see some other title substituted for that of Sarkin Bauchi, Sarkin Bornu, etc., held by minor Chiefs in various Provinces, since there is only one Chief who has a legitimate right to each of these titles. In the Southern Provinces, the old titles such as Alafin, Oba, Obaseki, Balogun, Bashorun, Bale, etc., should be preserved, but I imagine that the comparatively petty Chiefs who call themselves 'Crowned Kings' in the Western Provinces, have borrowed the title, which is altogether a misnomer, from a desire to emulate European dignities.

APPOINTMENT AND SUCCESSION TO PRINCIPAL CHIEFSHIPS

(a) *1st Grade*

35. The law of succession to Chiefships or Offices (other than that of Emir) in Moslem States is well defined by the Koran, and in Non-Moslem Communities by Native law and custom. A Resident should fully acquaint himself with the traditional methods practised in the case of every Chiefship of importance in his Province, and be able to report authoritatively to the Lieutenant-Governor, whether the nominee proposed has been selected in accordance with native custom. He should let it be clearly understood that the final nomination rests with the Governor or Lieutenant-Governor, in those cases which are reserved for the approval of one or the other. Succession to the Emirate was controlled by a combination of the hereditary with the elective principle, subject to the final choice of the Serikin Musulmi, precisely as now by the Governor.

Having ascertained who is the successor most likely to be elected or recommended, the Resident should (more especially of course in the case of the successor to a Paramount Chief) take every opportunity of gauging his character and ability, and of ascertaining the opinion of the Head Chief and influential men regarding him. If he is of opinion that a much better man (who is also in the line of succession) is available, and if in those cases where succession is usually be election—either popular or by a body traditionally invested with these powers—he wishes the succession to pass to a particular individual who has shown marked ability and loyalty, he will report fully in the annual Confidential Report on Chiefs. He should be able to inform the Governor whether the selection of the individual he recommends as successor to a Head Chief, would be acceptable to the community of all classes, and whether when the

G

succession is based on election, either by a constituted body or by popular vote, he would have any difficulty in securing his return. Though it is a matter of the first importance that the Government should be fully informed as to the comparative merits of rival candidates, and the grounds on which their election or claim is based, the name of the Government nominee should not be disclosed in a Mohammedan Emirate. It is obviously important that the Government should have come to as definite conclusions as possible in regard to the succession of a Paramount Chief, so that on the death of the holder of the office there may be no interregnum, and he may act in the place of the late Chief pending his formal installation by the Governor.

(b) *Minor Chiefs*

36. In the case of Minor Chiefs the selection should usually be by the people, subject to the approval of the Head Chief and of the Resident. If the Resident should be in doubt as to the wisdom of the Emir's selection, he can delay final approval by informing the Head Chief that he desires to consult the Lieutenant-Governor, which will give him time for a reversal of the election, if the person selected has in the meantime shown himself unsuitable for the post. It is very important that the Head Chief should fully acquiesce, and that the appointment should be made in his name, or friction and disloyalty may result later on. All minor Chiefs, including recognized office holders and Masu-ungwoi, will be formally installed by the Head Chief. In the absence of the substantive Resident the prior approval of the Lieutenant-Governor must be obtained. No person who still has the status of a slave will be appointed to any Chiefship or office.

(c) *District Heads*

37. District Heads must always live in their districts. When the principal town in a district is the residence of the Emir or Paramount Chief, the District Head will reside elsewhere. The men selected for appointment as District Headmen should be Chiefs with local influence, and it may often be advisable that as far as possible the appointment should be retained in the same family. District Heads will very rarely therefore be transferred from their own district to another, merely because the new appointment carries higher responsibility and an increased salary. For the new holder of office would know nothing of the district and a hardship is inflicted on the peasantry, in consequence of the customary *gaisua* (complimentary presents). It is still very necessary for Residents to check tendencies on the part of Emirs to favouritism and nepotism in the selection of Native Officials for responsible posts. . . .

EDUCATION OF CHIEFS

39. In my earlier Memo. I recorded the belief that 'it is from the rising generation that we must hope to produce the elements of real progress and enlightenment', and my successor with later experience strongly endorsed this view. I think, however, that all Residents will agree with me, that even the existing generation has proved wonderfully adaptable, and when one considers the methods to which they were accustomed in their youth, the progress made reflects the greatest possible credit alike upon the unceasing efforts and devoted ability of the British Staff, who have by precept and example made them what they are today. The importance, however, of training the character of the succeeding generation of Chiefs cannot be over-estimated.

A Political Officer should endeavour to interest the Native rulers in his Province in everything which tends to encourage progress, and the welfare of the people. Thus in the sphere of education he can point to the large number of posts as Clerks and Artisans, especially in the Northern Provinces, at present held by Aliens, which are available for youths who can read and write English. He should explain the economic advantages of afforestation and fuel plantations, the protection afforded against small-pox by Vaccination, the possibilities of prevention of epizootic diseases among cattle, and the increased returns from crops by cultivating improved varieties, and so on; and he should encourage them to devote all the funds they can spare to such objects, and themselves to set an example to their people.

NATIVE COUNCILS

41. The Judicial Council of a Paramount Chief is first of all a Native Court, upon which executive powers have been conferred to the extent stated in the Governor's Order which confers them. These Councils supersede the former Native Councils in the Southern Provinces, and the former Judicial Councils in Pagan areas in the Northern Provinces. The Governor may, however, under the Native Authority Ordinance, appoint a Native Tribunal to be a 'Native Authority', with Executive powers. I must impress upon Residents of Provinces in which there are primitive tribes, that they have no authority to set up Councils, but if, in spite of every endeavour, owing to the impossibility of selecting any Chief with power to enforce order, they desire to vest executive powers in a primitive Native Tribunal, they must obtain the consent of the Governor.

SCOPE FOR RULERS

42. In order that the Native rulers, in their role of Governors or

Wakils may find adequate scope for their energies, take a keen
interest in their duties, and command the respect and obedience of
their people, it is essential that they should be given the greatest
possible latitude and power compatible with the position they
occupy in relation to the Central Government. We wish to substitute
an ardour for progress and development for the former excitements
of war and slave-raiding. Our object should be to give them an
interest and an object beyond the routine performance of their duties,
to interest them in the scheme of Government, to show them
common interests, to engage their sympathies in our efforts for
secular education, and to promote a legitimate rivalry in civilized
progress and even in sports. In a word that, so long as they prove
themselves loyal and capable, it is through them that the people are
governed, and it is the desire of Government to uphold their authority and prestige in every possible way, and to encourage initiative
and a sense of responsibility. It is by bearing these principles constantly in mind that Residents in the Moslem States have achieved
the success which is manifest today. They are principles which must
be borne in mind wherever this policy is extended. Unnecessary
interference on the part of a Resident humiliates the Native ruler,
lowers his prestige, and robs him of interest in his work.

GENERAL ATTITUDE OF OFFICIALS TOWARDS NATIVE CHIEFS

43. It must be in fact remembered that the policy is to support
Native rule (within the limitations laid down in paragraphs 16–22),
and not to impose a form of a British rule with the support of Native
Chiefs—which is a very different thing. It will not be necessary to
describe how this policy—which will necessarily vary in accordance
with the ability and intelligence of the Chiefs—should permeate
every detail, but it may perhaps be useful to indicate a few instances,
e.g.:—

When a District Officer interviews a Subordinate Chief his
Superior Chief should if possible be present.

An Officer on tour should be accompanied by a representative of
the Paramount Chief, and make him the mouth-piece of any orders
given to Village Heads and other Native Officials.

Native Departmental Subordinates, such as Wardmen and Forest
Guards, should not give orders direct to Village Heads, or to
Chiefs.

The chain of responsibility from the Village Head to the Paramount
Chief should be maintained, and the Native Courts with their Staffs
of Scribes and Messengers, must work in harmony with, and not
interfere with the executive authority of the Chiefs.

SUMMARY

44. To summarize this part of this Memo:—the policy of the Nigerian Government is (a) To rule indirectly through the Native Chiefs, and in the North to maintain, strengthen and educate the Fulani and Kanembu ruling races, so that the regeneration of Nigeria may be through its own governing class and its own indigenous institutions. (b) To maintain the independence of free Pagan races, not to place them under Moslem rulers, and gradually to form them into tribal and racial Units under Paramount Chiefs of their own race and their own selection. (c) To maintain and develop all that is best in the indigenous methods and institutions of Native rule, to avoid as far as possible everything that has a denationalizing tendency, and to inculcate respect for authority, self-respect, and fair treatment of the lower classes, the weak and the ignorant. These are the ideals which have guided the policy of Nigeria in the past. Writing in 1909 my successor said that he 'did not dare to be positive as between Native and direct rule'. The days of hesitation are I hope ended, and my successors in Nigeria will I trust adhere to the policy which has now I think vindicated its claims to acceptance.

APPLICATION IN THE SOUTHERN PROVINCES

45. These principles are gradually and effectively being introduced into the Southern Provinces. It is inevitable that, in spite of much high sounding talk in the local Press, they should not be popular with the semi-educated portion of the coast population, for the man who has but a partial education considers himself superior to the illiterate Chief, and resents his authority. I am however convinced that those Native Gentlemen whose education has been on larger lines, and has broadened their horizon, recognize the soundness of this policy. . . .

CONTINUITY OF PROVINCIAL ADMINISTRATION

46. One essential condition for the success of this policy is continuity of Administration. To this end I have always insisted that as far as possible a Resident once posted to a Province should remain in charge of it. In the last few years this rule has been still further extended, and all Political Officers above the rank of Assistant District Officer are as far as possible permanently posted to particular Provinces. . . .

PART II: REVENUE AND EXPENDITURE

DEVELOPMENT OF NATIVE TREASURIES[1]

49. At the time I left Northern Nigeria in September, 1906, this policy has been clearly laid down. . . . The Native Revenue Proclamation had been enacted, but the collection of the tax had only just been inaugurated, and its total proceeds for the year 1904/05 were only £21,000—insufficient to pay the salaries of the Native Officials of a single important Province. The development of the Native Treasuries, under the title of *Beiyut el Mal*, was due to the initiative of Mr. Palmer and the fostering care of Mr. Temple in the succeeding years. The name was unfortunate for the Native Treasuries bear no real resemblance to the Egyptian Beit-el-Mal, to the abuse of which Slatin Pasha attributed the collapse of the Sudan Administration. Up to 1913 the whole sum collected under the Proclamation was paid into the Treasury, and a re-grant was made to the Native Administration. This system has now been abolished, and only that portion of the Tax which is credited to Colonial Revenue is paid to the Treasury. The Head Chief in whose name it is levied is bound by law to pay the remainder into the Native Treasury.

CONSTITUTION OF NATIVE ADMINISTRATION

50. Each Unit which possesses a Treasury of its own is called a Native Administration. Except among primitive tribes the Central Authority consists of the Paramount Chief with his Principal Officers of State, who usually form his Judicial Council. The Judiciary is represented by the Chief Alkali of the Central Native Court, and in Moslem States the Limam[2] is also a person of importance. The Native Treasurer is in direct charge of the monies received and accounts for their expenditure. Subordinate to this Central Administration are the various Officials, both at the Capital and in the districts . . . appointed by the Paramount Chief as already described. It is preferable that these posts should be filled by Natives who are subject to the jurisdiction of the Head Chief and Native Courts. If aliens of a different race and religion are required, e.g., for carrying out public works, etc. (even though the cost of the work is borne by the Native Treasury), it is preferable that they should be Government employees. Their pay can be re-imbursed by the Native Treasury.

NATIVE ADMINISTRATION AMONG PRIMITIVE TRIBES

51. Each independent Unit must of necessity have a separate Treasury, since the control and expenditure of the money is entrusted

[1] See Table on facing page.
[2] Deriving from the Arabic *el kadi* and *el imam* respectively.

THE ORGANIZATION OF NATIVE ADMINISTRATION IN THE NORTHERN PROVINCES, 1916

Province	Population	Area (sq. miles)	Divisions	N.T.s	Paramount Chiefs	Dist. Heads	Office Holders	Native Courts	Total Salaries £
First Class:									
Sokoto	1,250,381	32,600	4	3	4	67	104	39	51,914
Kano	2,846,984	29,500	4	9	9	88	204	60	79,543
Bornu	672,342	33,600	3	2	1	19	51	16	23,886
Bauchi	511,699	23,700	5	5	4	22	53	37	29,332
Zaria	402,371	13,320	3	1	1	28	39	17	16,676
Second Class:									
Niger	272,121	16,770	4	6	3	51	60	47	19,609
Nassarawa	229,185	16,710	4	8	5	43	30	27	10,544
Ilorin/Kabba	420,840	14,700	3	3	1	42	48	35	19,741
Muri	405,060	28,700	4	3	1	53	17	22	7,706
Yola	239,478	11,600	3	3	1	29	31	12	8,755
Kontagora	137,056	27,800	3	4	4	19	20	27	6,225
Bassa	202,377	6,700	3	1	–	15	14	17	3,383
TOTAL	7,589,894	255,700	43	48	34	476	671	356	£277,314

Notes: Paramount Chief is one having a Judicial Council. Office-holders include only those with a minimum annual salary of £50. There were additionally 123 independent District Heads, only 14 of whom were in the First-Class Provinces (Bornu 4, Bauchi 10).

to the Paramount Chief and his Councillors. In some cases in the Northern Provinces a number of loosely organized tribes have been combined into a single so-called Native Administration, with a common Treasury, but with doubtful success, since no responsible Native Officials exist. In such a case the control of the funds is in theory vested in the Chiefs collectively, though in practice, owing to their inability and ignorance, the control is entirely exercised at present by the Resident. So experienced a Resident as Mr. Palmer writes: 'I cannot see that their existence serves a useful purpose at present, there is no Central Native Administration in these instances, no promises have been made, and there is no intelligent public opinion, such as exists in Emirates, to check the Resident's or Emir's personal views; in fact Government itself is the one and only "Central Administration". In most of such areas there is one Assistant District Officer having already a sufficiency of office work and numerous small Native units to manage. The existence of a Native Treasury means simply that he must keep two sets of accounts instead of one, and that his personal Staff is increased since the so-called Native Administration Officials are really his Officials.' Going on to speak of 'the increased financial responsibility which it was Your Excellency's policy to bestow on the Native Chiefs as they proved their fitness to exercise it,' he adds 'my submission is that mixed Pagan areas are unfit for any such responsibility, and that in such areas all sums over and above the salaries paid to Chiefs and others should go to Government direct'. It was for this reason that only a small percentage of the Tax was, and in many cases still is, assigned to such primitive communities—enough to pay the salaries only.

On the other hand there are some ancient and well organized Communities such as the Emirates of Daura, Kazaure, Gumel, etc., in the Kano Province, whose population is so small that the proceeds of the Tax are barely sufficient to pay the salaries of the Native Officials. It is optional to them to coalesce with their wealthy neighbour Kano, but by doing so they would lose at any rate their financial independence, the Emirs would become practically District Heads, and the control of the funds would pass from their hands to those of the Emir of Kano. Such coalition would make for progress and development by the application of surplus funds to poorer districts, and avoids the multiplication of Treasuries, but I do not desire to press it in any case where it would be unpopular.

NATIVE TREASURIES EXPENDITURE

58. Expenditure is shown under 15 Heads[1]—not all of which may

[1] Though there are today 19 heads of expenditure in N.T. Estimates, the order of the original heads is unchanged.

be required in any particular Treasury. The first three heads deal with the salaries of the Central Native Administration, the District Heads and the Village Heads respectively. . . .

Head 1

Under Central is included the emoluments of the paramount Chief and his Judical Council, together with such scribes and messengers as are necessary. . . . Officials and Servants who are employed about the person of the Chief would be paid for out of the liberal salary allowed him. The total under this Head should not as a rule exceed 12 to 14% of the total Revenue in an advanced Administration under a paramount chief. In a primitive Community this Head does not appear at all.

Head 2

The Second Head comprises the District Headmen. The general proportion of the Revenue assigned to their salaries including scribes and messengers should not, I estimate, exceed 24% to 26%. . . . If on fixed salaries, District Heads will not draw any additional percentage on account of Jangali collection [cattle tax].

Head 3

The Third Head includes the emoluments of the Village Headmen including heads of *Rugas* (cattle herds) whether paid as fixed salaries or as a proportion of the tax they collect. The total to be spent on this Head should probably be about 15% to 16% of the total Revenue.

Head 4

The Head Judicial covers the pay of the Native Judges, the Court Clerks, maintenance of Witnesses, and other expenses incidental to the working of the Native Courts. . . . A Mallam classed as an 'Alkali' should not receive a salary less than £24 p.a. Expenditure under this Head should be about 7% and 10% of revenue respectively in settled and primitive communities. . . .[1]

[1] For the six emirates of Sokoto, Kano, Katsina, Zaria, Bornu and Bauchi, (Group A) and for nine non-emirate treasuries (Group B), the percentages in 1916 were:—

Group A		Group B
16%	Central Administration	nil
24%	District Administration	25.5%
16%	Village Administration	16%
6.5%	Judicial	10%

It is interesting to compare these percentages with those set up as a criterion of 'financial soundness' for Native Treasuries in today's emirates (*Financial Memoranda*, 1963).

FINANCIAL RESPONSIBILITY OF CHIEF

77. Although in the earlier stages it is necessary that the Resident should exercise close control (and even in the more advanced Native Administrations his close supervision can never be dispensed with), he must bear in mind that the Paramount Chief is the recognized Ruler, and that subject to the Resident's advice and the final approval of the Governor, the disposal of the Revenue of the Native Administration is entrusted to him. The Chiefs and their Councils should therefore as far as possible prepare the Estimates of expenditure themselves. All payments should be made directly to him and his Staff, and even when works are undertaken by the Public Works Department on behalf of the Native Administration his agency should be employed as far as possible.

Memo No. 1.
DUTIES OF POLITICAL OFFICERS AND MISCELLANEOUS SUBJECTS

THE OBJECT IN VIEW

3. The British role here is to bring to the country all the gains of civilization by applied science (whether in the development of material resources, or the eradication of disease, &c.), with as little interference as possible with Native customs and modes of thought. Where new ideas are to be presented to the native mind, patient explanation of the objects in view will be well rewarded, and new methods may often be clothed in a familiar garb. . . .

CONNOTATION OF NAMES OF RANKS

4. The term 'Resident' implies duties rather of a Political or advisory nature, while the term 'Commissioner' connotes functions of a more directly Administrative character. The former is therefore applicable to the Chief Government Officer in a Province of which large areas are under the immediate rule of a Paramount Chief, who, with Native Officials, himself administers a form of Government. The latter is more adapted to Provinces, or parts of Provinces, less advanced in civilization, where the authority of the Native Chiefs is small, and a large measure of direct Administration must devolve upon the Protectorate Government. The term 'Commissioner' is, however, already used in so many other connections, viz., a Commissioner of the Supreme or Provincial Court, a member of a

Commission of Inquiry, a Police Commissioner, etc., that for the sake both of distinction and of brevity, the term Resident has been adopted to denote the two highest grades in the Administrative or Political Department, and the term District Officer though strictly applicable only to the next two grades will be used in this Memorandum to include an Assistant District Officer.[1]

GENERAL NATURE OF ADMINISTRATIVE OFFICER'S DUTIES

5. It is the duty of Residents to carry out loyally the policy of the Governor, and not to inaugurate policies of their own. The Governor, through the Lieutenant-Governor, is at all times ready and anxious to hear, and to give full and careful consideration to the views of Residents, but, when once a decision has been arrived at, he expects Residents to give effect to it in a thorough and loyal spirit, and to inculcate the same spirit in their juniors. This does not mean a rigid adherence to the letter of a ruling. Among such diverse races in widely varying degrees of advancement, it is inevitable and desirable that there should be diversity in the application of a general policy by the Resident, who knows the local conditions and feelings of his people. It does mean, however, that the principles underlying the policy are to be observed and the Resident in modifying their application will fully inform and obtain the approval of the Governor.

Festina lente is a motto very applicable to Africa, provided that the coach is not set on the wrong rail, so that a wrong course—temporarily easy—is inaugurated. By shirking initial difficulties and yielding to prejudice far greater difficulties must be encountered later.

The Government relies on its Administrative Officers to keep in close touch with Native opinion and feeling, and to report for the information of the Governor. It is thus only that we can produce the best results,—that the Governor and Lieutenant-Governors can keep in touch and gain information, and the Political Officer can count on support and on recognition of his work.

DIFFERENCE OF METHOD IN ADVANCED OR BACKWARD COMMUNITIES

(a) *Advanced tribes*

6. The degree to which a Political Officer may be called upon to act in an administrative capacity, will thus depend upon the influence and ability of the Native Chiefs in each part of the Province, though in every case he will endeavour to rule through the Native Chiefs.

In those parts of Provinces which are under the immediate

---

[1] In the early years, 'District Commissioner' was used in the Southern Provinces and 'Assistant Resident' in the Northern.

authority of a Chief of the first or of the second grade, the primary duty and object of a Political Officer will be to educate them in the the duties of Rulers according to a civilized standard; to convince them that oppression of the people is not sound policy, or to the eventual benefit of the rulers; to bring home to their intelligence, as far as may be, the evils attendant on a system which holds the lower classes in a state of slavery or serfdom, and so destroys individual responsibility, ambition, and development amongst them; to impress upon them the advantage of delegating the control of districts to subordinates, while keeping a strict supervision over them; to see that there is no favouritism in such appointments; and to inculcate the unspeakable benefit of justice, free from bribery and open to all.

Where taxation exists the consequent duty of assessing all the towns and villages himself, will throw upon the Political Officer a considerable amount of purely Administrative work, even in such districts. In this work he should invite the co-operation of the Chief, and endeavour to enlist his cordial assistance by making it clear to him that his own interests are deeply involved.

(b) *Backward tribes*

In districts where there is no Chief of the first or second grade, a Political Officer's functions become more largely Administrative, and among uncivilized Pagan tribes he must assume the full onus of Administration, to the extent to which time and opportunity permit. In such communities he will constantly endeavour to support the authority of the Chief, and encourage him to show initiative. If there is no Chief who exercises authority beyond his own village, he will encourage any village Chief of influence and character to control a group of villages, with a view to making him a Chief of a district later if he shows ability for the charge. Native Court clerks or scribes, constables or couriers will never be allowed to usurp the authority of the Native Chief or Village Head.

POSITION AND DUTIES OF RESIDENT IN CHARGE

7. The Resident is the senior Government Official in the Province, and represents the Lieutenant-Governor in all Administrative matters. In the absence of a responsible officer of any Department it is his duty to report any dereliction of duty on the part of any departmental subordinate to the Head of his Department, or if of a serious nature to the Lieutenant-Governor. All such officers will be guided by the instructions and wishes of the Resident, so far as they are not incompatible with the orders they have received from the head of their department, to whom they will report the matter if the Resident's instructions conflict with departmental orders. The Head

of a Department issues his instructions direct to his subordinate officer, and it is the duty of the subordinate to keep the Resident fully informed of any orders he receives which it may be useful for him to know, as for instance a Public Works Department Officer who had received orders to commence the repair of houses, etc. If the subordinate is a Native clerk the District Officer will be regarded as the local representative, and communications from the Head of the Department will be addressed to him. . . .

The first and most essential duties of a Resident and his staff are those in connection with the conduct of Native Administration, including the close supervision of the Native Courts and the assessment for taxation. This work is sufficiently onerous, and it cannot be adequately performed if a Resident is charged in addition with work and correspondence of a general administrative nature. As the senior representative of Government in his province, he cannot be entirely relieved of all general administrative duties, but in the scheme of administration in Nigeria for which I am responsible, it has been my endeavour to relieve him of them as far as possible (a) by the creation of Lieutenant-Governors with an adequate Secretariat to undertake it, and (b) by the appointment of Station Magistrates charged with the Police Court work at large centres, and with the conduct of non-political questions and correspondence.

JUNIOR STAFF

11. Residents will spare no efforts to instruct young Officers posted to their Staff, and will see that all are familiar with the Ordinances, Regulations, General Orders, and Political Memos. These constitute the 'laws and usages' of the Protectorate, which all Political Officers are bound by their oath to enforce impartially. District Officers in charge of Divisions will send full reports to the Resident, from which he will extract any information useful for his half-yearly and Annual Report to the Lieutenant-Governor, to whom he will forward all assessment reports and any particular reports, or quote paragraphs from it, if of particular interest, so as to afford the Lieutenant-Governor an opportunity of gauging the abilities of Junior Officers. Assistant District Officers will submit their reports to or through their Divisional Officer as the Resident may direct. Junior Officers will not be employed at Headquarters on clerical or accounting work which the Native Staff is capable of performing. District Officers will reside at the administrative centre of the division to which they are posted, and not at the Capital of the Province. When there are any Assistant District Officers in excess of the establishment, they will be temporarily posted to the Secretariat for six months training.

NECESSITY FOR CONSTANT TRAVELLING

12. Political Officers must endeavour to preserve a proper equili-
brium between their Judicial and Executive duties, neither allowing
the former to engross all their time and to detain them at their
Headquarters, nor becoming so absorbed in assessment, and other
executive work, as to neglect Judicial duties and leave cases to the
Native Courts which would be more advisedly tried by the Provincial
Court.

'The work done by a Political Officer,' said Sir H. Lawrence, 'in
his district, surrounded by the people, is greatly superior to the work
done in office surrounded by untrustworthy officials.' A District
Officer should pass from place to place and endeavour to lessen
oppression and bribery, and to watch over and improve the Native
tribunals. He should when possible be accompanied by the local
Chief or district Head. He will of course at the same time hold his
Court wherever he may be, and take opportunity to do so in a formal
manner in the principal towns.

The primary object of travelling through the Province is that the
Political Officer may show himself to the people and hear their
complaints at first hand, not trusting to the reports which reach him
at Headquarters, where the villagers may possibly often fear to
carry complaints, especially if they refer to some petty oppression or
illegal exaction by the Chiefs. It is only by the advent of a British
Officer that scoundrels, misrepresenting the Government action, or
extorting what they will from the Natives in the name of Government,
can be caught; for the villagers in their ignorance, supposing them
to be genuine, dare not as a rule complain.

It has been abundantly shown by experience that 'unrest' . . .
inevitably take place . . . when districts are not regularly and systematically visited. By frequent touring, abuses are redressed before
they become formidable, the law-abiding people are encouraged to
restrain the turbulent and lawless elements, and trust and confidence
in Government is fostered.

In Provinces where there is direct taxation, officials should be
constantly passing from place to place, for the purpose of carrying
out the assessment of every village, or verifying and revising the
initial assessment. But whether there is direct taxation or not, it is
equally the duty of a Political Officer to travel constantly, in order to
record, or to add to the statistics required for the Provincial Records;
to verify or fix the areas of jurisdiction of each District Headman
and Chief, or Native Court; and to become personally acquainted
with the various peoples in his district. These duties are of primary
importance in the early stage of administration and organization . . ..
Travelling, it must be remembered, costs money for transport, and

is not undertaken for pleasure. Each journey, therefore, should achieve some definite and useful result. . . .

A Veterinary or Forestry Officer, or Public Works Department Officer, inspecting roads and buildings, and any other departmental officer who has occasion to travel in a Province should seize the opportunity of accompanying a Political Officer on tour. It is not however, essential that a departmental officer should be accompanied by a Political Officer, since such a course would frequently result in mutual delay, but he would generally be accompanied by one of the native political staff to facilitate his work.

LANGUAGES

13. All Officers of the Political Staff are required to pass an examination in the Ordinances and Regulations of Nigeria, in the General Orders, and in one of the chief Native languages of Nigeria. Proficiency in a Native language is an important qualification for promotion. Promotion will ordinarily be provisional only unless an officer has passed, and he will be liable to revert if he does not do so within the period prescribed. Assistant District Officers must pass the Lower Standard to qualify for promotion, and a Resident should have passed the Higher Standard, especially if the language he has adopted is Hausa.

CONTINUITY ESSENTIAL IN AFRICA

14. I regard continuity of Administration as a matter of paramount and indeed of vital importance in African Administration. It is only after many years of personal contact that the African—naturally reserved and suspicious towards strangers—will give his confidence unreservedly. More can often be accomplished in half-an-hour by an officer well known and trusted by the people, than by another, though his superior in ability, after months of patient effort.

It has, therefore, been my general rule, that the more senior an officer becomes the less liable he is for transfer from his Province. An Assistant District Officer may be posted to two or three Provinces in succession, in order that he may gain experience, and the Lieutenant-Governor may decide whether his abilities are best adapted for work in an advanced, or a backward Province. As a Second Class District Officer he has become more of a fixture, and finally when he becomes Resident in substantive charge of a Province he is never taken away from it.

These rules are of course liable to violation owing to sudden vacancies, etc., more especially of late under war conditions, but though a Senior Officer may be removed for a time he will be restored to the Province he knows and to the people who know and trust him as soon as circumstances permit. Now that there is a single Administrative roster for all Nigeria, a Southern Provinces Officer may find himself posted on promotion to the Northern Provinces and *vice versa*. But here again the change will not as a rule be permanent, especially amongst the Senior Officers, and I should endeavour to restore an Officer to the people whose language he has learnt, and among whom he can do more efficient work, as soon as an exchange could be effected. Residents in like manner will avoid changing their Staff from one division to another if it can be helped.

RELATIONS OF DEPARTMENTAL OFFICERS WITH RESIDENT AND NATIVE ADMINISTRATION

15. The Political Officer is the channel of communication between all Departmental Officers and the Native Administration. It is essential that a Resident shall be fully informed of any project which a Departmental Office proposes to inaugurate, and he will inform the Emir and enlist his assistance. If after consulting the Emir he considers that the project—or the manner in which it is proposed to carry it out—is inadvisable he will refer to the Lieutenant-Governor, and it will be held in abeyance until a reply is received. The general scope of the work having thus been discussed and approved, the Departmental Officer is at liberty to give orders as to details, but if he desires to introduce any new principle he will again consult the Resident. If the work is to be carried out at some distance from the Capital, a responsible Native official will usually be attached to the Departmental Officer, through whom he can make his requisitions for labour, etc., and issue his instructions. If the matter is urgent, and the Departmental Officer finds it necessary to issue instructions without delay, he will fully inform the Resident, in order that he in turn may inform the Native Administration.

While these instructions are of especial importance where the expenditure of Native Administration funds is involved, the general principal will also be observed in the execution of duties or works which are paid for from departmental votes. In the former case the Native Administration has the right to determine the priority in which different works shall be carried out and the method, subject to any technical objections. Thus, if with the approval of the Governor the Native Administration provides funds for the construction of several different sections of roads, the construction of which is placed in the hands of the Public Works Department, it is admissible that the Native Administration should decide which road should take priority, and if it is itself capable of carrying out the earthworks, it may request the Public Works Department to deal with the alignment, bridges, and culverts, and only to exercise a general supervision over the remainder. Since, however, the road may eventually become a metalled motor track under the Public Works Department charge, it is clear that the construction must be in accordance with technical instructions. On the other hand a Departmental Officer carrying out Government work from Departmental votes—such as the repair of telegraphs—will look to the District Officer to assist him in procuring the necessary labour and supplies, usually, as I have said, through the medium of an official of the Native Administration. Departmental Officers must bear in mind that, in order to obtain the full benefit of Native co-operation, the orders must be given not by the Resident or any of his Staff, but by the Head Chief. . . .

Where the duties of a Departmental Officer are educational, e.g., Medical and Sanitary, Forestry, Agriculture, and Veterinary—and he is engaged on a tour of instruction, it is desirable that he should inform the Resident of the nature of the advice he proposes to give, especially if it involves a specific course of action, in order that the Resident may instruct his Staff and the Native Administration to co-operate, and also in order that there may be no conflict of instructions. I recollect an instance in which two Departmental Officers, visiting the same town within a short time of each other, each with a different object in view gave diametrically opposite instructions on a specific point to the local Chief. In such a case the Resident would have been able to discuss the matter with both and to arrive at a clear course of action. Political Officers are, moreover, able to put a Departmental Officer in possession of local conditions and prejudices, and so to assist him in his objects. . . .

JUDICIAL FUNCTIONS

16. The Resident in charge of a Province has ex-officio full powers as Judge of the Provincial Court of the Province, of which his European Staff are 'Commissioners'.[1] The Judicial powers of a Commissioner may be increased at the discretion of the Lieutenant-Governor, irrespective of his rank, on the recommendation of the Resident and of the Legal Adviser, in accordance with the ability he shows in his judicial work. Evidence of judicial ability will necessarily count much in selection for promotion. . . .

NATIVE COURTS

17. A Resident will establish a Native Court in every city or district where it appears advisable to do so, and will constantly supervise its work, especially in the lower grades of Courts. He must of course carefully study the Native Courts Ordinance and Memo. 8.

[1] These Courts were abolished by Sir Donald Cameron.

H

In Courts of Grades A and B he will watch the integrity of the Native Judges, and note their comparative ability for promotion to more important centres, and see that their sentences are in accord with British conceptions of humanity. In the lower grades he will take care that the initiative of the Chiefs who compose the Court is not interfered with by the clerk or scribe, that they do not exceed their powers, and that their sentences and findings are free from bias.

THE 'PROVINCE', 'DIVISION', AND 'DISTRICT'

18. A Province is a single entity under the control of the Resident in charge. It is divided into 'Divisions' under District Officers responsible to the Resident. The Divisions must not be confused with the 'districts' under Native Headmen. The more important divisions will be under first-class, and the less important under second-class District Officers. The charge of a first or second-class division is an appointment notified in the Gazette, which forms the Treasurer's authority to disburse the duty pay which attaches to it.

The division in which the Headquarters of the Province is situated will usually be in charge of a District Officer, like any other division, so far as its routine work is concerned, but it is, I think, of great importance that in the more advanced Provinces the paramount Chief should deal direct with the Resident, and he is apt to feel slighted if referred to a subordinate Officer. He should not only have free access to the Resident at all times, but should not be debarred from consulting him in any matter, even of detail, regarding the 'Emirate Division' even though the matter may eventually and properly be dealt with by the District Officer. In Provinces where there is no Paramount Chief and only an embryonic Native Administration, the Resident will generally be able to take charge of the Headquarter division himself with the assistance of a District Officer who can take his place when on tour.

The number of divisions in a Province is subject to the approval of the Governor, and they will be notified in the Gazette, but their boundaries may at any time be altered by the Lieutenant-Governor subject to the stipulations in this paragraph. One or more Assistant District Officers will be attached to each division, either generally or to a particular district, as the Resident may decide. Each Divisional Officer will tour constantly in his division hearing complaints, recording statistics, inspecting Native Courts, checking native agents, surveying, and assessing, and supervising the collection of taxes where these are imposed. He will reside near the principal town of the division, and each division in turn will be visited by the Resident. The Divisional Headquarters (involving the erection of new buildings, as well as political considerations) will not be transferred to another place without the prior concurrence of the Governor. The Resident himself will reside at the Provincial capital, which will also usually be the Headquarters of the Military detachment (if any) and of the Medical and Police Officers. Wherever he wishes to go on tour the District Officer in charge of the Headquarter division will deal with any urgent correspondence addressed to him or any urgent matter as may be directed by the Resident, unless the 'relief Resident' is present. . . .

A Province, or even a Division, may comprise various units of Native Administration, but in no case will such a unit be comprised partly in one Province and partly in another; and the same applies as a rule to a Division. The limits of the jurisdiction and authority of Native Chiefs may not be altered, or one Emirate or Chieftainship placed under another, without the sanction of the Lieutenant-Governor, who will in any case of importance consult the Governor. Such reference is necessary when it is proposed to subordinate a Chief hitherto independent, and more especially an independent Pagan Community to a Moslem Emirate which should very rarely, if ever, be done.

DEPARTMENTAL FUNCTIONS OF POLITICAL OFFICERS

19. A Political Officer has to represent various Departments and to exercise diverse functions in the Province to which he belongs. He acts as *Postal Officer*, in the absence of a European Officer of the Department, and is responsible for the despatch of mails in transit, and for the various duties laid down in the Regulations under the Postal Ordinance. The Postal and Telegraph Clerks, under his general supervision, will undertake the duties of issuing stamps, and preparing receipts for parcels and registered letters, etc.

The *Police* in his Province are under the general orders of the Resident, whose relation to them and to the Commissioner or Assistant Commissioner of Police is laid down in Police Regulations and in General Orders and elsewhere. Isolated Police Constables should never be stationed in villages since it deprives the Village Headman of responsibility and initiative; and men placed in such a position of power are apt to misuse their authority. Detachments without a European are always to be deprecated. When in charge of the Government prison, the District Officer will inspect it frequently and check the prisoners with the warrants at least once a month.

Political Officers will also assist the *Customs* on those inland frontiers where it is not possible for the Department to have a European representative, and also in the collection of Customs dues on Postal parcels; and in such capacity they exercise the powers of Customs Officers, and any preventive staff is under their orders. . . .

EXTRA-PROVINCIAL AFFAIRS

22. Residents should read all Bills published in the Gazette, prior to enactment, and they should submit to the Governor, through the Lieutenant-Governor, any suggestions or emendations which they consider would improve the Ordinance—more especially if they have any bearing on questions of Native Administration. They should also make a point of reading the proceedings of the Nigerian Council, including the Governor's review of the year.

THE ANNUAL REPORT

23. As soon as possible after the close of each year, the Resident will submit to the Lieutenant-Governor, through the Secretary, a report of the work done in his Province, and on all matters of interest connected therewith for the past year. The report will be written by the Resident in substantive charge of the Province. If he is absent on leave at the end of the year he will write it on his return if he is due back before the end of February. Otherwise he will leave a draft completed as far as possible to the date of his leaving, and the fact that this draft was left and forms the basis of the report will be stated by the Officer who completes and signs it.

The report will be typewritten on foolscap paper, on one side of the page only, and a third margin will be left. The pages will be numbered, and fastened together at the extreme left-hand corner only. Paragraphs will be numbered *consecutively from beginning to end*. It will be on fairly strong paper and sent unfolded. One copy only will be sent to Headquarters (the duplicate being retained in the Provincial Office), but in order to avoid unnecessary re-typing, a copy of paragraphs relating to trade should be sent for transmission to the Officer charged with the duty of compiling trade statistics. Reports will be written in the first person, and the use of slang terms or of vernacular words such as 'Doki', 'Mammie', etc., where they have English equivalents should be avoided, as also the term 'Whitemen' instead of 'the Government' or 'boys' where men are meant.

It is desirable that the Annual Report should be complete and self-contained record for reference, and with this object in view it will contain a brief summary of any important correspondence which has taken place during the year, included under its appropriate heading, setting out the conclusions and decisions arrived at without too much detail. It will aim at being a full statement of facts and events—even though some repetition is involved—including any matters already reported in the interim half-yearly report. Recommendations, requisitions, questions, and discussions of policy and departmental criticism, should be reserved for separate correspondence, the report being as I have said limited to a statement of events, facts and conclusions.

The report should be in terse phraseology in order that the maximum information may be included within reasonable length. The progress of each division should be separately related as part of the single unit of the Province, when dealing with various subject-heads as a whole. Any passage of interest from the Divisional Officers' report may be quoted, but their reports should not be attached in their entirety, or the Resident's report becomes a mere bundle of attachments.

Reports on subjects which are dealt with by a Departmental Officer will not repeat the statistics and details which would find a place in the latter Officer's report, but will give a general summary, with especial regard to the bearing of the work of the Department on the Provincial Administration. The Annual Reports will be transmitted to the Governor with the Lieutenant-Governor's comments upon them.

The Governor's notes on these reports must necessarily be so terse, that they may sometimes possibly read as though they conveyed dispraise when no such intention existed. Residents will bear in mind that the pressure of work necessitates brevity in these replies, and that the report is only one of many (including all Departmental ones) with which the Governor has to deal. When answering the Governor's or Lieutenant-Governor's comments and questions, the context should be briefly stated in order to save reference. . . .

Special care must be taken in compiling this report, since it is the most-important of the Provincial archives, which in future years may become of great interest and value. . . .

COMMERCIAL DEVELOPMENT[1]

26. It is an important part of the duty of the Political Staff to encourage trade by every means in their power, informing primitive tribes of the value of neglected sylvan produce, encouraging the growth of cotton, and collecting data as to the output and possibilities of increase of all products, sylvan or cultivated—whether by improved methods of transport or otherwise. They will enforce the Adulteration of Produce Ordinance by prosecutions for fraudulent adulteration, and will endeavour to maintain a high standard of purity by explaining that inferior produce—rancid kernels, discoloured cotton, greased or gritty hides, etc.—commands only a lower price. It is advisable not to press too strongly the cultivation of

---

[1] I have included this section out of the score or so headings listed by Lugard because it is sometimes naively suggested that the early administration paid heed to nothing save law and order.

any particular crop, but to leave it to the discretion of the planters, after informing them as far as possible of the prices obtainable and the probable extent of the demand. District Officers will forward samples of actual and possible economic products for transmission to the Imperial Institute; they will make suggestions and proposals having for their object the increase of trade; and will report where the collection of sylvan produce is only partial, and is capable of development and extension. They will report also on the nature of the requirements of the people, and suggest any new article which might, if imported, find a ready sale, and stimulate production, and they will state what facilities for, or improvements in, means of transport of produce can be given by Government; what openings there are for new trading-stations; and whether the markets are well attended and well supplied. For this purpose, as well as for adminitrative reasons, they will do their utmost to promote road-making throughout their Provinces, and encourage the use of wheeled transport.

FORMATION OF NEW VILLAGES

36. When a new village is built, inquiry will be made as to the origin of the new community, and their reason for abandoning their former residence. If they do not belong to the tribe in occupation of the district, the sanction of the local Chief must be obtained, and it must be clearly understood that they come under his jurisdiction and control, and pay their taxes (if a tax is therefore enforced) through the District Headman in whose area they have settled. If the immigrants are from foreign territory, no tribute will be enforced for the first year. The Chief or District Headman, whom the new village will acknowledge, will be determined by the ownership of the site of the town, according to native custom and land tenure. The settlement will be laid out by the District Officer, with adequately broad streets and market-places. . . . A Government Station should be from ¾ to 1 mile from the nearest village. . . .

MEMO NO. 4.
EDUCATION

THE PRINCIPLES OF AN EDUCATIONAL POLICY

9. The primary function of education should in my judgement be to fit the ordinary individual to fill a useful part in his environment with happiness to himself, and to ensure that the exceptional individual shall use his abilities for the advancement of the community, and not to its detriment, or to the subversion of constituted

authority. We are today beginning to realize our failure in this respect both in India and in West Africa. If the local Press may be taken as a criterion of the feelings of the educated communities in all the West African Colonies we must admit that education has not brought them happiness and contentment. It should be the ideal of a sound educational policy to exchange this hostility for an attitude of friendly co-operation, and to train a generation which shall be able to achieve ideals of its own without a slavish imitation of Europeans, and be proud of a nationality with its own definite sphere of public work and its own future.

The education afforded to that section of the population whose lives will be spent in the towns and villages in Nigeria, instead of making them unsuited to and ill-contented with their mode of life, should enlarge their outlook, increase their efficiency and standard of comfort, and bring them into closer sympathy with Government, and it should in particular produce a new generation of Native Chiefs of higher integrity, a truer sense of justice, and appreciation of responsibility for the welfare of the community. As regards that smaller section who desire to enter the service of Government or of commercial firms, education should make them efficient, loyal, reliable and contented—a race of self-respecting Native gentlemen. Finally, the policy should popularize education, and increase the output of youths well qualified to meet the demand.

The whole-hearted and loyal acceptance of a definite educational policy by all concerned in carrying it into effect is essential to success. There are few subjects which lend themselves in a greater degree to controversy, upon which every thinking man has his individual views. But progress can only be made by concentration of effort upon well-defined lines. The present policy was discussed for three years, and all interested have had an opportunity of expressing their opinions, and of adding bricks to the structure. . . . I look with confidence to Residents to take a keen personal interest in the schools, to work in close co-operation with the Education Officers and with unofficial agencies, and to do all in their power to remove prejudices and to popularize the schools. Hitherto there has been a lack of co-operation between Government and unofficial efforts. The Government on its part is at all times glad to receive opinions and practical suggestions.

SPECIFIC OBJECTS IN VIEW IN NIGERIA[1]

10. The objects in view and the principles to which it was sought to give effect may be summarized as follows:—

[1] Lugard drafted the Education Ordinance in 1914, but it was not enacted until December 1916. The average attendance at the Government Schools in 1913 was 354 in the North and 4,600 in the South. Some 30,000 more pupils attended unassisted schools in the South, while the North had 43 mission s chool

(a) That the primary object of all schools should be the formation of character and habits of discipline, rather than the mere acquisition of a certain amount of book-learning or technical skill, and that the grant in aid should be in part based on success in this direction.

(b) That the teaching should be adapted to the needs of the pupils, whether they are intending to qualify for clerical or other like service, or desire to become mechanics or artisans, or on the other hand have no wish to leave their village and the pursuits their fathers had followed.

(c) That the proportion of teachers to pupils should be adequate, that they should be properly qualified and their status improved. Adequate grants must be given to assisted schools (from which Government and commercial clerks are largely drawn) to enable them to pay adequate salaries to their staff.

(d) That educational agencies, whether controlled by Government or by Missions, should co-operate with a common object, and as far as possible by similar methods of discipline and instruction.

(e) That continuation and evening classes for advanced and for specialized study, and institutions and classes for the training of teachers, should receive special encouragement.

(f) That the value of religion, irrespective of creed or sect, and the sanction and incentive it affords, should be recognized and utilized as an agent for this purpose, together with secular moral instruction.

(g) That Government should exercise some measure of control over all schools, even though not assisted by grants, and endeavour to bring them into line with the general policy.

THE THREE TYPES OF EDUCATION REQUIRED

16. It is the aim of Government to take the lead in the application of the principles I have described. Three separate objects for which Educational Agencies are employed are recognized, viz. (a) the literary training required for posts in which a good knowledge of English and accountancy is necessary; (b) the technical training of mechanics and artisans employed with power-driven plant, and other technical work; and (c) the teaching of crafts and agriculture and the very elementary schooling suitable to village life.

Schools are being established by Government at the Head-quarters of each Province, and at other important divisional Head-quarters, to supply the secondary education required by the first class, and also that lesser standard necessary to enable the second class to become really efficient workmen. For the technical training of the latter class a Technical Institute is being established in the North, and apprenticeships are provided in all departments, as well as certain departmental schools in such technical subjects as forestry, agriculture, surveying, etc. For the third class, rural or village schools, affiliated to the Provincial School, are provided, and also one or more Central Industrial Schools.

PROVINCIAL (SECONDARY) SCHOOLS

17. It is intended that the Provincial Schools shall afford a secondary education, including all standards, but in the North there are at present so very few (if any) who have passed the 5th and 6th Standards, that a single Secondary School will be temporarily established near the Technical Institute at Kaduna, to which the advanced pupils from all the Provincial Schools may be sent. Since they are all required as teachers, it will in fact be, and will continue in the future to remain, a Training Institute for Teachers. Perhaps at some future date the Normal Class at this 'Secondary School' may develop into a Teachers' Institute and the school itself may be able to afford a kind of post-graduate course for teachers and others who have improved their opportunities since leaving school. Together with the Technical Institute it may possibly, in years to come, develop into the University of West Africa.

The provincial school will be residential, in order that the boys may be detached from their home surroundings, and come continuously under the influence of the Staff. By this means only can character be formed and habits of discipline inculcated. For the same reason the school should be located a mile or two from the Native city. Until the authorized limit of boarders is reached, a few day-boys may be accepted, but they should be replaced as soon as possible. Any youths who desire an advanced education may be transferred to the provincial from the rural schools. When a boy has passed the 5th Standard he may elect to continue his literary studies; or he may become an apprentice in a Government Department, or may join the Technical Institute, or he may become a teacher in a rural school. The main object of these Government Schools is to train boys to meet the demand for Government clerks and junior employees, but they will not be precluded from accepting employment with commercial firms or as officials of the Native Administration.

There will be continuation classes in special subjects, in extension of or in addition to the curriculum of school studies, and a large normal class for the training of teachers, the supply of whom, especially in the North, is at present the most urgent need.

The school will be under the eye of the Resident and the paramount Chief, and each school will have its own Advisory Committee, upon which they or their representatives will sit. The English Public School will form the model, and the British Headmaster and his

Native Staff will reside at the school. Native dress will be worn in all Government Schools. Polo, cricket, football and other suitable games, in which the Staff will participate, will be encouraged alike for their effects on health and manliness, as for the opportunities they afford of bringing masters and pupils together on friendly terms. In some Provinces games are regarded with disfavour, in others the parents appreciate their value. Games should not, therefore, be made compulsory, and in such a matter the prejudices of the parents should be given the fullest consideration. The schools will be regularly inspected by the Director of Education and his Inspectorate Staff.

Rules will be drawn up by the Headmaster in consultation with the Resident in regard to school discipline—e.g., the school precincts, the punishments which may be awarded, the hours of instruction and of recreation, the period assigned for holidays, etc.—and submitted through the Director of Education to the Lieutenant-Governor.

The language of social intercourse will be English or Yoruba in the South, and English or Hausa (Yoruba in Ilorin) in the North, as the case may be. The medium of instruction will be English in the South, and in the higher standards in the North—in the lower standards in the North—Hausa. A boy who is found to be intellectually deficient or dull will not be retained at school. In addition to the recognized scholarships, free tuition may be given to promising boys who are unable to meet the school fees. The cost will usually be borne by the Native Treasury, and the number of boys for whom provision is made will be fixed by the Chief and his Council.

The buildings should be in the Native style of architecture, and usually in the form of a parallelogram. The classrooms will have windows for ventilation on both sides, but above the level of the boys' desks. The schools will be erected and maintained by the Native administration, if funds permit, on sites which afford sufficient space for a recreation ground. They should be located two or three miles from the Native city and from the Township, so that the boys may be quite detached. The British Headmaster, who will live on the premises, will still be able to bicycle in and to keep touch with his colleagues, and the Resident and Staff can easily visit the school. If, however, in any particular provincial capital the prejudice against a detached boarding school is still so strong as to endanger the co-operation of the Native Administration, the project must be temporarily abandoned, but no permanent buildings will in that case be erected, and the Resident will do his utmost to prepare the transfer later. The danger is lest such a temporary arrangement should tend to become permanent. Pupils come from all parts of the Province, and many will, therefore, be boarders in any case, and it will not be to their advantage, or in the interest of discipline, that they should be exposed to the temptations of a city. If the school is (temporarily) in or close to the city, such boys will be housed in the school precincts and never in the town.

A preferable alternative would be to erect the permanent school buildings on the selected site, and (until the Native prejudice is overcome) allow the boys from the city to attend as day-boys. It is, of course, essential that the British Master should live in the school and maintain discipline and order.

No boy will be admitted to the lowest standard of a provincial school under the age of 12 or over 14. They may be admitted to the higher standards at similarly appropriate ages, allowing about one year for each standard. These rules may be relaxed in the case of sons of Chiefs, or in other exceptional cases. Since teachers are very urgently required in the North, a special class of Mallams may be formed for this purpose, even though they are over age as ordinary pupils. Boys will not be allowed to have personal servants. One or two old women will be engaged to do the cooking and general cleaning, each boy being responsible for his own sleeping quarter. Pupils may not marry while at a provincial school without the special sanction of the Director of Education. For sanitary reasons horses should not be kept on the premises. Holidays will be limited to two months in the year. The Head Native teacher in charge is responsible for discipline and general cleanliness. . . .

A boy who attains the highest standard at a provincial school should be a competent teacher or clerk, able to read, write, and speak English fluently. For appointment as Native Court Clerks and Interpreters in their own Province, the highest standard will not be necessary. It is desirable that the provincial school should supply candidates for these appointments who would be able to speak the local dialect fluently. They would, moreover, probably be less likely to impose upon the Native Chiefs who have known them from childhood. Efforts will be made to attract to these schools the sons of local Chiefs.

PROVINCIAL SCHOOLS AMONG BACKWARD TRIBES

18. In Provinces where the population consists of primitive tribes, the object of the provincial school is:—

(a) To train the more promising boys from the rural schools as Clerks for the local Native Courts and as Interpreters.

(b) To train teachers for the rural schools.

No attempt will at present be made in such provincial schools, e.g., those in Provinces populated by backward tribes, to teach the higher standards. Boys from the pagan schools will not be sent to any Secondary or Industrial School of which the atmosphere is Mohammedan, nor will Moslem teachers be employed in those schools. Teachers for such schools in the North may be procured from the South, or Native-foreigners, and West Indians may be employed if necessary.

INDUSTRIAL CLASSES FOR VILLAGE SCHOOL TEACHERS

19. Even in a school established in a more advanced community a class will be formed for the same purpose, where Native crafts, industries, and agriculture will be taught, so that boys who wish to become teachers in the rural schools may qualify in these branches, which form the chief subjects of instruction in those schools. It must be noted that these classes are for the *training of teachers* and not for the teaching of arts and crafts to ordinary pupils. The Government model plantation or garden would be at the service of the school for instruction in agriculture. To qualify as teachers in the rural schools, boys must also pass the 4th or 5th Standard and the normal class for imparting instruction and enforcing discipline. In the North they will be taught Hausa, and in the South English.

RURAL SCHOOLS (ELEMENTARY AND INDUSTRIAL)

20. For the third class referred to—the peasantry who do not seek either a literary education to qualify them as Clerks, etc., or a technical training for power-driven workshops—rural or village schools are provided. Their object is to improve the village craftsmen and agriculturists, to raise the standard of life, comfort and intelligence in the village community, and to teach habits of discipline, industry and truthfulness. At these schools trades will be taught (carpentry, blacksmithing, agriculture etc.), together with some rudimentary schooling in elementary hygiene, colloquial English or Hausa, and such moral or religious instruction, whether Christian or Mohammedan, as may help to free the peasant from the cruel domination of superstitious and inhuman practices. In the higher classes some small knowledge of 'the 3 R's' may be added, which shall render him less liable to be the victim of misrepresentation and fraud, and enable him to understand the simple processes of the Native Courts, etc. The schools will, therefore, be mainly industrial in character, and the pupils will spend, say, half their time in such work until they have passed the elementary course, and after that almost their entire time in learning a trade.

The most important trade in the country is agriculture, but the teaching of it in village schools should be limited to very simple facts combined with manual work; as, for instance, the value of rotation of crops, and of leguminous crops and manures as renovators of the soil, in lieu of the wasteful processes of 'shifting cultivation' now practised. . . .

The teaching of other crafts would be carried on in the same practical and simple fashion. Instead of being taught to make folding chairs to loll in, or fancy boxes, they will be instructed how to make doors and windows, stout simple furniture, and improved agricultural implements, to burn and lay bricks, and to construct improved houses. The object in view will be to raise the standard of comfort and decency in the village, rather than to make articles for sale to Europeans at a small profit, and the grant to an assisted village school should be in proportion as it conforms to these principles. . . . I should favour the appointment of one or more travelling masters, who would stay for a month or more at any particular school and organize its work and instruct its teachers.

These village schools are not intended to develop into Secondary Schools. But though the majority of the pupils will continue to lead their village life, there will be no doubt be a certain number of superior intelligence who will desire to be transferred to the provincial school, where they can receive a higher education to qualify for Government or other employment. Others may desire to attain a higher proficiency in manual training by entering the Industrial School, or in agriculture at the departmental school. The village school will thus become a feeder to the provincial school, from which many will return as teachers in the village schools. It is very desirable that sons of Chiefs should attend these schools if they do not join the provincial school.

Village schools are day-schools, and boys will enter the lowest (infants) class at ages not below 9 or above 11. The medium of instruction in the lowest classes must of necessity be the vernacular. In the higher classes Hausa in the North and English or Yoruba in the South. The instruction in the infant classes will be of the Kindergarten type. In the more advanced classes not more than two hours per diem will be devoted to 'book learning', except in the case of boys in the highest class who desire to pass into the provincial school. As boys pass from the infant classes, they will be divided into groups according as they wish to learn industrial crafts (carpentering, blacksmithing, etc.), or to devote themselves to agriculture.

CENTRAL INDUSTRIAL SCHOOLS

21. The industrial section of the original class at Nassarawa (Kano) has been retained as a Central Industrial School under the control of the Native Administration, where Native arts and crafts are taught by the skilled craftsmen of Kano, and a British instructor

paid by Government exercises supervision, and teaches the use of imported tools, and better methods, as well as some useful innovations, such as the making and laying of bricks and the construction of carts and wheels. . . .

To these schools teachers and boys can come who desire to improve their knowledge of Native crafts and to learn new methods. Considering, however, the urgency of the demand for trained mechanics for the Railway and other workshops, Residents must avoid too provincial an outlook, and not allow these schools, or the industrial class at the provincial school, to draw away boys who might otherwise enter the Technical Institute. The two schools at Kano and Maidugeri [sic] will suffice for all present needs.

There is no classroom instruction, but pupils can of course attend evening classes at the neighbouring provincial school. Woodwork and carpentry, metalwork, including engraving on copper and brass, and smiths' work, leather work and the making of saddles and other articles of leather, weaving and embroidery on cloth and leather are taught in the school. It is under the general supervision of the Education Department and the Political Staff.

TECHNICAL EDUCATION

22. It has already, I think, been made clear that the term Technical Education as used in this Memo. does not include Native arts and crafts. It refers primarily to mechanics and workshop hands employed on plant driven by steam or electricity. There are of course other forms of technical education, such as telegraphy, surveying, dispensary work, etc. . . .

The skilled mechanic handling power-driven machinery requires an entirely different training from that afforded by an industrial school. Those who aspire to become Native foremen, engineers in charge of vessels, or competent skilled mechanics working to plan and scale, require a knowledge of English and of simple figures. They should have attended a Primary School and passed Standard IV or V before being accepted as apprentices. Their training should be conducted entirely by the technical departments, but, instead of being left to the chance assistance of Europeans engaged in work themselves, there must be an Instructor attached to each of the larger workshops, whose sole duty it will be to look after and instruct the apprentices. I propose that such Instructors should be attached to the principal Railway, Public Works and Marine shops. . . . For those who show special aptitude, continuation classes will be formed in which they can study simple theory and drawing, etc. These classes will be held by the Instructor before working hours, or in lieu of the earlier working hours, when the lads are not tired out physically.

Youths who have passed Standard V before completing their apprenticeship will be termed 'first grade' apprentices.

There is also a separate class, viz., casual labourers employed in the shops, who have shown intelligence and skill, and have gradually picked up knowledge, and been promoted to posts involving more and more skill, until they have become very valuable shop hands in charge of some particular machine. This is a very useful class deserving every encouragement. They are of course generally illiterate and can never aspire to the higher posts as foremen, etc. They may be engaged as 'second grade' apprentices. With the exception of these shop hands no boys will be accepted as apprentices unless they have passed the 4th Standard, when they can be engaged as 2nd Grade apprentices. . . .

In order to attract boys who have passed the 5th Standard to engage themselves as 1st Grade apprentices, the profession must be made more attractive. Mr. Carr, who is the best authority on such a point, asserts emphatically that the preference of the educated youths for clerical appointments does not arise from a contempt for labour, but because the clerical profession offers better pecuniary prospects and a better social position. If the new system produces good men who can replace the West Indians and other aliens now being imported, and even to some extent the European foremen, it will be a saving to the Government to appoint local men on good salaries. In the meantime something can be done to better the social status of these apprentices by providing recreation rooms and grounds, encouraging *esprit de corps* and promoting competitions between them and the clerical departments.

TECHNICAL EDUCATION IN NORTHERN PROVINCES

23. None of the intelligent Moslem population of the Northern Provinces has as yet been trained in the workshops of the Public Works Department or Railway in the North. The difficulty hitherto has been that the Government establishments are manned by coast men, whose language, religion, dress, and customs are entirely different from their's. The two classes will not readily amalgamate and the prospect of association would, I am informed, deter the better class Mohammedan youths from adopting this career.

In order to overcome this difficulty, the bequest made by Sir A. Jones was devoted to the foundation of a Technical Institute, for the training in mechanical engineering, etc., of pupils in the Northern Provinces. . . . Its proximity to the Central Railway Workshops, the erection of which at Kaduna has long been approved, will enable pupils to have practical demonstrations beyond the scope of the resources of the Institute.

It will be a Government institution . . . and boys who have passed Standard IV in the provincial schools will be eligible to enter between the ages of 14 and 16. They will spend about four years at the Institute, the two last being specialized in the line in which they show most aptitude, and will then be drafted to the Railway or Public Works Department workshops under a five years' indenture as apprentices on a progressive salary. A pupil who during the earlier part of his course at the Institute is found unsuitable intellectually or physically, or who desires to abandon it, either because he finds it distasteful or because he does not desire to become an apprentice, can either return to the 'literary' branch, or be transferred to the Industrial School or return to his village. The instructors in the Institute will be skilled British mechanics, and the medium of instruction will be English. Opportunity for improving his education in reading, writing, arithmetic and geometry will be afforded to the pupil by means of special classes (some of which may be obligatory) held by the instructors of the Secondary School. This school and the Institute will be side by side about a mile north of the Kaduna capital, and this proximity will, I trust, promote a friendly rivalry in sports and social interests, and prevent *ab initio* the idea that the clerk occupies a higher social sphere than the skilled mechanic. By such means only shall we succeed in producing skilled labourers who may later replace the British foreman, whose services are so costly, and are likely in the future to be difficult to obtain. The two schools together—the Secondary School for the higher education of Native officials and the Technical Institute for the training of skilled mechanics and foremen in every department of technical work—will form the 'Gordon College' of the Northern Provinces distinct in their aims yet closely associated in their social life, and both guided by a common policy in which the formation of habits of discipline, integrity and industry are the keynote.

CLERICAL APPRENTICES OR 'CADETS'

24. Parents deplore the tendency of young men to embark prematurely on an independent career, which in such circumstances can offer little prospect of success, and exposes them to temptation, and to the cost of maintaining a separate establishment beyond their means. It is very greatly to be desired that parental discipline should be supported in every way possible, and though a clerk in the Government Service must be available to be sent wherever his services are required, it will no doubt happen that a considerable number of juniors are or can be employed in the largest centres where their parents reside.

To effect the object in view I propose a scheme of clerical apprentices between the ages of 17 and 20, with salaries rising from £24 to £36 by increments of £4 during four years. They would reside during this apprenticeship with their parents, and would attend school for two hours in the day and one hour in the evening. They would be called 'Student Clerks' or 'Cadets', and if they pass the required tests at the end of their term they would have received a much better and more prolonged education than the ordinary clerk. They would be bound to enter the Government Service for a period of, say, five years, and would be eligible for accelerated promotion. Eventually the cadets might become a *corps d'élite* and aspire to high posts.

AGRICULTURE

28. The attempts to create an Agricultural School in the Southern Provinces have not been successful. The profession is not apparently attractive to the class which attends the schools, while the conservative agriculturist of the Interior is intolerant of new methods. Renewed efforts must be made to train boys as Instructors and as Overseers for the Department.

In the North a small class has been formed for tuition by the Departmental Staff, and I hope that more applicants will be available from the Provincial Schools.

SPECIAL SCHOOLS

(a) *King's College*

32. There are one or two special Schools which stand outside this general organization. King's College, Lagos, has a Staff of three British Masters, and is the highest Government educational establishment in Nigeria, but it has little chance of setting an example in the training of character, so long as its students are not boarders. It is important that it should be made a Boarding School as soon as possible. . . .

King's College should be able to give a boy the greater part of the Education he requires, preparatory to specialized study for the two professions which afford the best opening for the sons of wealthy Natives, who can afford to send their boys to England to take a degree in Medicine or Law. I hope that a scheme now under consideration for an African Hostel in London will facilitate the exercise of some measure of control in such cases, and shorten the period of exile. But before adopting these professions a young man will do well to consider the alternative of planting or farming, after a course of education in agriculture, or of starting as a trader or merchant. No doubt, a good income can be made in any of these

I

lines by those who prefer an independent life to service under Government or a commercial firm. . . .

(c) *The Aliens' school in Northern Provinces*

Since the Northern Provinces at present produce no clerks or artisans for the Government Service, there are at the Capital a very large number of Coast men, for whose children a special school has been established at Kaduna. It is a Christian school and the medium of instruction is English.

EVENING AND CONTINUATION CLASSES

33. The Regulations lay stress on the provision of Continuation, Vacation and Evening Classes, and every Government Provincial School will institute them. . . . No school can be considered thoroughly efficient which does not provide them. . . .[1]

MEMO No. 5.
TAXATION

MORAL EFFECT OF DIRECT TAXATION

(a) *Stimulates industry*

4. 'Experience (I wrote) seems to point to the conclusion that in a country so fertile as this, direct taxation is a moral benefit to the people by stimulating industry and production. . . .'

(b) *Inevitable corollary of abolition of forced labour*

5. In those communities in which forced labour, whether in the form of domestic slavery or of arbitrary exactions, formed the basis of the social system, 'direct taxation as being the State recognition of the rights and responsibilities of the individual is the moral charter of independence of a people'. It imposes on the freed slave, on the one hand, the obligation to render to the State, to which he owes his liberty, some portion, however small, of the labour or its equivalent which was formerly the sole property of his master, while the latter, deprived of the forced labour of his slaves, is compelled to lead a more useful life, either by personal effort, or by taking an active part in the labours of administration in return for a salary provided by means of taxation. . . . Direct taxation may be said to be the corollary of the abolition, however gradual, of forced labour and domestic slavery.

[1] This noble sentiment does not seem to have found favour with the subsequent Departments and Ministries of Education, though the Universities are reviving it.

DIRECT TAXATION: A UNIVERSAL NECESSITY OF
CIVILIZATION

6. There is no civilized State in the world where direct taxation
has not been found to be a necessity, and African communities
which aspire to be regarded as civilized must share the common
burden of civilization. Temporary expedients may be found in the
early stages of administrative organization to postpone the burden,
or transitory circumstances—such as the revenue from the liquor
traffic—may temporarily defer its necessity, but such postponement
can be but temporary if the ideal of the community is to tread the
path of progress and civilization. Postponement is, in my judgement,
a short-sighted and weak policy, and renders the eventual necessity
all the harder of accomplishment. . . .

SUPPORT OF NATIVE AUTHORITY AND PROTECTION OF
PEASANTRY

7. Apart from the beneficial results of taxation . . . the immediate
object of direct taxation is to provide a revenue, which, being
collected through the medium of the Native Rulers and in accordance
with Native law and custom, can therefore be properly shared with
them—not as a dole from Government, which would destroy their
self-respect, but as their proper dues from their own people in return
for their work as Rulers or Judges. They are thus provided with
legitimate incomes, and all other forms of exaction from the peasantry can be declared illegal and suppressed. In unorganized communities, where Native Rulers properly so-called cannot be said to
exist, the creation of salaried Chiefs affords a valuable means of
instituting and enforcing native authority. In States under organized
rule, such as the Moslem States of the North, or Benin, Yoruba-land
and Egba-land in the South, it is imperative to provide an adequate
income for the Chiefs and Officers of the Native State before it is
possible to put a stop to forced labour, heavy taxes on traders,
arbitrary exactions of all kinds from the peasantry, and the perversion
of justice by means of bribes or unjust fines. To effect this object the
Native Revenue Ordinance was enacted in the Northern Provinces,
while the Native Authority Ordinance was passed to support the
authority of the Chiefs, both in the collection of the authorized
taxes, and in the maintenance of order.

CONDITIONS IN THE SOUTHERN PROVINCES

8. It was sought by these means in the Northern Provinces to find a
solution for the difficulties attendant on the abolition of the legal status

of slavery, to support the ruling classes and to protect the peasantry. The two latter objects are becoming no less insistent in the Southern Provinces, where a new incentive to the re-organization of the Native Administration exists in the disintegrating influences exercised by alien settlers, who are apt to repudiate the control of the local Native authority. With the advent of the railway the Northern Provinces would for the first time have been seriously exposed to this new influence had not the system built up in previous years been strong enough to withstand it.

The influence of the various Missions in the Southern Provinces has in the past been no less destructive, I fear, of Native authority, for the converts considered themselves emancipated from the rule of their Chiefs and looked to their teachers alone. The Government itself, by allowing its district officials, however unwittingly, to aggrandize subordinate Chiefs, and by failing to substitute legitimate means of maintaining the position of Chiefs for those which it rightly abolished, and again by modelling its Native Courts on the procedure of the Supreme Court, with the result that the Court Clerk often usurped the authority of the Chief, and by giving the Supreme Court an unlimited jurisdiction (which tended to the supersession of Native law and custom) seriously contributed to the causes which led to the decay of Native authority. These causes are, I trust, already in process of amelioration, but without an assured revenue for the Native Administration, no effective reconstruction can be accomplished. . . .

RESULTS IN NORTHERN PROVINCES

9. The result in the Northern Provinces may be claimed as a success. The Chiefs and officials of the Native Administration are provided with adequate incomes, which they earn by taking an active, and very onerous, share in the administration of the country, while the peasantry are contented and prosperous as they have never been before, and are relieved from the uncertain exactions of the past. Slavery on the other hand is rapidly dying out, not by drastic action on the part of Government, but by voluntary liberation through the Native Courts, because in the new order of things owners are recognizing that it is not merely unnecessary, but an expensive and troublesome form of labour contract. . . .

The Administrative Staff of the Northern Provinces, to whose ability and indefatigable work, and above all to whose sympathy with the people these results are solely due, have life-long cause for pride in their achievement, the patent results of which need no exaggeration.

PROMOTES CLOSE TOUCH WITH THE PEOPLE

10. It is indeed by no means the least benefit of direct taxation, that it effects much more than the mere collection of revenue, and promotes an intimate touch between the British Staff and the Natives, whether the latter are officials of the Native Administration, and the assistants of the District Staff in the work of assessment, or whether they are inhabitants of remote and almost inaccessible villages whose very existence, but for this task of assessment, might have remained unknown. Though the District Officer comes at first as a tax-gatherer, the amount he claims is negligible and constitutes no burden, while his visit preludes the cessation of the horrible cruelties of witchcraft ordeal, the protection of the weak and aged, and the gradual substitution of order and justice for oppression and the law of the strongest. He must be constantly on tour, and the visit to each village should simultaneously involve the settlement of ancient disputes, the administration of justice, the collection of valuable statistics, and above all it will afford opportunity to the District Officer to explain to each village Head the obligation to refrain from lawless acts, the policy of Government, the allegiance owed to their own Chiefs (and the co-operation between Government and those Chiefs).

'Direct taxation ensures the selection of the most capable and most influential men as the Chiefs and Advisers, and invests them with authority and responsibility. Both in the assessment, collection, and disposal of the revenue they become a part of the Government of the country, and incompetence or dishonesty is soon exposed. With the advent of competent and responsible Native Rulers, discipline and good order are introduced.'

REVENUE FOR NATIVE ADMINISTRATION PURPOSES

11. The share of the general tax assigned to the Native Administration affords, not merely the means for providing an adequate income for its officials, but also a fund by the aid of which the Native Administration can take a direct part in such of the projects of Government as it is well fitted to co-operate in. . . . The Native Rulers and Officials will thus find fresh scope for their energies and a pride in the progress of their country.

RESPONSIBILITY OF GOVERNMENT

12. The Government is responsible that the taxes (in which it shares) are just and reasonable, and that the method of collection is such as will distribute the burden fairly, before it can pledge its power to enforce them if necessary. The object in view is to retain

as far as possible the ancient tribute as sanctioned by Native law and custom, and to preserve the individuality of the institutions of the country; to utilize the Native machinery for the purpose; and to introduce some uniformity and equality in the incidence of taxation in the different provinces. The result it aims at is to emancipate the people from indolence on the one hand and forced service on the other, and to raise them to a plane of greater communal and individual responsibility.

GENERAL CHARACTER OF THE CHANGE OF SYSTEM

13. The earlier memorandum thus summarized the change of system: 'the assessment is based upon the sum of the existing taxation (where taxation existed) modified by the Resident after careful personal inquiry and in accordance with the actual present wealth and ability of the village to pay. It was thus neither a mere consolidation of the existing taxes, nor was it an arbitrary assessment *de novo* by the Resident. Its merit, in my view, was that it partook of both characters. So far as it was based on tradition and custom it ensured a ready acceptance among a conservative people, and its collection presented no novel difficulties, while so far as it was modified by the Resident, consolidated, and fixed alternatively at a money value payable only once in the year, it inaugurated the beginnings of new principles, recognized in more advanced communities, and enabled the collection to be made in a manner in which the proceeds could best be utilized by the Administration, and accounted for in accordance with financial instructions, while it ensured a more just incidence and greater uniformity.'

NATURE OF THE 'GENERAL TAX'

14. . . . In no conceivable way can tax be raised more fairly than as a contribution by each individual according to his wealth, whether he be an agriculturist or a craftsman, a trader or a collector of sylvan produce, a nomad herdsman or a dweller in the cities, a Chief or a peasant. The tax in the terms of the Ordinance is to be levied as far as possible in accordance with Native custom, and Sir Percy Girouard writes that 'Mohammedan taxation as a whole has undoubtedly the basis of an income tax assessed upon the wealth of the individual'. 'As a result (he says) a rough income tax was imposed upon agriculturists, cattle-owners and industrials.' The task of arriving at how much each individual should pay is the joint duty of the British and Native Staff.

In my former Memorandum the tax was described as 'not levied on a man's hut or cultivated land, to neither of which has the State any right, and any claims to which he will cordially resent', but as levied 'on the income and profits of each individual' according to his ability to pay, regardless of the source from which he derives his income.

LAND RENTS

15. My successor in Northern Nigeria suggested in gradual substitution for this, a 'national income based on national land tenure, land rents and an income tax'. A great part of his Memorandum is concerned with this question of economic rent, which he directed should be 'kept quite apart from the improvements made'.

I desire to make it perfectly clear to all Political Officers in the Northern Provinces, that the Native Revenue Ordinance does not impose the duty of calculating an 'economic rent', and under the 'Lands and Native Rights Ordinance' there is no object or use in ascertaining the 'prairie value' of land unless it is proposed to grant a Right of Occupancy in respect of it to an alien, since the economic rent is included in the tax, and the Secretary of State has laid it down that there is no intention of charging rents to Natives of the soil under the Ordinance. The two subjects of Land and Taxation are kept quite distinct under separate Ordinances and must be so dealt with.

The taxation imposed by the Revenue Ordinance is an income tax, at a rate to be fixed by the Governor, while the rents imposed by the Land Ordinance are limited exclusively to Rights of Occupancy granted by the Governor. The suggestion . . . that the cultivator of the soil is liable to an economic rent under the Native Revenue Ordinance, for the land he occupies over and above the general income tax, has no legal sanction.

THE DISTRICT HEADMAN

36. The area ruled over by a paramount Chief is thus divided into districts, of which the Headman is the chief Executive Officer responsible to the Emir and Resident for its control and good order, and for the annual payment of the tax. He replaces the former fief-holder and also the Jekada or tax-gatherer. The duties of the latter as messenger or agent are now discharged by the accredited messengers of the Emir or the District Headman, or by Government or Court couriers carrying a symbol or wearing a dress of office. They are paid fixed salaries by the Native Administration, or by the District Head, and are not in any case authorized to make any demands whatever on the villagers. If not the former fief-holder, the District Head is a local Chief of influence and good repute, and must always be a freeman. The Head of a District may require a small staff to assist him in his duties. This will be fixed by the Emir and Resident

and submitted for approval with the estimates. In the Kano Emirate, where the population is extremely dense, it has been necessary in most districts to appoint a sub-district Headman, but these will, I hope be gradually eliminated. The accurate delimitation of these districts in consultation with the Emir, and their incorporation in the provincial map, was the first and most important task in the inauguration of the new system. They must not be confused with the 'district' of which an Assistant District Officer is in charge, which may include many Headman's districts (or a portion of one), and is a part of one of the 'Divisions' into which a Province is divided.

On the completion of the collection of the tribute the District Head will personally bring it to the Emir with his own statement kept as nearly as possible in the form of the Tribute Register, showing the amount paid by each village, and those in default (if any). In his capacity as Executive Chief it is also his duty to arrest criminals and bring them before the Native Court, and to see that estates of deceased persons are administered by the same tribunals. It is his duty to collect the fines imposed by the Native Court, of which he is notified by the Alkali.

In primitive districts where there is no paramount Chief the District Head may himself be the highest Native authority representing an independent community. In that case he will bring the tribute to the Divisional Officer, who will pay him his salary. The Village Heads are paid their percentage of the tax through the District Head.

AGRICULTURISTS—TAKI

40. For the diversity of taxes [described in paragraph 18], a single tax is substituted called the 'General Tax' or 'Haraji'. It has transpired that even so late as the present year many taxes were being paid in one Province to the Village Head, in addition to the Government tax. Residents must, therefore, keep a watchful eye on Native officials and prosecute them if discovered in such practices.

As regards the agricultural section of the community, the new consolidated tax is paid equally by the estate-owner or the peasant, since it is based on the usufruct enjoyed by each. There are, however, few, if any, estates now in the Northern Provinces which are claimed to be privately owned by a landlord class. The estates formerly held as appanages of office are now replaced by fixed salaries, and the peasants who cultivated them have become small independent occupiers. . . .

Since the value per acre under cultivation of the ordinary produce, exclusive of specially valuable crops on irrigated land, varies but little in different holdings—though its average value may be greater or less in different districts according to the proximity of good markets and the Railway—the simplest way of assessing the income of a cultivator is to measure the land he holds and charge the tax on the income which should be derivable from it. The rate will not vary (being 1/10th), but the amount realized by the tax will vary according to the market value of the produce. To effect this I had at one time hoped gradually to institute a Cadastral or Revenue survey, but this very expensive scheme has been rendered unnecessary for the present, by the use of Mallamai trained in the simple processes of land survey. This system of Native land survey, known as 'Taki Survey', has afforded excellent results in Kano. It is only required where the population is dense, and practically the whole of the land surveyed is under cultivation. If applied in sparsely populated areas it may lead to the curtailment of cultivation. . . .

Some of the junior officers (it seems to me from reading various assessment reports) appear to regard 'Taki' as a rent for land which once fixed is constant, no matter what the annual yield of crops may be. A moment's reflection will convince them of the fallacy of this idea, for 'Taki' is professedly calculated on the usufruct or yield of the land. Land rents may be imposed, but this is a different matter from the tax on the annual income derived from them, which is all that we are at present concerned with. That tax, as Mr. Arnett points out, and as I have emphasized in this Memorandum, is dependent on the yield and on market prices. The Ordinance goes further and says that the yield may be calculated on what the land should produce if cultivated to a normal standard. It needs no 'Taki system', therefore, to penalize the lazy farmer, who prefers a small yield from a large area rather than to make the most of his land, but it is in the enforcement of this liability that the 'Taki' system has its main value, for without it the assessing officer cannot tell what area the individual holds, and what should be his income. . . .

PASTORALS AND STOCK

41. The 'Jangali' (livestock tax) is shown in the returns separately, but it is in reality only that part of the General Tax which falls on owners of livestock. If they own nothing else, as in the case of nomad herdsmen, their contribution to the General Tax consists of Jangali only, and the rate fixed is approximately the same as on other forms of property or wealth, viz., at present one-tenth of the annual value. If on the other hand the livestock is only part of the property (as in the case of village cattle) the owner pays on it equally with land and crops, but for convenience of collection and statistics the payments are separately classified as 'General Tribute' and 'Jangali', each being one tenth of the annual value of the property.

It is in principle immaterial whether the tax is levied as Jangali or included in the taxable income assessed under the General Tax. Herds and flocks would usually be dealt with under the former, and sheep and goats individually owned under the latter.

The collection of the tax on stock will be made between July 1st and October 31st, when the flocks and herds have returned from the *Fadama* frequented in the dry season. During these wet season months the herds are as a rule in the districts in which their owners reside and the Emir will in his own interest be careful to see that the herds have returned. In no case may collectors be sent into other Provinces—a procedure which is apt to lead to disputes and to excessive exactions. . . .

Residents must make arrangements to collect from every herd or flock in their Province, irrespective of ownership, during the period named, unless the owner can produce a permit stating the number of cattle on which Jangali has been already levied. Such permits can be given in respect of oxen used for pack transport, or cattle en route to a market for slaughter. The District Head in whose district herds or flocks happen to be at time of collection will report the presence of every herd, and its ownership and numbers. If any departure from this procedure seems necessary in any Province, the Resident will report the circumstances and ask for instructions. The Revenue collected will always be credited to the Province which makes the collection. This system of territorial collection, which at first presented many difficulties has now become both necessary and feasible, as I anticipated in my earlier memorandum that it would, with the inevitable evolution from clan jurisdiction to territorial jurisdiction.

FORCED LABOUR—ROADS, ETC.

44. The single duty which the law imposes upon the people without remuneration is the maintenance of roads and waterways. The Ordinance of 1916 does not include the making of new roads, nor are the people called upon to maintain metalled roads unless used by wheeled vehicles belonging to Natives. Their obligation is limited to the 'sweeping' of the roads, e.g., keeping down weeds, patching up holes, or ruts, and clearing the drains. Where long stretches of road intervene between villages a grant may be made by the Native Administration to assist.

Forced (e.g., unpaid) labour for building town walls or Chief's residences is prohibited. The Native Treasuries in the one case, and the liberal salaries given to Chiefs in the other, can well afford to bear such charges. No taxes, licences, dues, or royalties, unless sanctioned by Ordinance, may be levied by any Chief or collected by Government officials, and no unpaid labour may be employed other than that authorized by law as already described. All these are now included in the General (Income) Tax, and the collection of a tax merely because it existed in former times (as was stated in reply to recent questions regarding a butcher's tax and *Kurdin Rua*) is wholly unauthorized. Licences and dues levied for a specific privilege are of course not 'taxes' and are expended on the service for which they are raised.

ASSESSMENT REPORTS

49. The assessment returns and map will be accompanied by a report on the area assessed. The Assessing Officer in the prosecution of this work is brought into such close relations with the local Chiefs and people, and, in obtaining the information has opportunities of learning so much about their history, origin and affinities, that the occasion should be taken to write a concise historical and ethnological account of the people. The data already collected in this way in the districts of the Northern Provinces which have an approved assessment are extraordinarily interesting and surprisingly complete. . . .

The Assessing Officer will give full particulars of the method by which he arrived at the census of population, and at his appraisement of the taxable capacity of the villages, and whether he estimates that it is higher or lower than the former obligations (if any) imposed on the people. He should also state to what extent he anticipates that the tax will be paid in cash, and, if any part is in kind, what is its nature and whether any difficulty in realization is likely to occur.

DUTY OF THE VILLAGE HEAD

51. The village is the unit of collection, and the village Head is responsible for collecting the tax and taking it to the District Head. There is, of course, only one Head recognized as such by Government in any village. He should be encouraged to keep a full record of the individuals and the amount paid by each. In preliminary assessments he must be mainly responsible for apportioning the tax to each individual according to his relative degree of prosperity; nor is this task as difficult as it would seem at first sight, for in the previously taxed districts the people are accustomed to an assessment and have a shrewd sense of equity. In 'approved assessments' the goal at which we aim is that each individual should be assessed according to his wealth, and informed of the amount he has to pay. The tax-payer must clearly understand that the demand contains, and is not in addition to, the old taxes, and if these are collected in addition, the Village Head is liable to imprisonment.

The Village Head should, when possible, associate with himself other influential men on the lines of the Indian 'Panchayet', for in India the appraisement of the income and taxable capacity of each individual in the village is still, I believe, left to the Village Headman, even after some centuries of British rule. These alone have knowledge of the income of each man, and on a revision they alone can say whose wealth has increased or decreased, or whether the population has grown greater or less. The statements of the Village Head and his 'Panchayet' can be usefully and effectively checked by the District Head. . . .

An assessment based on a properly graduated Income Tax can only be achieved by the careful training of the District and Village Heads. 'The education of the Native Administration in the assessment of the individual's share of the total demand on the basis of a rough Income Tax is (wrote Sir P. Girouard) a most important part of the British official's work'. It is not advisable to wait till a Village Head 'is proved to have acquired sufficient knowledge and education to carry out the system of assessing individual wealth' before attempting to graduate the tax. His education can only be achieved by actual training and practice. It is surprising how few complaints have hitherto been received.

INDIVIDUAL ASSESSMENT IN ADVANCED COMMUNITIES

54. I have in the preceding paragraphs described the method by which the individual will be assessed, and the amount made known to him. In brief the village tax list with the liability of each individual —or at any rate of those who pay a heavier tax than the average—is inaugurated by the District Officer at the original assessment. It is kept up to date and enlarged by the Village Head, and may be seen by any individual on demand. . . .

THE TAX RECEIPT

56. As an additional check on the Village Head and in order to verify the statement of an appellant, it is desirable that he should give to each taxpayer a receipt for the amount he has been called upon to pay, coloured differently for successive years, and perhaps different in shape for men and women. Failure to produce a receipt will prove evasion of payment, and the Village Head must be strongly supported in such case. . . .

COLLECTION BY DISTRICT STAFF IN PRIMITIVE AREAS

59. Among the more primitive tribes, where the central authority is still weak or non-existent, the District Headman can only be evolved at the cost of much labour and time, and even the Village

Head will have but little authority and be of little use. In such cases the tax must be not only assessed but also collected under the personal supervision of the District Staff, but in no circumstances are police to be used in assisting to collect the tax either directly or indirectly. If the Assessing Officer considers it necessary to have a police escort with him, the Resident will obtain the prior sanction of the Lieutenant-Governor. Since it will, in most cases, be practically a Capitation Tax the task will not be difficult. If the tribe had been conquered by Moslems and already taxed, the nature and extent of the taxation should be recorded. Independent tribes have as a rule shown themselves willing to pay, provided they can do so direct to Government and not through an over-lord or Native tax-gatherer.

The independence therefore of tribes which have maintained it against all Native aggression should be respected by allowing them to pay direct to Government through their own Village Heads. In the course of time, District Heads can be created for groups of villages, and whenever any Chief can be found who can exercise some authority, he will be made a District Head (however inefficient at first) and placed on a fixed salary.

TAX ASSISTS IN PROGRESS OF THE TRIBE

60. Thus I hope that the tribute will assist in accomplishing the main object of the administration, by grouping communities under responsible heads, through whom Government may rule and de-centralize its powers and functions, always endeavouring to push each community a step further up the ladder of progress, and of individual and municipal responsibility. At the foot of the ladder are the primitive tribes without cohesion, and recognizing no tribal authority, who must at first pay their small tax village by village direct to Government, in contrast with the organized Native Administration which collects its tax through its own salaried and responsible officials, and accounts for it in its own Native Treasury.

IMPORTANCE OF TAX HOWEVER SMALL IN AMOUNT

62. Even though the collection of the small tribute from primitive tribes may at first seem to give more trouble than it is worth, it is in my view of great importance as an acknowledgement of British Suzerainty, involving abstention from murdering traders and general lawlessness—which they recognize to be prohibited. It is, also, though negligible today, the nucleus of a future revenue on a basis of population and wealth, to which from their earliest contact with Government they will have become accustomed, and which with the increase of wealth and trade will some day become of great importance. It is, moreover, a matter of justice that all should pay their

share alike, whether civilized or uncivilized, and those who pay are quick to resent the immunity of others. Finally, and in my judgement the most cogent reason, lies in the fact that the contact with officials, which the assessment and collection necessitates, brings these tribes into touch with civilizing influences, and promotes confidence and appreciation of the aims of Government, with the security it affords from slave raids and extortion.

ANNUAL REVISION

64. The approved assessment should, so far as possible, be checked and brought up to date annually. Increase of population; of cultivated land, and of livestock; improvement in value of produce by development of means of communication, transport, and markets; and growth of trade; may all have tended to increase the wealth of the community, and hence the amount due as tax. On the other hand, migration, famine, or other causes, may necessitate a temporary decrease. The value of the crops will vary from year to year.

Among the more advanced communities this revision may be effectively carried out by summoning the district and Village Heads to the provincial or divisional headquarters, where the paramount Chief in discussion with them, will be able to arrive at a very fair estimate of any necessary changes, as is done annually in Sokoto. As time permits, the District Officer would check this revision on the spot and re-assess the individual taxes. In less advanced communities the lack of intelligent and trained Native assistance will often necessitate the continued adoption, perhaps for several years, of an assessment once made, subject to such rough and ready modifications as may obviously be necessary. The application to the individual of the modifications made in the annual revision will necessarily fall chiefly on the Village Head, until such time as the District Officer is able to visit the place and readjust the tax list; nor is it conceivably possible that the British Staff could annually revise the taxes of each individual among some ten million souls. He should be instructed to explain the cause of any increase to the people, lest they should fear that increased industry would involve them in disproportionate taxation. It is only by thus testing his ability, that a Village Head can learn his work and become efficient.

When revision is due to some sudden change, such as a failure of crops, or a large increase or decrease of the population due to migration or sickness, etc., the necessary changes in taxation may amount to a re-assessment but in the vast majority of cases the annual revision will involve but small change. . . .

The paramount Chief will keep his own register separately, and the Resident will consult him as to whether any revision of an approved assessment is advisable. No pledges of immutability should be given, as the amount is liable to variation each year according to seasonal variation in the value of the crops, etc. Sir P. Girouard anticipates that it will be possible for the Resident 'each year just after the rains, when the probable amount of the crop can be foretold with fair accuracy, to call the District and Village Heads to his headquarters', and fix the tax for the year.

DISPOSAL OF TAX

66. The tax is paid into the Native Treasury, and, except in the case of the most primitive tribes, one-half is retained by the Native Administration, the other half being credited to Revenue. In the case of primitive tribes where the salaries are very low, 25 per cent. may be assigned but if there is no Native Treasury 5 per cent. or 10 per cent. will suffice for the payment of the Village Heads, who are the only Native officials to receive a share. Of the revenue accruing to a Native Treasury from the General and Jangali Taxes, the percentage now passed to 'Central', 'District Heads', and 'Village Heads' in different Provinces varies extremely. As a rough and ready rule I think that, in an advanced Emirate, the total of all three should not exceed from 50 per cent. to 60 per cent. of these taxes roughly in the proportion of 12, 24, 15, to Central, District and Village, respectively.[1] The proportion in Pagan Treasuries will be less.

SALARIES OF NATIVE ADMINISTRATION OFFICIALS

67. When the system was first inaugurated, all Chiefs and officials of the Native Administration were paid a percentage of the tax, but this was only a temporary expedient until the scheme should have become fully operative, and it should be clear what incomes were required in order to enable them to maintain their positions, when the percentages would be converted into fixed salaries.[2] This has now been done in all cases except the Village Heads, and even they are in some Provinces being paid salaries. 'As long (writes Mr. Palmer) as the Chiefs took a share, it was almost impossible to lay stress on the distinction between the Government share and the collector's

[1] Cf. page 93 and n.

[2] The original percentages were: Paramount Chief 22%; District Head 17%; Officials 6%; Village Head 5%; Government 50%.
Where there was no Paramount Chief, a District Head who paid direct to Government received 22%, the Village Head 8%, and Government 70%. Where there was no District Head, the Villages Heads received 5–10% and Government 90–95%. On *jangali*, the principal chief was paid 35%, the head of the *ruga* or cattle-camp 10%, the collectors 5% and Government 50%.

share; but, when they are salaried, Chiefs are bound to bring their full tribute to account, and it is more difficult to conceal temporary financial expedients. They must now collect accurately and account accurately, or be found out'.

Each independent unit has a Treasury of its own, from which are paid the salaries of the Principal Chief, the office holders and officials, the District and Village Heads and the Officers of the Native Courts. Any alterations or additions proposed by the paramount Chief, with the consent of the Resident, are approved by the Governor if recommended by the Lieutenant-Governor when the annual estimates are passed. There are at present fifty such Treasuries in the Northern Provinces.

The salaries of the paramount Chiefs were fixed on a generous scale, the more important Emirs receiving £4,800 per annum.[1] With the disappearance of the superfluous office-holders, and Court slaves, formerly dependent on his bounty, and the payment of all police and minor officials by the Native Treasuries, the personal income of the Emirs has substantially increased, and it is possible that these salaries may err on the side of liberality. Chiefs in recept of a salary are not allowed to receive any *Gaisua, Kurdin Sarauta, Gado* or other of their former perquisites. These must now be paid into the Native Treasury. A Chief must pay for repairs to his residence. The result of this system has been to cement the loyalty of the Chiefs by bonds of self-interest, since they know that they could not themselves enforce the tax, and are dependent for their wealth and power on the British Administration.

CASH AND KIND

70. The tax must be collected in cash wherever possible in order to avoid the transport of bulky produce, and the difficulty of its conversion into currency. Cash is now obtainable throughout Nigeria, even in the remotest parts, if a little trouble is taken, and, in order to bring pressure on the tax-payers to collect cash for their tax, the District Officer should always insist on the villagers who have none transporting the produce they pay to the nearest market and witnessing its conversion into cash. The tax thus promotes the circulation of currency with its attendant benefits to trade. Payment in cash is now almost universal in the Northern Provinces. When payment is received in kind the District Officer should, of course accept only what is most easily convertible into cash, such as cotton,

---

[1] In 1904, the Emir of Kano's personal net income, including traditional payments of *Gado*, etc., was estimated at £8,500, followed by the Sultan of Sokoto at £5,515 and the Shehu of Bornu at £5,009. Today these are in the region of £10,000 each, exclusive of the salary as a Member of the House of Chiefs.

livestock, produce which can be sold for export, or possibly food which can be issued as rations to soldiers or police.

I am averse to accepting labour, or the equivalent of labour (such as steamer fuel) in lieu of the tax. It is better to pay for such things in cash and receive the cash back as tax, lest an ignorant people should confuse the moderate annual demand with forced labour, and may see that Government pays for labour. Such a course, moreover, lessens the chance of the whole tax falling on the poorer classes, while the Chiefs escape by forcing the villagers to do the work. If horses (for mounted infantry) or livestock or food for issue to troops, is accepted it will be paid for at market prices from the vote on the estimates, and the proceeds credited to the tax. . . .

MODE OF PAYMENT

71. The tax will be collected in the name of the Emir by the Village Headmen and paid by them to the District Head, who will bring it to the Emir at the capital, accompanied when possible by a representative from each village. If there is no District Head the Resident will, of course, accept the tax at each village or at a central camp. Wherever there is a paramount Chief, therefore, the collection is entirely by officials of the Native Administration and never by Government agents. . . .

The paramount Chief is thus recognized as the authority by whom the taxes which constitute the revenue of the Native Administration are imposed, and as the agent of Government in respect of the share accruing to Revenue. . . . His dignity and prestige are maintained, and the peasantry are led on the one hand to feel that they pay their taxes to their own Chief and not to an alien Suzerain, and on the other hand in case of injustice they can appeal to the Residents.

PRECAUTIONS AGAINST ILLEGAL EXACTIONS

73. Village Headman will be warned that if any demand of any kind whatever should be made which is not in accord with the assessment of which they have been informed, whether for goods, cash or labour (other than the statutory obligation to repair the roads), they must at once inform the Resident. If the persons who made the demand are *bona fide* emissaries of the paramount Chief, or other Chief, or of the former Fief-holder, or of the District Head, inquiry will be made, and the person who issued the orders will be dealt with. If, however, they are merely criminals, passing themselves off as emissaries from Government or the Native Administration, they will be prosecuted under the Criminal Code.[1] The District

---

[1] *Sojan gona* still persists as a crime.

K

Staff will do their utmost to detect all such secret and illegal exactions and see that the Village and District Heads strictly carry out the authorized assessment.

SUMMARY OF OBJECTS OF TAXATION

74. The general result which it was hoped to obtain from this system of taxation, and which may fairly be said to have been realized in the Northern Provinces, may be summarized as follows:—

(a) A substantial revenue has been secured to the Native Chiefs and officials to replace the loss of slave-raiding and slave-trading, the levies on traders which crushed trade, the extortions from the peasantry and the fines and bribes which perverted justice. As individuals they have adequate salaries which they earn by discharging responsible duties for the Administration, and as rulers they have revenue for the progress of the country.

(b) A considerable and increasing revenue has been secured to Government, due to better organization and collection of tax and its universality, while coin currency with its immense influence for trade and progress has been promoted and has largely replaced cowries.

(c) The peasantry has been emancipated in the true sense of the word to an even greater extent than would be the case by the abolition of domestic slavery. The tax they pay is very moderate, and they are freed from arbitrary exactions. Industry and personal initiative are encouraged instead of being the mark for spoliation.

(d) The absentee ruler or landlord is replaced by the District Headman, who has responsible executive duties, delegated by the Emir, instead of being an idle place-holder. Decentralization of powers relieves the Emir of work he could not properly perform, limits opportunities for mal-administration by him, increases the Resident's opportunities for supervision, and facilitates the delegation of powers by Government, with confidence that they will not be abused, and so enables the Government to rule through the Chiefs.

(e) The old Fief-holders, who had deteriorated by the exercise of unchecked licence, have either had to accept responsible duties as District Heads or Officers of State, or have had to take to trade or agriculture and lead a life dignified by personal exertion.

(f) The multiplication of titular office-holders and others, including the tax-gatherers, who lived on industry of the peasantry, and the tendency of the Emirs to grant such offices to relatives or favourite slaves, has been checked, and only such officials are appointed as have substantial duties to perform, and as have been selected for their ability.

EXPENDITURE ON PUBLIC WORKS DEFERRED IN DISTANT
PROVINCES

75. Distant Provinces, like Sokoto and Bornu, must not feel
aggrieved if the annual direct expenditure upon them at the present
time is not the equivalent of the tax they pay to Government. The
stem and main branches of a tree must receive the bulk of the sap
and be developed before its outlying limbs. The main trunk railways
and roads must first connect the centres of trade, and of mineral and
other development, with the ports. Later the bulk of the expenditure
may in return be devoted to the development of the outlying Provinces, which, meanwhile, benefit indirectly by the general efficiency
and improvement in all departments, including those of education,
forestry and agriculture.

ANCIENT TRADITIONS AND CUSTOMS PRESERVED

78. The chief object in view when this policy was inaugurated was
'to introduce some uniformity of system throughout the Protectorate at the cost of as few changes as possible', and wherever the system
may be extended, the same object will be held in view, in order that
the prejudices of the people, and the force of custom and tradition
may be auxiliary, and not antagonistic, to the improved methods, so
long as they are not opposed to the principles. . . .

QUALIFICATIONS FOR PROMOTIONS

79. An Officer who has achieved success in the assessment of a
district is valuable therefore, not primarily because he has secured
an increase of Revenue. 'The primary test of the value of a District
Officer, and his fitness for promotion (as I wrote in 1906) is the
content and satisfaction prevailing in his division, the absence of
crimes of violence, and the efficiency of the Chiefs and Native
Court.' I concur heartily with my successor's addendum of August,
1908, that 'the genuine recognition of the absolute necessity of
governing this country through the Native Administrations' is an
essential for promotion to the higher grades, and that the sacrifice
of these principles to 'unknown and unappreciated British notions'
(among which I would include theories of land taxation foreign to
Native thought) is incompatible with that recognition.

Nor in the case of juniors do I undervalue the essential necessity
for a knowledge of the Native Language, and of a 'sound knowledge
of British Law and of Native Law and Custom, and the effective
use of this knowledge for the guidance of the inhabitants of their
districts.' These qualifications for promotion are, I think, inherent
in what I have written, and the policy I have consistently furthered.

MEMO No. VII.
NATIVE COURTS[1]

GENERAL POLICY

2. The objects in view may be outlined as follows:

(a) That the Native Courts shall consist entirely of Natives, administering Mohammedan law or Native law and custom, as the case may be, together with such alien law, as they are expressly authorized to administer (e.g., the 'Revenue', 'Native Authority', 'Public Health', and similar Ordinances), or as may be embodied in 'Rules' drawn up by the Court with the concurrence of the Head Chief and Resident, or drawn up by the Head Chief and issued as Rules approved by the Governor-General;

(b) To increase their influence, and to make them effective instruments of justice, by teaching them the elementary rules of evidence, and by enforcing strict impartiality and integrity;

(c) That the Provincial Staff, while closely supervising them with these objects in view, shall avoid unnecessary interference, so as to promote a sense of independent responsibility and initiative;

(d) That there shall be an adequate number of Courts so that complainants may be able to obtain redress without travelling prohibitive distances, and the difficulties of summoning witnesses may be reduced as far as possible;

(e) To promote a close co-operation between the Native and the Provincial Courts, as component parts of a single judicial system, and to relieve the latter of work which can be better done by the Natives themselves;

(f) To afford to the Natives of Nigeria tribunals which fully understand their own customs and modes of thought, and will command their confidence, and to promote co-operation between the Head Chief and those tribunals.

DESCRIPTION OF COURTS

(a) *Moslem Courts*

3. The Mohammedan Courts in the Hausa States and Bornu are presided over by Alkalai, who administer the Sheria under Koranic sanction, and are sometimes very learned in the law, with considerable reference libraries at their command. Ruxton's translation of Perron's Treatise on the Maliki Code forms the text-book for Administrative Officers. Powers of varying degree are conferred on

[1] This should be read in conjunction with Memorandum III, 'Judicial and Legal'. Both provide a useful historical background to the recent reorganization of the judiciary at all levels in the Northern and Western Regions.

these Courts in accordance with the ability and reputation of the presiding Alkali. The language is Hausa throughout the Fulani States, which renders supervision easy. The Emir's Court is transformed into a 'Judicial Council' by order of the Governor-General, and certain executive powers may be conferred upon it. In dealing with non-Moslem litigants these Courts modify the strict application of Mohammedan law by recognition of Native law and custom. Where the population is mixed, the Alkali should sit with non-Moslem assessors when dealing with 'Pagan' cases. During the dozen or more years since these Courts were re-established under British rule they have constantly improved, and are now for the most part extremely efficient tribunals.

(b) *Non-Moslem Courts in Native States* *note*

4. In those non-Moslem States which recognize a single Head Chief, of which there are several in the North, and the Egbas, Yorubas and Benis in the South, it is possible to set up Native Courts and Judicial Councils similar to those in the Moslem States, but even among these more advanced communities there is no professional class of judges administering a written code of Native law, as in the Moslem States.

(c) *Non-Moslem Courts in tribal areas*

5. Finally, there are the Courts set up among primitive Pagan communities, both in the North and South, in substitution for the arbitrary will of a Chief, or the operation of mob law. It is with these latter that the greatest difficulties are to be encountered, and it is with them that this Memo. is chiefly concerned.

FORMER SYSTEM IN SOUTHERN PROVINCES

6. Prior to the enactment of the Native Courts Ordinance, 1914, the Major and Minor Native Courts in the Southern Provinces were presided over by the District Officer when he was able to be present, and each village in the area over which the Court had jurisdiction sent probably two Chiefs to sit as members. There was little to distinguish between the District Officer's 'District Court' (affiliated to the Supreme Court) sitting with Native assessors, and the 'Native Court' presided over by the District Officer with attendant Native Chiefs. In both, the European was predominant, and there was little scope for initiative or responsibility for the Native Judges. As Dr. Maxwell observes, 'The District Commissioner or Assistant District Commissioner was the Court, and the Native members were merely figure-heads. He took the evidence when he was present, he gave judgement, and in practice he frequently gave judgement without

consulting the Native members, and the more experienced he was
the less important were the Native members'. In one case a District
Commissioner adjourned the Court till its members should concur
in his view. . . .

Since appointment as a member of a Native Court was the sole
Government recognition of the status of a Chief, selection to be a
'Warrant Chief' was naturally very popular, irrespective of the sitting
fees paid for attendance. The Courts therefore consisted of a very
large number of Chiefs—as many as 65 in some cases—and they sat
by rotation.

In these Courts semi-educated clerks were appointed to keep the
records and issue the processes of the Court, and in many cases,
as the Chief Justice has stated, these clerks, and the interpreters who
were necessary for the European who sat as President, became the
real power, and received bribes, while they terrorized the Native
Chiefs. . . . Their procedure was modelled on the Supreme Court,
with all its paraphernalia of printed writs and forms of summons,
and it is recorded that they were 'more or less of a caricature of an
English Court'.

In such conditions the law administered became of necessity a
hybrid between English law as known to the District Commissioner
or as laid down in his absence by the Native Court clerk, and Native
law as known to the Warrant Chiefs. 'Native custom was (it is said)
being steadily destroyed'. The receipts, which were very large (since
very heavy fines were imposed) were credited to a Native Court
Fund, which was subject to no audit. The members of Native Courts
in the old Lagos Protectorate, after paying half the receipts into the
Native Court Fund, or in some cases nothing at all, divided the
balance amongst themselves, a system which naturally led to the
imposition of heavy fines. . . .

At the time when Native Courts were first established in the
Eastern part of the Southern Provinces, the tribal system and
authority had already broken down, and had been succeeded by
anarchy, under the disintegrating influences of successful middlemen traders, and of the Aros. The latter were professional slave-
traders, and ruled by the terror of their Juju. The Courts no doubt
did much to re-establish authority, at a time when it had almost
disappeared, and their usefulness is shown by their growing influence,
and the number of cases with which they dealt.

FORMER SYSTEM IN NORTHERN PROVINCES

7. In the North the Native Courts set up among the primitive
Pagan tribes were 'Judicial Councils' of Elders and Chiefs, who were
entrusted with small powers to settle their own small causes. They

were purely Native, under the close supervision of the Resident. When possible a scribe was attached to the Court, but as a rule few records were kept.

THE NEW COURTS   *The Rise of Customary Court.*

8. The New Ordinance sets up Native Courts which may consist:

(a) of a single Native Judge, sitting with or without Assessors, and Advisers, or

(b) of a body of Chiefs, presided over by one of their number.

They are of various grades, according to the power conferred upon them in the warrant establishing the Court. The title of 'Judicial Council' is now reserved to the Court of the Head Chief, upon which executive powers are usually conferred. The Courts consist solely of Natives, and administer only Native law and custom, but they have the power of adding to that law, by means of 'Rules' which must be approved by the Governor-General. They may also be empowered to enforce specified Ordinances. These Rules and Ordinances then become part of the Native law legally enforceable by the Court. In using the phrase 'Native Law and Custom' throughout this Memo. I include Mohammedan law in Moslem districts.

EXECUTIVE POWERS OF COURTS

10. A Native Court other than a Judicial Council exercises no executive or legislative functions whatever other than that of making 'Rules'. In advanced communities Rules may also be drawn up by the Head Chief and enforced by the Court when approved by the Governor. I desire, as far as possible, to preserve the distinction between the Native Executive and the Native Judicial Authorities. In exceptional cases, however, a Native Tribunal may be appointed a 'Native Authority' by the Governor under Section 4 of the 'Native Authority Ordinance, 1916'....

JUDICIAL COUNCILS

(a) *Constitution*

11. The Judicial Council is a Native Court consisting usually of the Chief Officers of a Native State, presided over by the Head Chief, upon which executive powers have generally been conferred by the Governor-General....

The appointment of a Native Court to be a Judicial Council does not affect its judicial functions, which continue to be those defined in the warrant under which it was established as a Native Court. The mere appointment of a Native Court to be a Judicial Council does not in itself confer the right to exercise executive functions, and the title could be conferred as a compliment upon a Head Chief's Court without any executive powers. . . .

(b) *Function and Powers*

12. A Judicial Council is only set up in a Native State which has made some progress in advancement. Its executive functions are usually more important than its judicial functions, the ordinary judicial work being left to the Alkali's Court. It is not always necessary or wise to attempt to define the executive powers conferred on a Judicial Council. If undefined they will be assumed to be such as are conferred by Native law and custom, and necessary to the maintenance of law and order. If the Resident considers that in any case a Judicial Council has assumed powers which conflict with the prerogative of Government, or constitute a danger to enlightened progress and rule, he will represent the matter to the Lieutenant-Governor.

(c) *Especial Judicial Powers*

13. The judicial functions of the Council may, if so desired, be limited to 'political' offences and quasi-judicial cases, in which the executive and judicial functions are more or less combined. . . .

I directed in May, 1915, that the functions of the Judicial Council should as a rule be limited to the following matters (or some of them), leaving to the Alkali's Courts all ordinary criminal cases dealt with in the law books. Residents of the Northern Provinces were unanimous in their agreement—one suggesting that Pagan cases heard by a Moslem Court should be added to the list:—

(a) Defaults by Officers of the Native Administration;

(b) Boundary disputes and claims to land and property where ancient titles are involved;

(c) Offences against 'Rules' incorporated in Native Law (see paragraphs 46, 47);

(d) Questions of succession. (Ordinary inheritance can best be dealt with by the Alkali);

(e) Causes between Moslems and Pagans—in special cases;

(f) Cases in which the Alkali's authority is questioned;

(g) Sedition by fanatical preachers.

I have added offences against the 'Native Authority Ordinance', but these should usually be dealt with by the Provincial Court, in order to show that Government intends to uphold the Native Authority. I have already suggested that in certain cases the two Courts should practically sit together, by the summoning of the

Alkali to the Emir's Judicial Council. Residents will use their own discretion as to which of these powers they desire to recommend when submitting the warrant for the constitution of a Judicial Council.

(d) *Relation to Alkali's Court*

14. The Chief Alkali's Court exercises general powers over all matters, and is an Appeal Court from all Native Courts other than the Judicial Council.

If the Judicial Council is vested with powers of inflicting the death sentence, a well-qualified Alkali must be one of the members, in deference to the Moslem theory of government that it is the peculiar prerogative of the ruler to pass sentence in cases of homicide, unless the Emir himself or another of his council is so qualified. There is no objection to the Chief Alkali being an ex-officio member of the Judicial Council; it is, in fact, very advisable that he should be—or the death sentence of an Alkali's Court may be pronounced by the Emir. When serious cases are tried by a Judicial Council, it should be stated in the report who were present, and whether the Alkali concurred in the sentence.

There is no objection to the existence of both an Alkali's Court and a Judicial Council in the same city, and in cities of the Hausa and Bornu Provinces this would commonly be the case. They would have concurrent jurisdiction, and the members of either Court would be amenable to the other—as both are to the Provincial Court. An Alkali therefore who was accused of accepting bribes or other offence, could be dealt with by the Judicial Council. Similarly any of the Officials of State who had a seat on the Council would be amenable to the Alkali's Courts. . . .

NON-MOSLEM COURTS IN NATIVE STATES

15. Turning now to the constitution of Non-Moslem Courts, there are a few non-Moslem States in which it may be possible to set up a Native Court with large powers, under a capable Native Judge with competent members. In Egba-land, such Courts existed under the former 'independent Government', but it is important in such cases to remember that the law to be administered is 'Native law and custom', and not English law, and that offences against Nigerian Ordinances (including the Criminal Code), which are not offences against Native law, must be tried by the Provincial Court, unless Native Courts have been expressly authorized by any particular Ordinance to enforce that Ordinance, or unless they have been incorporated in the local Native law and custom in Non-Moslem districts, and cannot be enforced by a Native Court. The

law must be such as is known to and accepted by the people. The constitution of such Courts as regards members, assessors, etc., does not differ materially from an Alkali's Court, to which they approximate in type.

NON-MOSLEM COURTS IN TRIBAL AREAS

16. The Native Courts of the lowest grades—no longer called 'Judicial Councils'—set up among the primitive Pagan communities, which form about half of the population of the Northern Provinces, and the greater part of that of the Southern Provinces, form of course the bulk of the Courts of the Protectorate. It is important, therefore, to form a clear conception of the policy we have in view in regard to this type of Court and the means by which we hope to attain it.

In brief, the Courts will be purely Native institutions under the close supervision of the Administrative Staff, entrusted at first with the smallest powers, but steadily increasing in power and responsibility, with the progress of education and as the result of training. It will probably be found preferable to increase the number of Courts—which will always sit at the same place—rather than to have an excessive number of members. But I would impress upon the Administrative Staff of the Southern Provinces in this connection the maxim, which I regard as vital in all African Administration, that only harm and distrust is wrought by sudden and radical changes and dislocation of procedure. The old system in the Southern Provinces was beyond doubt a great advance upon the chaos which preceded it, and the volume of work done in the Courts proves that they were of use and met a need. The time is now, in my opinion, ripe for a change, but the changes must be gradually introduced if they are to be effective, and not alienate the confidence of the people. When therefore it has been the custom for each town to have one or more representatives on the Court, there is no necessity to alter this procedure, if it is in the judgement of the Resident advisable to retain it, and if it adds to the confidence felt in the Court.

SUGGESTIONS *RE* FORMATION OF PAGAN NATIVE COURTS IN SOUTH EASTERN PROVINCES

17. On the other hand superfluous members can, if desired, be given certificates as 'Recognized Chiefs' in lieu of their warrants as Members of the Court. They can also be appointed as the 'Native Authority', under the Native Authority Ordinance, and would then exercise certain limited executive powers as indicated in that Ordinance, but would have no authority to try cases. The new Native

Court would then consist of tribal or clan Chiefs, including persons who exercised great local influence and commanded confidence by their superior intelligence. They would, if considered advisable, be elected either by the whole community or by the 'Recognized Chiefs', and in their capacity as members of the Native Courts would of course exercise judicial powers solely, leaving the executive authority wholly in the hands of the 'Native Authority', and confining themselves to the settlement of matrimonial, family, and tribal disputes. . . . The President should always be the most influential tribal Chief.

The members should be representative of all the principal districts and towns comprised in the area of the Court's jurisdiction, and a member should not be appointed as the successor of a deceased member, merely because he is his son or heir. These are mere suggestions, based on but little knowledge of local tribal conditions, and it is left to the individual experience and ability of each Resident in charge of a Province, to evolve the system best suited to the conditions of each district of his Province.

VALUE OF EVEN THE CRUDEST OF COURTS

18. It may hardly seem worth while to set up a crude Tribunal consisting of naked Pagans, who can hardly be called Chiefs, and have but a limited control over a few families, but from such small beginnings alone is it possible to create the rudiments of law and order, to inculcate a sense of responsibility, and evolve among a primitive community some sense of discipline and respect for authority. A Resident in such cases will doubtless feel that it would be much less trouble to do the work himself, than to place even the smallest reliance upon so ineffectual an instrument, but I desire earnestly to impress upon every Administrative Officer that, even though the judicial work be not so well done as it would be by himself, it is only by the patient training of such a Court that better Tribunals can be evolved and real progress achieved. The close supervision of such a Court will involve more labour and personal effort than direct administration, but it is worth the effort.

ALIEN NATIVES AS PRESIDENTS

19. A more rapid road to progress may seem to present itself by the appointment of a superior Native alien to the Presidency of such a Court—whether he be a 'Mallam' in the North, or a Native clerk in the South. I do not assert that such a procedure is inadmissible as a temporary and educational experiment, but it must be used with caution. The appointment of a Mallam may not improbably mean that the whole community will shortly declare itself to be

Moslem, and it is not the business of Government to make itself an agent for the spread of Islam, while the appointment of an alien and semi-educated clerk may undermine the authority of the Chiefs and do more harm than good in the long run. . . .

THE EXPERIMENT IN BASSA

20. The history of the Native Courts in the Northern Province of Bassa is interesting in this connection. It is a Province of very primitive communities, with the additional disadvantage that its population consists of a number of remnants of tribes, all with widely different customs, and more or less antagonistic to each other—such as the Bassa Komos, the Bassa-Ngwe, the Igara, and others. A Court of Pagan Chiefs was found unworkable, as the President invariably favoured the party who belonged to his own tribe. They were also corrupt. A Hausa President was then tried, but he was ignorant of the Native law and custom of each tribe, and the Pagan Chiefs lost authority. So the Hausa was made sole Judge and the Pagan Chiefs sat as assessors, but their quarrels brought the Court into disrepute, and if a Chief of a litigant's tribe was not present, the President was ignorant of the Native law which affected him. Finally the alien President was instructed to sit with two assessors only—one from the tribe of each litigant. Apart from the questions of religion to which I have alluded, this system has worked well. If the assessors agreed, the President gave judgement accordingly. If they differed he heard the Native law on both sides and used his discretion.

It may possibly be found useful to try this system in some cases in the Southern Provinces.

NON-MOSLEM (TRIBAL) COURTS

21. To return to the constitution of these Courts. With an increase in their number, and a diminution in the number of members, it may be feasible to appoint permanent Presidents, instead of making the office tenable by rotation as is often the case in the Southern Provinces at present. In the Owerri Province, where the average number of members is 25, the President and Vice-President are appointed quarterly, and the members sit for a month at a time. This arrangement . . . has worked well as a transitional expedient. The members are appointed during pleasure, but may not be dismissed without the approval of the Lieutenant-Governor. The Administrative Officer has access to the Court at all times, and may transfer a case at any stage to his own Court or may quash it or order a re-hearing. He may amend the sentence, and he may likewise order the transfer of any case from his own to a Native Court. He may not, however,

order the Court to award any particular penalty, for that would destroy its independence.

CLERK OR SCRIBE OF THE COURT

22. Under the former system in the Southern Provinces, any person who desired to report a criminal matter, or who wished to take out a civil summons, applied to the Court clerk, who if the matter was serious referred it to the Administrative Officer, or if in his opinion it was not serious, issued a summons on his own authority. He was also in immediate charge of the lock-up where persons awaiting trial (and witnesses) were confined.

It has been freely alleged that some of these clerks were guilty of peculation, or receiving bribes, and of influencing the Court on behalf of their client. It is alleged that they intimidated the Native members by their better knowledge of Court procedure and English law, and by threatening to report cases which they said had been wrongly tried. If this were true, gross injustice would result and the endeavour to teach the Chiefs to administer justice to their own people would be nullified and brought into disrepute. I cannot impress upon Residents too strongly the vital necessity of taking every precaution to prevent this.

WARRANT OF CONSTITUTION

26. A Native Court is constituted by a warrant which:—
(a) States the names of the President and members.
(b) Defines the area of the Court's jurisdiction.
(c) States its grade—viz.: the powers conferred upon it.

. . . New Courts should only as a rule be set up by the substantive Resident. There is no limit laid down as to the number of the members who form a Court, and in those of the third and fourth grades, constituted among primitive tribes, it may be necessary to have a large number of Chiefs as members of the Court, who may be ordered to sit by rotation; but this system should never be adopted where there is a Chief of real importance, and it appears to be foreign to the ideas of the Yorubas and Benis.

AREA OF JURISDICTION OF NATIVE COURTS

27. In districts to which the Native Revenue Ordinance applies, the area of jurisdiction of the Court will usually be identical with the area under the executive charge of a 'District Headman', but if it is too large or too densely populated, two or more Courts may share it between them. In other parts of the Protectorate, or where district Headman have not yet been appointed, the area will be determined by boundaries well known to the Natives, and in no

case should a Court take in portions of two distinct tribes. Each clan should if possible have a Court of its own. The whole area of every Province will be parcelled out under the jurisdiction of one or other of the Native Courts. The object in view will be to create such a number of Native Courts as will allow of easy access by all to one or other. The areas over which Courts of the same class exercise original jurisdiction should not overlap, except when the Warrants constituting the Courts confer exclusive jurisdiction in respect of different classes of cases. A Superior Court may, however, include in its jurisdiction the areas of any number of inferior Courts, the distribution of work being arranged by the Courts. As a general rule, a case should be tried in the lowest Court which has power to deal with it.

CLASSES OF CASES TO BE DEALT WITH BY NATIVE COURTS

31. As a general rule, offences against the person may be dealt with by a competent Native Court, while offences against public order are dealt with by a British Court. Obviously the Provincial Court should try all offences under Ordinances, which are not offences under Native law, and have not been made so by a Rule by the Native Authority, also offences among primitive tribes where superstition may be likely to pervert the course of justice, or where the Native Court appears unwilling to inflict adequate punishment, or where the position and influence of the accused is likely to affect the impartiality of the Court. A Native Court in a primitive tribe would not in point of fact have the requisite powers to deal with any serious case of these classes. Civil actions arising from the marriage relation, debts, inheritance, and petty assaults, should usually be dealt with by Native Courts. The functions of the lower grade Courts are primarly to deal with civil matters by Native law, leaving criminal cases for the Provincial Courts.

(a) *Lands*

32. Since Government does not interfere with the ancient rights of occupancy of lands held by Natives, a Native Court is competent to decide disputes relating to such lands. The Provincial and not the Native Court will deal with land cases of the following classes:—

(a) Acquisition of land by Non-Natives and Native foreigners.
(b) Taking up of waste lands by fugitive slaves.
(c) Acquisition of Pagan lands by neighbouring Moslems.

All important decisions of the Native Court in regard to lands should be recorded in a separate book, and indexed for reference.

If they are of importance, they should be dealt with by the Emir's Judicial Council. . . .

PROVINCIAL COURT NOT TO BE SUPERSEDED

38. While the very best Native Courts, such as those at Kano or Sokoto, may be trusted with these large powers in criminal cases, I do not wish to see the Provincial Courts ousted from jurisdiction in all Native cases. Though it is a matter of comparatively minor importance, the loss to revenue is considerable if the Provincial Court receipts are reduced to a vanishing point, and the general sanitation of townships and other work suffers if the prison population is transferred to the Native prisons.

CO-OPERATION WITH PROVINCIAL COURTS

39. It is a matter of great importance that the Native Courts, whatever their grade, should be encouraged to regard themselves as an integral part of the judicial system of Nigeria, and that they should co-operate in every way with the Provincial Courts. This can sometimes be promoted by Native Courts undertaking a preliminary investigation into a serious case brought for trial in the Provincial Court, and by members of a Native Court sitting as assessors in the Provincial Court as expert advisers in Native law and custom.

APPEALS

40. There is no appeal from a Native Court to a British Court, but a person who considers himself wronged by the decision of a Native Court can apply to the Resident in his capacity as Judge of the Provincial Court, and he has power to reduce, modify, or suspend the sentence, to order a re-hearing, or to transfer the case to his own Court at any stage. . . .

SUPERVISION OF COURTS

41. There is no more important duty imposed upon an Administrative Officer than that of keeping the closest touch with the Native Courts of his Province—whether they be Moslem or Pagan Courts. He should frequently attend the sittings especially of the latter, and impress on the Court the necessity of granting a patient hearing, and of listening to all the evidence. He should avoid intervention during the proceedings, so as not to lower the prestige of the Court, or appear to try the case himself. If an unjust decision has been given from corrupt influence, the Judge will of course be dealt with and the case transferred to the Provincial Court. The Resident should personally, when possible, investigate any complaint or charge against a Native Court on the spot where he can hear the reasons

for their action by the members themselves. In exercising this power of revision in the numerous petitions which an Administrative Officer receives, he will be guided by the following principles. If the complaint is that the Court arrived at a wrong decision on the facts, he would as a rule refuse to interfere, unless there were a palpable miscarriage of justice, on the grounds that the Court which heard the case is the best judge, and the Administrative Officer's intervention, unless to prevent manifest injustice, lowers the prestige and influence of the Court. If, however, the Court has exceeded its powers, or if corrupt motives can be shown, revision is of course imperative. In all cases revision, while remedying any injustice, will be as unobtrusive as possible, in order that the position of the Court may not be impaired in the eyes of the Natives. If a Political Officer has occasion to cancel the judgement or sentence of a Native Court, he should do so in the Court, and explain the reason to the Chiefs.

A book should be kept in every Native Court-house, in which the Political Staff will enter the date of their visits, and any particular instructions they may have found reason for giving.

In supervising the Courts and overlooking their reports, the points of importance are:—(1) to see that the Court does not exceed its powers, and that its sentences are reasonable and just; (2) to verify that the fees and fines are correctly entered, and a corresponding sum has been deposited in the safe; (3) to see that the Court is properly constituted, and the finding and sentence are those of the President and members, without influence or interference on the part of the clerk; (4) to see that the offence was one triable by the Native Court and the accused was a person amenable to the Court. To effect this, an Administrative Officer should question the members of the Court separately and also the clerk, regarding each entry, and he should also question some of the parties who have appeared before the Court, and ascertain whether the fees and fines they have paid correspond with the counterfoil receipts. Where a Court is composed of illiterates, the President may find it useful to keep a notched stick as a tally of the number of cases tried and a check on the clerk. . . .

1922: LUGARD'S POLITICAL TESTIMONY

The extracts are taken from F. D. Lugard, THE DUAL MANDATE IN BRITISH *TROPICAL AFRICA, London, 1922, pp. 94–113; 193–234. The chapters quoted from are entitled 'Some General Principles of Administration', 'Methods of Ruling Native Races' and 'Taxation'.*[1]

. . . Liberty and self-development can be best secured to the native population by leaving them free to manage their own affairs through their own rulers, proportionately to their degree of advancement, under the guidance of the British staff, and subject to the laws and policy of the administration.

But apart from the administration of native affairs the local Government has to preserve law and order, to develop the trade and communications of the country, and to protect the interests of the merchants and others who are engaged in the development of its commercial and mineral resources. What, then, are the functions of the British staff, and how can the machinery of Government be most efficiently constituted for the discharge of its duties in those countries in Africa which fall under British control?

The staff must necessarily be limited in numbers, for if the best class of men are to be attracted to a service which often involves separation from family and a strain on health, they must be offered adequate salaries and inducement in the way of leave, housing, medical aid—or their equivalents in money—for their maintenance in health and comfort while serving abroad, and this forms a heavy charge on the revenues. Policy and economy alike demand restriction in numbers, but the best that England can supply. . . .

The administrative branch is concerned with the supervision of the native administration and the general direction of policy; with education, and the collection and control of direct taxes, which involve assessment and close relations with the native population; with legislation and the administration of justice in courts other than the Supreme Court; and with the direct government and welfare of the non-native section of the population.

The departmental staff is charged with duties in connection with transport, communications, and buildings (railways, marine, and

---

[1] The *Dual Mandate* should be studied together with Lugard's *Political Memoranda*; and, as a useful commentary on both, with Sir Charles Orr's *The Making of Northern Nigeria*, 1911, repr. 1965 with an Introduction by A. H. M. Kirk-Greene, where the administrative problems are analysed.

L

public works); with the development of natural resources (mines, collieries, forestry, agriculture, and geology); with the auxiliary services of government (medical, secretarial, accounting, posts and telegraphs, surveys, etc.); and the collection of customs duties.

The task of the administrative branch is to foster that sympathy, mutual understanding, and co-operation between the Government and the people, without which . . . no Government is really stable and efficient. Its aim is to promote progress in civilization and justice, and to create conditions under which individual enterprise may most advantageously develop the natural resources of the country. The task of the departments, on the other hand, is to maintain the Government machine in a state of efficiency, and to afford direct assistance in material development. Their motto is efficiency and economy. The two branches work together, and their duties overlap and are interdependent in every sphere. The efficient discharge of those duties in combination constitutes the white man's title to control.

There are in my estimation two vital principles which characterize the growth of a wise administration—they are Decentralization and Continuity. Though, as Lord Morley said of India, 'perfectly efficient administration has an inevitable tendency to over-centralization', it is a tendency to be combated. It has indeed been said that the whole art of administration consists in judicious and progressive delegation, and there is much truth in the dictum, provided that delegation of duties be accompanied by public responsibility. This is not applicable to the head of the Government alone or in particular, but to every single officer, from the Governor to the foreman of a gang of daily labourers. The man who is charged with the accomplishment of any task, and has the ability and discrimination to select the most capable of those who are subordinate to him, and to trust them with ever-increasing responsibility, up to the limits of their capacity, will be rewarded not only with confidence and loyalty, but he will get more work done, and better done, than the man who tries to keep too much in his own hands, and is slow to recognize merit, originality, and efficiency in others. His sphere of work becomes a training school, and he is able to recommend his best men for promotion to greater responsibility than he himself can confer. The Governor who delegates to his Lieutenant-Governor, Residents, and heads of departments the widest powers compatible with his own direct responsibility to the Crown, will witness the most rapid progress.

But delegation to an individual who is not equal to the responsibility obviously means disaster, and it is therefore often advisable to entrust extended powers to the individual rather than to incorporate them as a part of the duties of his office. His successor, who must obviously have less experience, and may or may not be his equal in ability, will not then automatically enjoy the same latitude, until he has proved his capacity in the higher office. . . .

The African is slow to give his confidence. He is suspicious and reticent with a newcomer, eager to resuscitate old land disputes—perhaps of half a century's standing—in the hope that the new officer in his ignorance may reverse the decision of his predecessor. The time of an officer is wasted in picking up the tangled threads and informing himself of the conditions of his new post. By the time he has acquired the necessary knowledge, and has learnt the character of the people he has to deal with, and won their confidence, his leave becomes due, and if on his return he is posted elsewhere, not only is progress arrested but retrogression may result.

It is also essential that each officer should be at pains to keep full and accurate records of all important matters, especially of any conversation with native chiefs, in which any pledge or promise, implied or explicit, has been made. It is not enough that official correspondence should be filed—a summary of each subject should be made and decisions recorded and brought up to date, so that a newcomer may be able rapidly to put himself *au courant*. The higher the post occupied by an officer, the more important does the principle become.

It is especially important that the decisions of the Governor should be fully recorded in writing, and not merely by an initial of acquiescence or a verbal order. This involves heavy office work, but it is work which cannot be neglected if misunderstandings are to be avoided and continuity preserved. The very detailed instructions regarding the duties of each newly-created department which were issued when the administration of Northern Nigeria was first inaugurated, served a very useful purpose in maintaining continuity of policy, till superseded on amalgamation by briefer general orders.

In the sphere of administration there are obviously many subjects —education, taxation, slavery and labour, native courts, land tenure, etc.—in which uniformity and continuity of policy is impossible in so large a country, unless explicit instructions are issued for guidance. By a perusal of the periodical reports of Residents, the Governor could inform himself of the difficulties which presented themselves in the varying circumstances of each province, and think out the best way in which they could be met, and could note where misunderstandings or mistakes had been made. By these means a series of Memoranda were compiled, and constantly revised as new problems came to light, and as progress rendered the earlier instructions obsolete. They formed the reference book and authority of the Resident and his staff.

In a country so vast, which included communities in all stages of development, and differing from each other profoundly in their customs and traditions, it was the declared policy of Government that each should develop on its own lines; but this in no way lessens the need for uniformity in the broad principles of policy, or in their application where the conditions are similar. It was the aim of these Memoranda to preserve this continuity and uniformity of principle and policy. . . .

The superstructure may vary in its details, some of which may perhaps be ill-designed, but the stability of the edifice is unaffected. You may pull down and re-erect cupolas, but you cannot alter the design of the foundations without first destroying all that has been erected upon them. . . .

It may be said that as Faith, Hope, and Charity are to the Christian creed, so are Decentralization, Co-operation, and Continuity to African Administration—and the greatest of these is Continuity. . . .

If continuity and decentralization are, as I have said, the first and most important conditions in maintaining an effective administration, co-operation is the key-note of success in its application—continuous co-operation between every link in the chain, from the head of the administration to its most junior member,—co-operation between the Government and the commercial community, and, above all, between the provincial staff and the native rulers. Every individual adds his share not only to the accomplishment of the ideal, but to the ideal itself. Its principles are fashioned by his quota of experience, its results are achieved by his patient and loyal application of these principles, with as little interference as possible with native customs and modes of thought.

Principles do not change, but their mode of application may and should vary with the customs, the traditions, and the prejudices of each unit. The task of the administrative officer is to clothe his principles in the garb of evolution, not of revolution; to make it apparent alike to the educated native, the conservative Moslem, and the primitive pagan, each in his own degree, that the policy of the Government is not antagonistic but progressive—sympathetic to his aspirations and the guardian of his natural rights. The Governor looks to the administrative staff to keep in touch with native feeling, and to report fully to himself, in order that he in turn may be able to support them and recognize their work. . . .

Lord Milner's declaration that the British policy is to rule subject races through their own chiefs is generally applauded, but the manner in which the principle should be translated into practice admits of wide differences of opinion and method. Obviously the extent to which native races are capable of controlling their own affairs must vary in proportion to their degree of development and progress in social organization, but this is a question of adaptation and not of principle. Broadly speaking, the divergent opinions in regard to the application of the principle may be found to originate in three different conceptions.

The first is that the ideal of self-government can only be realized by the methods of evolution which have produced the democracies of Europe and America—viz., by representative institutions in which a comparatively small educated class shall be recognized as the natural spokesmen for the many. This method is naturally in favour with the educated African. Whether it is adapted to peoples accustomed by their own institutions to autocracy—albeit modified by a substantial expression of the popular will and circumscribed by custom—is naturally a matter on which opinions differ. The fundamental essential, however, in such a form of Government is that the educated few shall at least be representative of the feelings and desires of the many—well known to them, speaking their language, and versed in their customs and prejudices.

In present conditions in Africa the numerous separate tribes, speaking different languages, and in different stages of evolution, cannot produce representative men of education. Even were they available, the number of communities which could claim separate representation would make any central and really representative Council very unwieldy. The authority vested in the representatives would be antagonistic . . . to that of the native rulers and their councils,—which are the product of the natural tendencies of tribal evolution,—and would run counter to the customs and institutions of the people.

An attempt to adapt these principles of Western representative Government to tropical races is now being made in India. . . . Though the powers entrusted to the elected representatives of the people are at first restricted under the dyarchical system (which reserves certain subjects for the Central Authority), the principle of government by an educated minority, as opposed to government by native rulers, is fully accepted. . . . The experiment has so far shown much promise of success, but the real test is not merely whether the native councillors show moderation and restraint as against extremists of their own class, but whether, when legislation has to be enacted which is unpopular with the illiterate masses and the martial races of India, there may be a reluctance to accept what will be called 'Babu-made law', though it would have been accepted without demur as the order of 'the Sirkar'—the British Raj.

It is, of course, now too late to adopt to any large extent the alternative of gradually transforming the greater part of British

India into native states governed by their own hereditary dynasties, whose representatives in many cases still exist, and extending to them the principles which have so successfully guided our relations with the native States in India itself, and in Malaya in the past. It is one thing to excite an ignorant peasantry against an alien usurper, but quite another thing to challenge a native ruler.

Such a system does not exclude the educated native from participation in the government of the State to which he belongs, as a councillor to the native ruler, but it substitutes for direct British rule, not an elected oligarchy but a form of government more in accord with racial instincts and inherited traditions. . . .

The second conception is that every advanced community should be given the widest possible powers of self-government under its own ruler, and that these powers should be rapidly increased with the object of complete independence at the earliest possible date in the not distant future. Those who hold this view generally, I think, also consider that attempts to train primitive tribes in any form of self-government are futile, and the administration must be wholly conducted by British Officials. This in the past has been the principle adopted in many dependencies. It recognized no alternative between a status of independence, like the Sultans of Malaya or the native princes of India, and the direct rule of the district commissioner.

But the attempt to create such independent States in Africa has been full of anomalies. In the case of Egbaland, where the status had been formally recognized by treaty, the extent to which the Crown had jurisdiction was uncertain, yet, as we have seen, international conventions, including even that relating to the 'Independent' State, and powers quite incompatible with independence were exercised by the Suzerain.

The paramount Chief might receive ceremonial visits from time to time from the Governor, and even perhaps be addressed as 'Your Royal Highness', and vested with titular dignity and the tinsel insignia of office. His right to impose tolls on trade, and to exact whatever oppressive taxes he chose from his peasantry, was admitted, but his authority was subject to constant interference. The last-joined District Officer, or any other official, might issue orders, if not to him, at any rate to any of his subordinate chiefs, and the native ruler had no legal and recognized means of enforcing his commands. He was necessarily forbidden to raise armed forces—on which in the last resort the authority of the law must depend—and could not therefore maintain order.

The third conception is that of rule by native chiefs, unfettered in their control of their people as regards all those matters which are to them the most important attributes of rule, with scope for initiative and responsibility, but admittedly—so far as the visible horizon is concerned—subordinate to the control of the protecting Power in certain well-defined directions. It recognizes, in the words of the Versailles Treaty, that the subject races of Africa are not yet able to stand alone, and that it would not conduce to the happiness of the vast bulk of the people—for whose welfare the controlling Power is trustee—that the attempt should be made.

The verdict of students of history and sociology of different nationalities . . . is unanimous that the era of complete independence is not as yet visible on the horizon of time. Practical administrators (among whom I may include my successor, Sir P. Girouard, in Northern Nigeria) have arrived at the same conclusion.

The danger of going too fast with native races is even more likely to lead to disappointment, if not to disaster, than the danger of not going fast enough. The pace can best be gauged by those who have intimate acquaintance alike with the strong points and the limitations of the native peoples and rulers with whom they have to deal.

The Fulani of Northern Nigeria are, as I have said, more capable of rule than the indigenous races, but in proportion as we consider them an alien race, we are denying self-government to the people over whom they rule, and supporting an alien caste—albeit closer and more akin to the native races than a European can be. Yet capable as they are, it requires the ceaseless vigilance of the British staff to maintain a high standard of administrative integrity, and to prevent oppression of the peasantry. . . .

'Festina lente' is a motto which the Colonial Office will do well to remember in its dealings with Africa.

The system adopted in Nigeria is therefore only a particular method of the application of these principles—more especially as regards 'advanced communities',—and since I am familiar with it I will use it as illustrative of the methods which in my opinion should characterize the dealings of the controlling power with subject races.

The object in view is to make each 'Emir' or paramount chief, assisted by his judicial Council, an effective ruler over his own people. He presides over a 'Native Administration' organized throughout as a unit of Local Government. The area over which he exercises jurisdiction is divided into districts under the control of 'Headmen', who collect the taxes in the name of the ruler, and pay them into the 'Native Treasury', conducted by a native treasurer and staff under the supervision of the chief at his capital. Here, too, is the prison for native court prisoners, and probably the school, which I shall describe more fully in the chapter on education. Large cities are divided into wards for purposes of control and taxation.

The district headman, usually a territorial magnate with local connections, is the chief executive officer in the area under his charge. He controls the village headmen, and is responsible for the assessment of the tax, which he collects through their agency. He must reside in his district and not at the capital. He is not allowed to pose as a chief with a retinue of his own and duplicate officials, and is summoned from time to time to report to his chief. If, as is the case with some of the ancient Emirates, the community is a small one but independent of any other native rule, the chief may be his own district headman.

A province under a Resident may contain several separate 'Native Administrations', whether they be Moslem Emirates or pagan communities. A 'division' under a British District Officer may include one or more headmen's districts, or more than one small Emirate or independent pagan tribe, but as a rule no Emirate is partly in one division and partly in another. The Resident acts as sympathetic adviser and counsellor to the native chief, being careful not to interfere so as to lower his prestige, or cause him to lose interest in his work. His advice on matters of general policy must be followed, but the native ruler issues his own instructions to his subordinate chiefs and district heads—not as the orders of the Resident but as his own—and he is encouraged to work through them, instead of centralizing everything in himself—a system which in the past had produced such great abuses. The British District Officers supervise and assist the native district headmen, and make any arrangements necessary for carrying on the work of the Government departments, but all important orders emanate from the Emir, whose messenger usually accompanies and acts as mouthpiece of a District Officer.

The tax—which supersedes all former 'tribute', irregular imposts, and forced labour—is, in a sense, the basis of the whole system, since it supplies the means to pay the Emir and all his officials. The district and village heads are effectively supervised and assisted in its assessment by the British staff. The native treasury retains the proportion assigned to it (in advanced communities a half), and pays the remainder into Colonial Revenue. There are fifty such treasuries in the northern provinces of Nigeria, and every independent chief, however small, is encouraged to have his own. . . . The native treasurer keeps all accounts of receipts and expenditure, and the Emir, with the assistance of the Resident, annually prepares a budget, which is formally approved by the Lieutenant-Governor.

In these advanced communities the judges of the native courts administer native law and custom, and exercise their jurisdiction independently of the native executive, but under the supervision of the British staff, and subject to the general control of the Emir, whose 'Judicial Council' consist of his principal officers of State, and is vested with executive as well as judicial powers. No punishment may be inflicted by a native authority, except through a regular tribunal. The ordinances of government are operative everywhere, but the native authority may make by-laws in modification of native custom—e.g. on matters of sanitation, etc.—and these, when approved by the Governor, are enforced by the native courts.

The authority of the Emir over his own people is absolute and the profession of an alien creed does not absolve a native from the obligation to obey his lawful orders; but aliens—other than natives domiciled in the Emirate and accepting the jurisdiction of the native authority and courts—are under the direct control of the British staff. Townships are excluded from the native jurisdiction.

The village is the administrative unit. It is not always easy to define, since the security to life and property which has followed the British administration has caused an exodus from the cities and large villages, and the creation of innumerable hamlets, sometimes only of one or two huts, on the agricultural lands. The peasantry of the advanced communities, though ignorant, yet differs from that of the backward tribes in that they recognize the authority of the Emir, and are more ready to listen to the village head and the Council of Elders, on which the Nigerian system is based.

Subject, therefore, to the limitations which I shall presently discuss, the native authority is thus *de facto* and *de jure* ruler over his own people. He appoints and dismisses his subordinate chiefs and officials. He exercises the power of allocation of lands, and with the aid of the native courts, of adjudication in land disputes and expropriation for offences against the community; these are the essential functions upon which, in the opinion of the West African Lands Committee, the prestige of the native authority depends. The lawful orders which he may give are carefully defined by ordinance, and in the last resort are enforced by Government.

Since native authority, especially if exercised by alien conquerors, is inevitably weakened by the first impact of civilized rule, it is made clear to the elements of disorder, who regard force as conferring the only right to demand obedience, that government, by the use of force if necessary, intends to support the native chief. To enable him to maintain order he employs a body of unarmed police, and if the occasion demands the display of superior force he looks to the Government—as, for instance, if a community combines to break the law or shield criminals from justice, a rare event in the advanced communities.

The native ruler derives his power from the Suzerain, and is responsible that it is not misused. He is equally with British officers amenable to the law, but his authority does not depend on the caprice of an executive officer. To intrigue against him is an offence punishable, if necessary, in a Provincial Court. Thus both British and native courts are invoked to uphold his authority.

The essential feature of the system (as I wrote at the time of its inauguration) is that the native chiefs are constituted 'as an integral part of the machinery of the administration. There are not two sets of rulers—British and native—working either separately or in co-operation, but a single Government in which the native chiefs have well-defined duties and an acknowledged status equally with British officials. Their duties should never conflict, and should overlap as little as possible. They should be complementary to each other, and the chief himself must understand that he has no right to place and power unless he renders his proper services to the State'.

The ruling classes are no longer either demi-gods, or parasites preying on the community. They must work for the stipends and position they enjoy. They are the trusted delegates of the Governor, exercising in the Moslem States the well-understood powers of 'Wakils' in conformity with their own Islamic system, and recognizing the King's representative as their acknowledged Suzerain.

There is here no need of 'Dyarchy', for the lines of development of the native administration run parallel to and do not intersect those of the Central Government. It is the consistent aim of the British staff to maintain and increase the prestige of the native ruler, to encourage his initiative, and to support his authority. That the chiefs are satisfied with the autonomy they enjoy in the matters which really interest and concern them, may be judged by their loyalty and the prosperity of their country.

Comparatively little difficulty, it may be said, would be experienced in the application of such a system to Moslem States, for even if their rulers had deteriorated, they still profess the standards of Islam, with its system of taxation, and they possess a literate class capable of discharging the duties I have described. No doubt the alien immigrants in the northern tropical belt afford better material for social organization, both racially and through the influence of their creed, than the advanced communities of negro stock which owe nothing to Islam, such as the Baganda, the Ashantis, the Yorubas, the Benis, and others. But the self-evolved progress in social organization of these latter communities is in itself evidence that they possessed exceptional intelligence, probably more widely diffused among the peasantry than would be found among those over whom an alien race had acquired domination. They too had evolved systems of taxation and of land tenure, and had learnt to delegate authority. The teaching of missions through many decades had in most cases produced a class who, if their energies were rightly directed to the service of their communities instead of seeking foreign outlets, would form a very valuable aid in the building up of a 'Native Administration'. That these communities are fully capable of adopting such a system has been proved in recent years in South Nigeria.

They have not produced so definite a code of law, or such advanced methods of dispensing justice, as the Koran has introduced, and they lack the indigenous educational advantages which the use of Arabic and the religious schools have conferred on the Moslem. On the other hand, many . . . have benefited greatly by the Christian schools, and a wider range of knowledge, including English. Some of their chiefs . . . have been remarkable men. Among many of these communities the chiefs exercise an influence different in its nature from that accorded to an alien ruler, and based on superstitious veneration.

The limitations to independence which are frankly inherent in this conception of native rule—not as temporary restraints to be removed as soon as may be, but as powers which rightly belong to the controlling Power as trustee for the welfare of the masses, and as being responsible for the defence of the country and the cost of its central administration—are such as do not involve interference with the authority of the chiefs or the social organization of the people. They have been accepted by the Fulani Emirs as natural and proper to the controlling power, and their reservation in the hands of the Governor has never interfered with the loyalty of the ruling chiefs, or, so far as I am aware, been resented by them. The limitations are as follows:—

(1) Native rulers are not permitted to raise and control armed forces, or to grant permission to carry arms. . . .No one with experience will deny the necessity of maintaining the strictest military discipline over armed forces or police in Africa if misuse of power is to be avoided, and they are not to become a menace and a terror to the native population and a danger in case of religious excitement —a discipline which an African ruler is incapable of appreciating or applying. For this reason native levies should never be employed in substitution for or in aid of troops.

On the other hand, the Government armed police are never quartered in native towns, where their presence would interfere with the authority of the chiefs. Like the regular troops, they are employed as escorts and on duty in the townships.

(2) The sole right to impose taxation in any form is reserved to

the Suzerain power. This fulfils the bilateral understanding that the peasantry—provided they pay the authorized tax (the adjustment of which to all classes of the population is a responsibility which rests with the Central Government)—should be free of all other exactions whatsoever (including unpaid labour), while a sufficient proportion of the tax is assigned to the native treasuries to meet the expenditure of the native administration. . . .

(3) The right to legislate is reserved. That this should remain in the hands of the Central Government—itself limited by the control of the Colonial Office . . . cannot be questioned. The native authority, however, exercises very considerable power in this regard. A native ruler, and the native courts, are empowered to enforce native law and custom, provided it is not repugnant to humanity, or in opposition to any ordinance. . . .

(4) The right to appropriate land on equitable terms for public purposes and for commercial requirements is vested in the Governor. In the Northern Provinces of Nigeria (but not in the South) the right of disposing of native lands is reserved to the Governor by ordinance. In practice this does not interfere with the power of the native ruler (as the delegate of the Governor) to assign lands to the natives under his rule, in accordance with native law and custom, or restrict him or the native courts from adjudicating between natives regarding occupancy rights in land. No rents are levied on lands in occupation by indigenous natives. Leases to aliens are granted by the Central Government.

If the pressure of population in one community makes it necessary to assign to it a portion of the land belonging to a neighbour with a small and decreasing population, the Governor (to whom appeal may be made) would decide the matter. These reservations were set out in the formal letter of appointment given to each chief in Northern Nigeria.

(5) In order to maintain intact the control of the Central Government over all aliens, and to avoid friction and difficulties, it has been the recognized rule that the employees of the native administration should consist entirely of natives subject to the native authority. If aliens are required for any skilled work by the native administration, Government servants may be employed and their salaries reimbursed by the native treasury. For a like reason, whenever possible, all non-natives and natives not subject to the local native jurisdiction live in the 'township', from which natives subject to the native administration are as far as possible excluded. This exclusive control of aliens by the Central Government partakes rather of the nature of 'extra-territorial jurisdiction' than of dualism.

(6) Finally, in the interests of good government, the right of

confirming or otherwise the choice of the people of the successor to a chiefship, and of deposing any ruler for misrule or other adequate cause, is reserved to the Governor.

The revenue of a native administration consists, as I have said, not of an arbitrary sum assigned to it by the Governor. Thus though the Suzerain power imposes the taxes (whether direct in the form of an income tax or indirect as customs dues, etc.), and the general rate of the former is fixed by the Governor, the actual assessment is in the hands of the native ruler and his representatives—the district and village heads—guided and assisted by the British staff. It therefore appears to the taxpayer as a tax imposed by his own native ruler, though he knows that the vigilant eye of the District Officer will see that no unauthorized exactions are made, and that any injustice will be remedied. Since the salaries of the ruler and the officials of the 'Native Administration' are paid out of their own native treasury funds, they cannot be regarded by him as officials paid by Government.

The proportion assigned to the native administration in advanced communities is a half of the general income and cattle tax,—the proportion is less in pagan communities. On the inauguration of the tax in Nigeria the proceeds were quite insufficient to meet even the necessary salaries of chiefs; but with improved assessment, a more honest collection, and increased prosperity, the sum, without additional burden, has become so large that in the more wealthy Emirates there is a considerable surplus, when all the salaries of the very largely-increased establishments of native officials, police and prison staff, etc., have been paid.

The revenues of the native administrations do not appear in the colonial budget of revenue and expenditure, and are dependent of colonial treasury or audit control. The proper expenditure of these large sums—obtained by taxes imposed and enforced by the Suzerain Power—must obviously depend in part on the ability of each native ruler, and in part on the Resident who advises him. 'Unfettered control' may in some cases mean that a Resident, and not the ruling chief, disposes of large revenues independent of the Lieutenant-Governor; in other cases it may mean a tendency to multiply offices and pay high salaries, which either overburden the finances of other less wealthy treasuries, or cause discontent among its employees, and ultimately enhance the cost of labour throughout the country— a result which is inimical to production and progress, unless necessitated by economic causes. It is a tendency which a Resident, however much he has identified himself in the interests of the native administration, may not find it easy to resist, though he sets his face against nepotism and the reckless exercise of patronage and display—

which are so apt to be regarded as the symbol of power by a native ruler.

Pending the growth of a fuller sense of public responsibility and of an enlightened public opinion, some check may be afforded by the preparation of annual estimates of revenue and expenditure in a very simple form. . . . While refraining as far as possible from interference in detail, the Lieutenant-Governor can, by suggestion and comparison, effect some co-ordination and uniformity where desirable, and can best discriminate between the scope which may be allowed to an individual, and the grant of extended powers of universal application.

The habits of a people are not changed in a decade, and when powerful despots are deprived of the pastime of war and slave-raiding, and when even the weak begin to forget their former sufferings, to grow weary of a life without excitement, and to resent the petty restrictions which have replaced the cruelties of the old despotism, it must be the aim of Government to provide new interests and rivalries, in civilized progress, in education, in material prosperity and trade, and even in sport.

There were indeed many who, with the picture of Fulani misrule fresh in their memory, regarded this system when it was first inaugurated with much misgiving, and believed that though the hostility of the rulers to the British might be concealed, and their vices disguised, neither could be eradicated, and they would always remain hostile at heart. They thought that the Fulani as an alien race of conquerors, who had in turn been conquered, had not the same claims for consideration as those whom they had displaced, even though they had become so identified with the people that they could no longer be called aliens.

But there can be no doubt that such races form an invaluable medium between the British staff and the native peasantry. Nor can the difficulty of finding any one capable of taking their place, or the danger they would constitute to the State if ousted from their positions, be ignored. Their traditions of rule, their monotheistic religion, and their intelligence enable them to appreciate more readily than the negro population the wider objects of British policy, while their close touch with the masses—with whom they live in daily intercourse—mark them out as destined to play an important part in the future, as they have done in the past, in the development of the tropics.

Both the Arabs in the east and the Fulani in the west are Moham-medans, and by supporting their rule we unavoidably encourage the spread of Islam, which from the purely administrative point of view has the disadvantage of being subject to waves of fanaticism, bounded by no political frontiers. In Nigeria it has been the rule that their power should not be re-established over tribes which had made good their independence, or imposed upon those who had successfully resisted domination.

On the other hand, the personal interests of the rulers must rapidly become identified with those of the controlling Power. The forces of disorder do not distinguish between them, and the rulers soon recognize that any upheaval against the British would equally make an end of them. Once this community of interest is established, the Central Government cannot be taken by surprise, for it is impossible that the native rulers should not be aware of any disaffection.

This identification of the ruling class with the Government accentuates the corresponding obligation to check malpractices on their part. The task of educating them in the duties of a ruler becomes more than ever insistent; of inculcating a sense of responsibility; of convincing their intelligence of the advantages which accrue from the material prosperity of the peasantry, from free labour and initiative; of the necessity of delegating powers to trusted subordinates; of the evils of favouritism and bribery; of the importance of education, especially for the ruling class, and for the filling of lucrative posts under Government; of the benefits of sanitation, vaccination, and isolation of infection in checking mortality; and finally, of impressing upon them how greatly they may benefit their country by personal interest in such matters, and by application of labour-saving devices and of scientific methods in agriculture.

Unintentional misuse of the system of native administration must also be guarded against. It is not, for instance, the duty of a native administration to purchase supplies for native troops, or to enlist and pay labour for public works, though its agency within carefully defined limits may be useful in making known Government requirements, and seeing that markets are well supplied. Nor should it be directed to collect licences, fees, and rents due to Government, nor should its funds be used for any purpose not solely connected with and prompted by its own needs.

I have throughout these pages continually emphasized the necessity of recognizing, as a cardinal principle of British policy in dealing with native races, that institutions and methods, in order to command success and promote the happiness and welfare of the people, must be deep-rooted in their traditions and prejudices. Obviously in no sphere of administration is this more essential than in that under discussion, and a slavish adherence to any particular type, however successful it may have proved elsewhere, may, if unadapted to the local environment, be as ill-suited and as foreign to its conceptions as direct British rule would be.

The type suited to a community which has long grown accustomed to the social organization of the Moslem State may or may not be suitable to advanced pagan communities, which have evolved a social system of their own, such as the Yorubas, the Benis, the Egbas, or the Ashantis . . . .. The history, the traditions, the idio-syncracies, and the prejudices of each must be studied by the Resident and his staff, in order that the form adopted shall accord with natural evolution, and shall ensure the ready co-operation of the chiefs and people. . . .

Native etiquette and ceremonial must be carefully studied and observed in order that unintentional offence may be avoided. Great importance is attached to them, and a like observance in accordance with native custom is demanded towards British officers. Chiefs are treated with respect and courtesy. Native races alike in India and Africa are quick to discriminate between natural dignity and assumed superiority. Vulgar familiarity is no more a passport to their friendship than an assumption of self-importance is to their respect. The English gentleman needs no prompting in such a matter—his instinct is never wrong. Native titles of rank are adopted, and only native dress is worn, whether by chiefs or by schoolboys. Principal chiefs accused of serious crimes are tried by a British court, and are not imprisoned before trial, unless in very exceptional circum-stances. Minor chiefs and native officials appointed by an Emir may be tried by his Judicial Council. If the offence does not involve deprivation of office, the offender may be fined without public trial, if he prefers it, in order to avoid humiliation and loss of influence.

Succession is governed by native law and custom, subject in the case of important chiefs to the approval of the Governor, in order that the most capable claimant may be chosen. It is important to ascertain the customary law and to follow it when possible, for the appointment of a chief who is not the recognized heir, or who is disliked by the people, may give rise to trouble, and in any case the new chief would have much difficulty in asserting his authority, and would fear to check abuses lest he should alienate his supporters. In Moslem countries the law is fairly clearly defined, being a useful combination of the hereditary principle, tempered by selection, and in many cases in Nigeria the ingenious device is maintained of having two rival dynasties, from each of which the successor is selected alternatively.

In pagan communities the method varies; but there is no rigid rule, and a margin for selection is allowed. The formal approval of the Governor after a short period of probation is a useful precaution, so that if the designated chief proves himself unsuitable, the selection may be revised without difficulty. Minor chiefs are usually selected by popular vote, subject to the approval of the paramount chief. It is a rule in Nigeria that no slave may be appointed as a chief or district headman. If one is nominated he must first be publicly freed.

Small and isolated communities, living within the jurisdiction of a chief, but owing allegiance to the chief of their place of origin—a common source of trouble in Africa—should gradually be absorbed into the territorial jurisdiction. Aliens who have settled in a district for their own purposes would be subject to the local jurisdiction.

There are some who consider that however desirable it may be to rule through the native chiefs of advanced communities, such a policy is misplaced, if not impossible, among the backward tribes. Here, they would say, the Resident and his staff must necessarily be the direct rulers, since among the most primitive peoples there are no recognized chiefs capable of exercising rule. The imposition of a tax is in their view premature, since (they say) the natives derive no corresponding benefit, and learn to regard the District Officer merely as a tax-collector. Moreover, refusal to pay necessitates coercive expeditions—scarcely distinguishable from the raids of old times. To attempt to adapt such methods—however suitable to the Moslem communities—to the conditions of primitive tribes, would be to foist upon them a system foreign to their conceptions. In the criticisms I have read no *via media* is indicated between those who are accounted to rank as advanced communities, entitled before long to independence, and direct rule by the British staff.

Let us realize that the advanced communities form a very minute proportion of the population of British Tropical Africa. The vast majority are in the primitive or early tribal stages of development. To abandon the policy of ruling them through their own chiefs, and to substitute the direct rule of the British officer, is to forgo the high ideal of leading the backward races, by their own efforts, in their own way, to raise themselves to a higher plane of social organization, and tends to perpetuate and stereotype existing conditions.

We must realize also two other important facts. First, that the British staff, exercising direct rule, cannot be otherwise than very small in comparison to the area and population of which they are in charge. That rule cannot generally mean the benevolent autocracy of a particular District Officer, well versed in the language and customs of the people, but rule by a series of different white men, conveying their orders by police and couriers and alien native subordinates, and the quartering of police detachments in native villages. Experi-

M

ence has shown the difficulty in such conditions of detecting and checking cases of abuse of office, and of acquisition of land by alien and absentee native landlords. There is a marked tendency to litigation, and the entire decay of such tribal authority as may previously have existed.

The changed conditions of African life is the second important fact for consideration. The advent of Europeans cannot fail to have a disintegrating effect on tribal authority and institutions, and on the conditions of native life. This is due in part to the unavoidable restrictions imposed on the exercise of their power by the native chiefs. They may no longer inflict barbarous and inhuman punishments on the individual, or take reprisals by force of arms on aggressive neighbours or a disobedient section of the community. The concentration of force in the hands of the Suzerain Power, and the amenability of the chiefs to that Power for acts of oppression and misrule, are evidence to primitive folk that the power of the chiefs has gone. This decay of tribal authority has unfortunately too often been accentuated by the tendency of British officers to deal direct with petty chiefs, and to ignore, and allow their subordinates to ignore, the principal chief.

It has been increased in many cases by the influx of alien natives, who, when it suited them, set at naught the native authority, and refused to pay the tribute which the chiefs were given no means of enforcing, or acquired lands which they held in defiance of native customary tenure. . . .

Here, then, in my view, lies our present task in Africa. It becomes impossible to maintain the old order—the urgent need is for adaptation to the new—to build up a tribal authority with a recognized and legal standing, which may avert social chaos. It cannot be accomplished by superseding—by the direct rule of the white man— such ideas of discipline and organization as exist, nor yet by 'stereotyping customs and institutions among backward races which are not consistent with progress.'

The first step is to hasten the transition from the patriarchal to the tribal stage, and induce those who acknowledge no other authority than the head of the family to recognize a common chief. Where this stage has already been reached, the object is to group together small tribes, or sections of a tribe, so as to form a single administrative unit, whose chiefs severally, or in Council as a 'Native Court' may be constituted a 'Native Authority', with defined powers over native aliens, through whom the district officer can work instead of through alien subordinates. His task is to strengthen the authority of the chiefs, and encourage them to show initiative; to learn their difficulties at first hand, and to assist them in adapting the new conditions to the old—maintaining and developing what is best, avoiding everything that has a tendency to denationalization and servile imitation. He can guide and control several such units, and endeavour gradually to bring them to the standard of an advanced community. In brief, tribal cohesion, and the education of the tribal heads in the duties of rulers, are the watchwords of the policy in regard to these backward races. . . .

To this end the institution of the tax is the first beginning. It marks the recognition by the community of the Suzerainty of the protecting Power, and the corresponding obligation to refrain from lawless acts. Failure to impose it is regarded as a sign of weakness or of fear. The payment of 'tribute' to a chief marks the transition from the patriarchal to the tribal stage. It forms no burden, and is only refused if a community deliberately desires to throw off all restraint and revert to lawlessness, in which case coercive measures become inevitable for the protection of the law-abiding. The most experienced Residents declare that it is not resented, and is a definite curb on the impulse to attack traders. . . .

The inauguration of a treasury, in like manner, though admittedly beyond the grasp of such peoples, is the embryo conception which will later develop with education, and they are quick to realize that the salaried chiefs and sub-chiefs are not merely paid officers of the Government, but receive a portion of the funds which they themselves collect from the people. They do not exist merely to collect an alien tax as the agents of Government, but are selected as men who will be trusted and followed by their people, and capable of expressing their opinions. Among the primitive communities it suffices that the share of the tax should be sufficient to meet their salaries only, so long as they are incapable of understanding or exercising any judgement regarding other expenditure. Without a tax there can be no treasury, and without a treasury no real eventual measure of self-rule. The imposition of a tax at a later stage of development would be resented as a breach of faith, and would generally lead to trouble.

It is not necessary that these embryo administrations should follow closely the model adopted for the Moslem communities, if any more natural line presents itself. Experience in the advanced pagan communities will suggest divergencies. For, as I have said, there is no desire to impose on the people any theoretically suitable form of government, but rather to evolve from their own institutions, based on their own habits of thought, prejudices, and customs, the form of rule best suited to them, and adapted to meet the new conditions.

Direct British rule among primitive tribes, unaccompanied by any tax, may perhaps, if a fully adequate staff is provided, be the least troublesome, and temporarily at any rate the most efficient—albeit the most costly—method. But it shirks the more difficult task of education, and when the time comes—as it inevitably will come—and the people demand a voice in the control of their own affairs, we shall find . . . that we have destroyed the natural institutions of the country, that we have sapped the foundations of native rule, and have taught them only the duty of obedience. We can then only offer an alien system, evolved by Western nations to suit wholly different circumstances, moulded on European and native habits of thought.

It is of the first importance that the chiefs should be elected by the community from among themselves, and be men of influence and strength of character, neither middlemen traders selected for their wealth nor Moslems. It is preferable also not to employ the latter as judges of the courts, or teachers in the schools, even though progress be slower. If the selection of an alien is inevitable he should not be allowed to retain any armed following. The District Officer must be tolerant of misrule due to inexperience in a chief who promises well, and avoid damaging his prestige and influence.

In order to develop a system suited to their needs, the District Officer must study their customs and social organizations; for without a knowledge of their institutions the result must be failure. . .

These primitive tribes—as we shall see when discussing the courts—are capable, even in their present stage, of settling ordinary social disputes in a tribunal composed of chiefs—which, in default of rulers of sufficient individual importance and prestige, it is often necessary to endow with executive powers as the 'Native Authority'.

Turning now from the detailed discussion of the application of this system to advanced communities on the one hand, and to primitive tribes on the other, let us glance at its results and the criticisms it has evoked. I think that there are very hopeful possibilities for the future in the development of the 'Native Administrations' of Nigeria. . . .

The system described has, of course, like every other possible system, found its critics and opponents. The educated native very naturally dislikes it, for it places the native chief, who has no schoolroom education, and is probably ignorant even of the English language, in a position of authority over his people, and tends to make him independent of the educated native lawyer or adviser.

The criticism of Europeans is, so far as I am aware, chiefly confined to those who have not had personal experience of its working, or adequate opportunity to examine for themselves the truths of statements they have read in the native press. Bishop Tugwell, whose long and faithful service in West Africa has chiefly lain in the coast area and its immediate hinterland, writes: ' "Indirect rule" is direct rule by indirect means. The Emir's position and salary are secure. His sway, backed by British authority, is rendered absolute, while his people become his serfs, or those of the British Government. Their life is thus robbed of all initiative or desire for progress—intellectual, social, moral, religious, or political.' The Emir, he adds, who is appointed by the Government, is the instrument of the Resident, and 'the name of Christ must not be proclaimed lest this blighting system should be overturned'.

The statement is inaccurate, for there are very many cases on record in Nigeria, extending from the earliest beginnings of British rule in the north up to the present day, where not only the highest officials of the native administration have been deprived of their positions and subjected to the rigours of the law for misconduct, but even Emirs and principal chiefs have been deposed for misrule. As regards the peasantry, it is incontestable that they have never enjoyed such liberty and material prosperity as they now possess, such security of land tenure and immunity from oppression.

But Bishop Tugwell, unconsciously perhaps, gives imperfect expression to an aspect of the matter on which I have already touched. It was naturally a cause for anxiety and misgiving that the British Government, by supporting native rule, and the authority of the native courts, should accept some measure of responsibility for evils which its meagre staff of British officials was unable to control adequately, seeing that the one was exercised by men who had behind them a century's tradition of such tyranny and oppression as I have described, and the other had become corrupt and inflicted barbarous sentences. To overthrow an organization, however faulty, which has the sanction of long usage, and is acquiesced in by the people, before any system could be created to take its place—before, indeed, we had any precise knowledge of Moslem methods or of native law and custom,—would have been an act of folly which no sane administrator could attempt. The very necessity for avoiding precipitate action, and the knowledge that reform could only be effective, and enlist native co-operation, if it was gradual, made the responsibility all the more onerous. To infer that it was not realized, or was lightly regarded, is to do a great injustice to the administrative staff of the early Government of Northern Nigeria, who struggled to cope with a burden which fixed them beyond their strength. Some died, and some left with health impaired.

That the supervision exercised was insufficient, in spite of their efforts, is a reasonable criticism, for the staff was quite inadequate. In the year 1903–4, in which the whole of the Moslem States first came under British control, Northern Nigeria provided in its budget for forty-four administrative officers. Of these, we can only assume that a half were actually at work. Thus in the fourth year after the administration was inaugurated there was only about one officer available for each 11,600 square miles and 400,000 head of population—and most of them very young and new to the work! . . .

That the system is inapplicable to communities of Europeanized natives educated on Western lines is admitted. The method of their progress towards self-government lies . . . along the same path as that of Europeans—increased participation in municipal affairs until they prove themselves fitted for the larger responsibilities of Government of their own communities, by a majority vote in the councils, by popular election. and by appointment to posts of responsibility in the Civil Service.

A local criticism is that the natives are taught to look to the District Officer only, that the latter is intolerant of any departmental officer exercising authority in his district, and that it is impossible for a departmental officer to feel a keen interest in his work, and achieve the best results, if he is practically dependent on a junior administrative officer, and can get nothing done without reference to him.

The reply is that orders to the local headman emanate, not from the District Officer, but from his own chief (to whom any wishes of Government in the matter are communicated by the Resident). The District Officer, who knows the headmen personally and speaks their language, is the natural and best means that the departmental officer can employ for making his demands known, and obtaining the services of an agent from the chief to procure labour, etc. In technical details he gives his orders direct. In case of difficulty it is not to the District Officer but to his own chief that the headman appeals for instructions. The chief in turn only invokes the advice of intervention of the Resident if he needs it. . . .

The object of substituting for British rule, in which the chiefs are mere agents of the Government, a system of native rule under the guidance and control of the British staff, whether among advanced or backward communities, is primarily educative. Among backward tribes the chiefs have to learn how to exert and maintain authority, and establish a chain of responsibility reaching down to the village head.

Among the more advanced their interest is directed to education, forestry, sanitation, prevention of disease, and public works. In all alike the endeavour is to prevent denationalization, to develop along indigenous lines, to inculcate the principal that the function of the ruler is to promote the welfare of his people and not to exploit them for his own pleasure, and to afford both to rulers and people the stimulus of progress and interest in life.

No system of rule can be effective—whether governmental or municipal—unless it enjoys some measure of financial independence; and . . . the fundamental basis upon which the policy . . . is the assignment to the native rulers of a definite revenue with which to pay the salaries of their officials, and to inaugurate schemes of development.[1] This revenue must obviously be found by taxation, and in Nigeria . . . it is derived from a direct tax—based on the principle of an income tax—collected through the machinery of the native administration, in accordance with native law and custom, and under the close supervision of the British staff. The native rulers and others who share it are not therefore salaried officials of Government, but derive their incomes as proper dues from their own people, in return for their work as rulers, or judges, or employees of the native administration. They, and even the more intelligent of the peasantry, can see that a substantial portion of the tax is spent by themselves in their own immediate interests, and can appreciate the necessity of devoting the remainder to the central Government. They thus have an interest in its collection in full, and there is no perennial complaint of an insufficient grant for the maintenance of the native administration, disproportioned to their particular claims.

Moreover, it is obvious that the native rulers must have some means of livelihood, and of maintaining their position. If there be no legal and recognized tax, the necessary income must be obtained by arbitrary levies on the peasantry, subject to no control by Government. In the Moslem States the tax is the corollary of the abolition of slavery.

It has been asserted that, with the exception of those communities which have accepted the Koranic system of taxation, the natives of Africa are unaccustomed to, and radically opposed to, direct taxation and that it is therefore better to adopt indirect taxation, the incidence of which they do not understand.

The African is not peculiar in disliking taxes, but as soon as any degree of tribal cohesion is reached, the obligation to pay tribute to the head chief—generally in the form of slaves, concubines, food, and unpaid labour—is recognized. As the tribe advances in organization, and its rulers become more powerful and luxurious . . . the demands become increasingly heavy. It is probable that the Moslem conquerors in Northern Nigeria merely superimposed the Koranic tithe upon the pre-existing scheme of taxation among the Habes. Mohammedan rule merely admitted of a more systematized method.

Only among the most primitive peoples, where the authority of a paramount chief has not yet emerged, do we find an entire absence

[1] As so much of this chapter on taxation repeats Lugard's Memorandum No. 5 (see p. 118), I have quoted here only the introductory pages.

of taxation, for there is no authority to demand or enforce it. Such communities regard the payment of tribute as the token of acknow-ledgment of a Suzerain, with the consequent obligation to refrain from murders and robberies. Provided that it is not collected by alien native tax-gatherers, and is not unduly onerous, they do not appear to resent its imposition; and, as I have said in the last chapter, refusal to pay is usually a formal and deliberate prelude to an outbreak of lawlessness.

A direct tax is not therefore contrary to native custom or prejudices among those who have reached the tribal stage, and the dislike of it is not due to any objection to the principle, but to the imposition of a tax in addition to, instead of in substitution for, the tribute. The Yorubas, who at first resented it strongly, asked for its imposition when they understood the system, and the hostility of the Fulani was similarly converted to a whole-hearted co-operation. . . .

The payment of direct taxes is in Africa, as elsewhere, an un-welcome concomitant of progress. It marks the recognition of the principle that each individual in proportion to his means has an obligation to the State, to which he owes security for life and property, and his increased wealth,—due to fair wages for his labour, improved transport, and a large competitive market for his produce.

By its means the upper classes can be paid salaries for public work; slavery, forced labour, and all other forms of exactions from the peasantry can be declared illegal without reducing the ruling classes to poverty. The freed slave, on his part, renders to the State a small and fixed proportion of the profits of his industry. The tax may thus in a sense be regarded as a means of promoting the recognition of individual responsibility, which is inseparable from liberty, but is destroyed by the system of slavery. It was by this means that in Nigeria we sought a solution of the difficulties atten-dant on the abolition of the legal status of slavery, and to support the ruling clases while protecting the peasantry.

It emancipates justice by freeing the salaried native judge from the temptation of bribes and unjust fines. It lightens the heavy burdens on trade, both by rendering possible the abolition of the tolls levied by native rulers, by decreasing the amount which must be raised by customs, and by promoting, as no other agency can, the introduction of coin currency. The task of assessment promotes an intimate touch between the British staff and the native officials who assist in it on the one hand, and the inhabitants of remote and almost inaccessible villages on the other hand, who but for this assessment might have remained unknown. The District Officer comes as the herald of a just and equitable tax to replace extortion.

Among unorganized communities, not previously subject to tax, where native rulers cannot be said to exist, the tax affords a means to creating and enforcing native authority, of curbing lawlessness, and assisting in tribal evolution, and hence it becomes a moral benefit, and is justified by the immunity from slave-raids which the people now enjoy. . . .

1922: THE CLIFFORD MINUTE

The extracts are taken from the Minute addressed in Kaduna by the Governor of Nigeria, Sir Hugh Clifford, to his Honour the Lieutenant-Governor of the Northern Provinces on 18 March, 1922, and published for the benefit of all officers in the Political and Educational Services.

1. Before quitting the Northern Provinces, the inspection of which by me has been completed by the journey just concluded, I desire officially to record the sense of obligation under which I feel myself to be to you for the assistance that Your Honour has throughout afforded to me, and for the manner in which you have so freely placed at my disposal your unrivalled knowledge of the country and of its inhabitants. . . .

Everywhere throughout this wide expanse of country. . . . I found a profoundly peaceful, diligent, prosperous and thriving peasantry, tilling their fields in complete confidence and security, governed by their own hereditary rulers, and living under forms of government which are the natural growth of their own political genius, and which owe nothing to exotic systems that have no sanction in local custom and tradition. That an enormous change— a change almost incalculably great—has been effected, since the beginning of the present century, in the character of the Governments under which these millions of human beings live and move and have their being is, of course, a fact. The salient feature, however, of the system of administration which was inaugurated by Sir George Taubman Goldie in the days when the Niger Company exercised administrative functions, and which, during the past five and twenty years, has been gradually extended over the Northern Provinces, is that the change which has been wrought has entailed no abrupt violent departure from established custom or tradition;[1] none save minor alterations in the administrative machinery which had been developed by the people centuries before our Protectorate over them was established; no material modification even in the laws under which they live, save only that the traffic in slaves is no longer sanctioned by them. The change, which is so great as to amount to an absolute transformation, affecting alike the social, material and many of the moral conditions amid which these people live, abides wholly in the manner in which the indigenous system of

[1] Interestingly enough, this 'gradualism' and refusal to break abruptly with a proud past form the theme of many current addresses by the Premier of the North, Sir Ahmadu Bello. See, for example, *My Life* and his published speeches.

government is today being made to function, and in the wholly new spirit in which Emirs and their Chiefs and Officials, from the Waziri and Galadima to the smallest Village Head, are being gradually and patiently taught to discharge the responsibilities and to carry out the duties which devolve upon them under that system.

2. I have spoken of the peasantry of the Mohammedan Emirates, as thriving and prosperous,—adjectives which, at the present time, it is possible to apply with accuracy to very few, and to none save specially favoured populations. These terms, however, exactly fit the conditions under which the *talakawa* who inhabit the country which we have visited are today living. The culture and civilization which have been developed among them through Arabian and Fulani influence, are in their own way, singularly complete and self-sufficing. . . .

3. While, therefore, my admiration is second to none for the work that has been performed, and for the achievement already attained in the Northern Provinces by the Political Staff of which Your Honour is today the Head, I feel it to be my duty, alike to my colleagues in the Political Service and to the native population, the supervision of whose affairs is committed to their charge, to exhort the former to the exercise of a sleepless vigilance, and to impress upon them the necessity of rendering themselves at all times accessible to any who may seek their counsel or their aid, and of doing all that in them lies to maintain the closest personal touch with every class of the populations among which they are living.

5. Nonetheless, and in this I have the satisfaction of knowing that Your Honour is in the fullest agreement with me, there must be no yielding to the temptation to rest upon laurels already won, or to judge that the success so far achieved calls for no betterment. The problem which every Political Officer is called upon, almost daily, individually to face, in those parts of the country where native administrative machinery has happily been preserved intact, and where the hereditary Rulers and their Councillors, Ministers and Officials are the actual, *de facto* governors of the land is one of considerable complexity and difficulty. As is too often the case when perfection is sought in human affairs, the fairway that should be followed is flanked on either hand by its Scylla and Charybdis,—too frequent and too personal or direct interference with native administrative methods being, in its own way, scarcely less mischievous in the results it is apt to produce, than is the converse policy of blind confidence in the integrity and trustworthiness of Mohammedan officials, and the reluctance to intervene, the slackness of supervision, and the consequent toleration of, or failure to detect, abuses that commonly result therefrom.

6. It must be the aim of the efficient Political Officer attached to a Native Administration to steer a middle course between these two extremes. He should keep steadily before him, in the first place, the cardinal fact that all executive authority is vested, not in him, but in the Native Administration; and that his proper functions are primarily advisory and for the rest are supervisory. He must recognize from the outset that, in all transactions between himself and the ruling classes in the Mohammedan States, he is dealing with a proud, sensitive and timid people, and that the timidity to which they are a prey is due, not so much to moral cowardice, but to an instinctive shrinking from the embarrassment and humiliation that are produced by the impatience, the roughness of manner, the loss of temper, the discourtesy, or any apparent contempt of, or disregard for, their accepted usages and traditions which they may, from time to time, think that they detect in those whom they recognize as occupying positions of authority over them. This feeling of timidity and uneasiness is immeasurably enhanced if any doubt is felt as to the ability of a European officer completely to understand all that is said to him; or by a corresponding doubt upon their part as to how far they are interpreting accurately the orders or ideas which he is endeavouring to impart to them through the medium of the vernacular. Upon this point I shall have something further to say in a later paragraph of this minute.

7. The Political Officer must also keep well in the foreground of his mind the fact that the folk with whom he is dealing are, or believe themselves to be, quite pathetically impotent; that they very rarely believe themselves to be in a position to resent openly any affront that a European may put upon them, no matter whether it be the result of set intention, or the mere blunderings of ignorance and indifference. It is therefore incumbent upon the efficient Political Officer to adopt toward all Mohammedans of standing, whether they are or are not officials in the employment of a Native Administration, what I can only adequately describe as a certain chivalry of manner, treating them with a measure of dignity and courtesy corresponding as nearly as possible to that which usually inspires their own behaviour, and scrupulously avoiding violent gestures, loudness of speech, or even the unnecessary raising of the speaking voice when addressing them. It must be one of the primary objects of every Political Officer to inspire the Africans of all classes with whom he has to deal, not only with respect, but with confidence; and neither the one nor the other is to be won by the European whose faults of manner are calculated to convey to the natives about him the idea that he is either a hectoring bully, a mannerless oaf, or, it may be, merely a buffoon. Similarly, it is very rarely safe to venture upon

anything resembling a humourous sally when talking to Mohammedans of the superior classes, unless the individual addressed is
exceedingly well known to the speaker. No one could dream of
denying to the Hausa or the Fulani the possession of a sense of
humour; and, indeed, I make no doubt that this has not infrequently
been employed to convulse delighted local audiences with admirably
rendered accounts of interviews with the more experienced members
of the Political Staff during which, at the time, the latter have
flattered themselves that they had succeeded in creating no mean
impression. The Mohammedan of the upper classes, however,
usually reserves his quips and jests for his intimates, and he is apt to
regard any departure from this rule by a European as undignified,
or if, as not infrequently happens, the point of the pleasantry be
missed, as something which is embarrassingly incomprehensible, or
possibly even offensive.

8. Finally, Political Officers should make a painstaking study of
the innumerable little details governing the everyday demeanour
and comportment of the Mohammedans among whom they are
living which, taken together, constitute in their eyes the difference
between good and bad manners. Had this been done in Nigeria at
an earlier stage by all the Europeans who came into the country, we
should not today be so frequently treated to the deplorable spectacle
of well-meaning Mohammedans throughout the whole Dependency
baring their heads as an intended token of respect (which in their
own eyes it can never be) when greeting or addressing Europeans.
This study should be extended to the predilections and prejudices
of the people; and wherever possible, these should be carefully and
even scrupulously respected. To give a concrete instance of what I
mean. Some Political Officers living among Mohammedans should
never for an instant forget that, according to the teaching of the
Mohammedan religion, the dog ranks next after the pig on the list of
'unclean' animals; that physical contact with a dog, no matter how
accidental, to an orthodox Mohammedan, is or should be, an
unspeakable pollution; that he instinctively feels, not only repulsion
but contempt, at the sight of a European fondling his pet dog; and
that mere elementary courtesy and respect for one's neighbour's
feelings, to say nothing of one's own self-respect, should restrain a
Political Officer, whose duty brings him into close daily intercourse
with cultured Mohammedans, from wantonly offending prejudices
of this character. During a visit which was paid to me at a Residency
in the Northern Provinces by one of the leading Fulani Emirs in
September, 1919—that is to say, within a very few weeks of my
arrival in Nigeria,—I was horrified to see two or three dogs, the
property of the Political Officer in whose house the meeting was

taking place, being allowed to run at large in and out among the Mohammedan officials who had their seats upon carpets spread upon the floor. I at once interfered; but that such an incident could be *possible*, showed either gross ignorance of Mohammedan feelings and prejudices, or a no less gross callousness and indifference to them; and either the one or the other, and still more a combination of both, argue the possession of qualities which are of a character effectually to bar those sentiments of mutual respect and confidence without which it is not feasible for a European to establish really intimate and sympathetic relations with cultured Mohammedans.

9. To Your Honour and to many of the senior Political Officers in the Northern Provinces, all this may appear very rudimentary. My object in addressing to you this Minute, however, is to impress upon the very large number of young officers, who have recently joined the Political Service of the Northern Provinces, two elementary but essential facts—viz., the great importance of cultivated good manners in their dealings with Mohammedans of all classes; and the impossibility of achieving this without first undertaking a careful and sympathetic study of native ideas, standards of courtesy, prejudices and predilections.

10. Some young Englishmen newly arrived in the country, and even, it is to be feared, some Political Officers of much longer standing, may perhaps ask: 'Why should I bother myself about what the natives think about me and my manners? Why should I be at pains to study their ideas and prejudices? If my way of comporting myself is good enough for me, it has got to be good enough for them.' The answer is that, for every European, the shy confidence of a primitive Mohammedan people is hedged about by barriers as formidable as those which guarded the Palace of the Sleeping Beauty; and that if any attempt is to be made to scale or penetrate them, the initiative must come from the white man. Unless, therefore, he be prepared scrupulously to refrain from raising fresh and unnecessary barriers of his own creation—such as are so easily reared up by faults of manner and of taste, as such things are judged from the native standpoint—he must be content to abandon at the very outset of his career, what should be one of the main objects of his ambition. This in turn means that he must resign himself for all his official life to the fate of one who is groping his way about an imperfectly lighted room, filled with unfamiliar, puzzling and often singularly angular objects. He will be condemning himself to *guessing*, in circumstances in which sure and intimate *knowledge* should guide him by its clear light to absolute certainty: and his guessing will often be at fault. Yet upon his reading of a situation, and upon the advice that he may tender to Government may depend

the difference between justice and injustice (as such things are judged by the natives concerned); the difference between the honour and the dishonour of the Government which he is serving; the difference between good, honest work accomplished, such as may be held to justify any man's existence, and a piece of slipshod, indifferent, fudged make-shift, the poor quality of which must be manifest even to its uncritical author. For really first-class political work in this country, it must be remembered, cannot be done by the light of nature, on the spur of occasion, or without long preliminary preparation. Knowledge, sure and unerring knowledge of the people, of their character, of their point of view, of their customs, traditions, habits, modes of thought, is needed as the solid foundation upon which alone really sound political work can be reared up; and this has to be garnered slowly, patiently, painfully, little by little. It is not to be acquired as occasion requires. It is the fruit of the labour of years: it can never come as the happy inspiration of the moment.

11. More than a quarter of a century ago, at the end of a period of some thirteen years' service most of which I had spent as a Political Officer almost entirely alone among a Mohammedan population, with only one spell of fifteen months' sick-leave to break its sequence, I tried to put into words, in a book long out of print, some of the lessons which that somewhat unusual experience had taught me. I would ask Your Honour and the more senior members of the Political Service in the Northern Provinces to bear with me if, more especially for the benefit of the young men who have recently joined the Service, I here quote a few passages from the book in question. I was writing of the Political Officer whom fate sets down in an isolated position among natives, and who, I claimed, can find a study of inexhaustible interest lying ready to his hand, if only he can be brought to realize its extraordinary interest and fascination.

'Almost unconsciously he begins to perceive that he is sundered from the people of the land by a gulf which *they* will not[1] attempt to bridge. If he is ever to gain confidence the work must be of his own doing. They cannot come up to his level; he must go down to the plains in which they dwell. He must put off many of the things of the white man, and must forget many of his airs of superiority. . . .
'He must start by learning the language of his fellows, as perfectly as it is given to a stranger to learn it. That is the first step in a long and often weary march. Next he must study, with all the eagerness of Browning's Grammarian, every native custom, every native con-

[1] This word was omitted from the original Minute, but its insertion is clearly required by the text and is to be found in some Secretariat file copies of the Minute.

ventionality, every one of the ten thousand ceremonial observances to which the natives, among themselves, attach so vast an importance. He must grow to understand each one of the hints and *doubles ententes* [sic], of which natives make such frequent use; every little mannerism, sign and token; and most difficult of all, every motion of the hearts and every turn of thought of those whom he is beginning to call his own people. He must become acutely conscious of native public opinion, which is often diametrically opposed to that of his race-mates on one and the same subject. He must be able unerringly to predict how the slightest of his actions will be regarded by the natives, and he must shape his course by the light of that knowledge, if he is to maintain his influence over them and to win their sympathy and their confidence. He must learn to place himself in imagination in all manner of unlikely places and situations, and thence instinctively to feel the native point of view. That is really the whole secret of governing natives,—a quick and accurate perception of their point of view in all conceivable circumstances; a rapid process whereby a European places himself in the position of the native with whom he is dealing; an instinctive and instantaneous apprehension of the precise manner in which that native will be affected, and a clear vision of the *man*, of his feelings, his hopes, his desires and his sorrows,—these, and these alone, mean that complete sympathy and understanding, without which a white man among natives is apt to be but a sounding brass and a tinkling cymbal.

'It does not come all at once. Months, perhaps years, pass before the exile begins to feel that he is winning any grip upon his people; and even when he thinks that he knows as much about them as is good for any man, the native soul shakes itself in its brown casing, and comes out in some totally unexpected and unlooked-for place to his no small mortification and discouragement. But, when he has got thus far, discouragement matters little, for he has become bitten by the love of his discoveries, and can no more quit them than can the morphiamaniac abandon the drug that is killing him.

'Then he gets deep set in a groove and is happy. His fingers are between the leaves of the Book of Human Nature, and his eager eyes are scanning the lines of the chapter which in time he hopes to make his own. The natives about him have learned to look upon him as almost one of their own people. His speech is their speech; he can think as they do; he can feel as they feel, rejoicing in their joys, sorrowing in their pains. He can tell them wonderful things, and of a philosophy of which they had not dreamed. He never offends their susceptibilities, never wounds their self-respect, never sins against any of their innumerable conventions. He has shared their sports, doctored their ills, healed their sick, protected them from oppression, stood their friend in time of need, done them a thousand kindnesses, and has helped their dying through the strait and awful pass of death. Above all, he *understands*; and in manner they love him. A new white man, speaking with them in a strange tongue, seems to lift him for the time out of their lives. The stranger jars upon the natives, who are the exile's people; and he looking through the natives' eyes which are no longer dim for him, sees where his race-fellow offends and in his turn is jarred, until he finds himself wincing at his own countryman, as once the natives winced at him. Coming out of the groove hurts badly, and wedging oneself back into it again is almost worse; but when a man is once well set in the rut of native life, these things do not disturb him, for he has found happiness and has no need of other or wider interests.'

12. Conditions have altered vastly throughout the Tropical Possessions of the Crown during the two and a half decades which have elapsed since those words were written, red-hot from a personal experience. In the Northern Provinces of Nigeria today, men do not spend year after year in continuous isolation or pass month after month without seeing a white face or speaking a word of their own language, and the opportunities for acquiring a deep and intimate knowledge of the people among whom we are working are proportionately restricted. What I would seek to impress upon young men now entering the Service, however, is that the possession of that knowledge is today as vitally important to England, and to the tremendously responsible work which she has undertaken to do in her Tropical Possessions, as it was five and twenty years ago; that to every one of them a splendid opportunity is vouchsafed of learning more about the people among whom he is living than is known to the rank and file of his fellows; that here, ready to his hand, is one of the most fascinating studies upon which it is given to any man to have the supreme good fortune to embark,—a study which is not only compellingly engrossing in itself, but which is bound enormously to enhance the value of the student to the Government he is serving, and proportionately to enlarge his individual power for good and his ability to serve faithfully both England and the pathetically defenceless people, the control or management of whose affairs England has given to him in trust.

13. In a very peculiar degree, we Political Officers in these distant lands have the honour of our country in our keeping; and I should like to see every man in the Service realizing this to the full and sparing no pains to fit himself by constant study and self-discipline for the adequate discharge of that sacred duty. . . . It is a cheap fashion of our time to mock at enthusiasm, to be rather shy of confessing to such a weakness as the possession of ideas, to be a little ashamed of appearing to be actuated by any save purely selfish and material motives. That is, however, in many cases, I am convinced, a mere surface pose that is often designed to hide far more serious sentiments and ambitions which, precisely because they are

N

serious and deeply felt, are not easy of expression by the average Englishmen. . . .

14. Turning now from the question of the spirit and the manner in which the work of a Political Officer in this country should be done, and from the consideration of the study and self-discipline which must be his if he is to equip himself efficiently for its discharge, there are a few matters connected with the character of that work and with objects at which it aims, concerning which I should like to place a few considerations upon record for the guidance of Political Officers.

15. In paragraph 5 of this Minute, I have made mention of the difficulty wherewith every Political Officer, who has dealing with a Native Administration which is the *de facto* Government of the State which it controls, is constantly confronted, of avoiding undue interference with native methods and procedure, on the one hand, and on the other, of playing so inactive a part that his presence ceases to exert any practical restraining influence.

16. In order to maintain an even course between these two extremes, there are certain facts that every Political Officer should bear steadily in mind.[1] . . .

17. It is well to bear such facts as these in mind, because it is neither fair nor right to judge men and methods in a Mohammedan Emirate, which has only been subjected to our influence for a couple of decades, too rigidly by the standards which have been set up in our midst, which we have all learned in our cradles unquestioningly to accept but which a very few generations ago would have been regarded by the average, cultured Englishman as almost impossibly idealistic. I would not be understood as suggesting that these standards are not to be the guides of our judgement, far less that our constant aim and object should be anything less than their establishment throughout Nigeria in all their integrity. The fact that we accept them, and that we are bent upon forcing their acceptance upon the people among whom we are working, should not be allowed to blind us, however, to an appreciation of their extreme novelty and of their almost revolutionary character in the eyes of many of those people; nor should the discovery, that many cultured Mohammedans in this country extend to our views on such subjects only a limited comprehension and sympathy, cause us to regard them as folk who are inflicted by an incurable moral obliquity of vision, far less as being in any true sense depraved. Instead, recognizing that these people are the natural products of their environment and of centuries of inherited tradition, we should use a generous tolerance in

[1] Here follows a literary comparison with mediaeval Europe and England in the 18th century.

our judgement of them. We should realize that while, as I have already pointed out, a Political Officer living among these people has an immense number of difficult things to learn, that which he has to *teach* must be imparted slowly, cautiously, and with the utmost patience, his every act and judgement being inspired by a thorough appreciation of the native, rather than of the European, point of view. It is his primary business to insure that life, liberty and property are safeguarded, and to prevent both the old customary powers of chiefs being abused, and new forms of extortion and oppression from becoming prevalent. To this end he should be ubiquitous, accessible at all hours to the meanest suitor, patient with a patience far exceeding that of the Patriarch, and at once firm and just in all his dealings, alike with the rulers and with the folk they rule. Yet throughout he should not judge the wrong-doer by standards not his own for it is quite easy through an over-zeal for justice, to be betrayed into acts that are unjust. This being so, he must never suffer his vigilance to relax. When, however, facts come to his knowledge which show that evil has been done, he should not allow disappointment or indignation to influence him. He should realize that he is engaged in working a very radical revolution in facts and in ideas that have held undisputed sway for hundreds of years; that great, even astounding, progress in the desired direction has already been made; but that we are trying in fact to crush into the space of a few years moral and ethical changes which, even among our own energetic countrymen, have been the slow growth of centuries. Such a process must necessarily be gradual, not abrupt. Time alone can work its fulfilment—time and infinite patience. Also he should remember that punishment should never be vindictive, and that the only use it has lies in its deterrent effects. To be equitable, moreover, it must be meted out in proportion, not so much to the nature of the offence committed, as to the moral responsibility of the individual who has been found guilty of that offence. The crime of an Englishman who embezzles public funds, for example, must be judged by quite other standards than those which would be appropriate in the case of a Village Head who has failed to account for all the tax-money collected by him; and a Fulani official who has committed some oppressive act,—though he and his fellows must be actively and effectively discouraged, and if possible prevented, from repeating the offence,—cannot be treated as would be, say, a modern British landlord who sought forcibly to exercise *le droit du seigneur* over his tenantry.

18. Similarly, Political Officers must not be too contemptuous or too intolerant of local superstitions; nor should they regard as 'extraordinary' people who hold views very similar to those which

were entertained by John Wesley only a hundred and fifty years ago. Some day, no doubt, many of these ideas will be discarded by the natives of Nigeria, as they have now been discarded by ourselves; but the process must inevitably be a very gradual one, and in the the mean time the actuality of the native's belief in witchcraft and magic, rather than the soundness or otherwise of his judgement in such matters, should be the fact that should chiefly engross the attention of a Political Officer, since it lends a new meaning and value to acts which are in themselves grossly and inexcusably criminal, if they be judged only from the standpoint of the modern, educated European.

19. In all that he does or leaves undone in his control or management of the administration of a Native State by its own local Government, the Political Officer must be careful, whenever possible, to lend his support to the authority of the Emir and his officers. They, and not he, constitute the *de facto* Government of the country over which their operations extend; and this is a fact that should be made manifest upon all occasions to the people living under their rule. If punishment has to be meted out, it is the Emir who should award it; if anyone is deserving of commendation, it is the Emir who should allot the praise or announce the reward. The Political Officer should be the Whisper behind the Throne, but never for an instant the Throne itself. Similarly, as regards less prominent native officials, he should take care never publicly to discredit any man occupying a position of authority,—even if it be only that of the Head of an insignificant village—unless his removal from office has already been finally determined upon. To do so is to weaken the Native Administration in one of its parts, and the cumulative effect of such actions may be to reduce to impotence the whole machine of local government. A tool should never be wantonly blunted if it be not intended forthwith to consign it to the scrap-heap.

20. The Native Administration of the Northern Provinces are, as I have said, the *de facto* Governments of the country today. They are, we are all convinced, the form of government most fitted to the needs of the populations that have evolved them; but surely, if gradually, those populations are themselves undergoing a process of change and evolution, and the Native Administrations, must keep pace with them. They cannot stand still, if they are to endure.

21. The *laudator temporis acti* is an inevitable figure in every primitive tropical country of which I have any knowledge wherein, through the advent of European influence, great changes have been wrought in the space of a very few years; and no man who has himself witnessed the passing away of a state of things which, however abominable it might be in many ways, yet had about it the

glamour of age, of simplicity, of the unmoral and of the picturesque, can fail to experience, as he watches it, some sentimental, if illogical, regrets. The school of thought, however, which pins its faith to the rigid maintenance of the *status quo* in the Mohammedan Emirates, as the only means of securing their perpetuation, is doomed, I am convinced, to failure and to disappointment. Any attempt to keep these Native Administrations 'unspotted from the world'—the modern world of which they form a part—by sheltering them from outside influences and from the influx of strangers and of extraneous and exotic ideas, cannot possibly prove successful for any prolonged period. It is like trying to stay a torrent with the hand; and if the attempt were persisted with, the Native Administrations of the Northern Provinces would presently be reduced to a condition of frailty comparable to that of the mummy-groups, occasionally brought to light by excavators in Egypt, that, at the first breath of air, are said to vanish, crumbling into dust.

22. We, I feel strongly, must work for more solid ends than these. We must not be content merely to purify the Native Administrations, and to render them efficient and justice-dealing machines for the government of the populations living within their borders. We must go further than that, and must watch over and stimulate their growth and their gradual evolution, recognizing that, as time goes on, they must so develop as to command the respect and the confidence, not only of their own subjects, but of all who may visit or settle within the territories under their rule. On such terms only can they be made permanently to endure; but I am persuaded that, if the policy above indicated is clearly appreciated and steadily pursued, there can be secured to the Native Administrations of the Northern Provinces at least as fair a chance of permanency as that which is enjoyed by the great Native States of British India, many of which stand on more firm foundations today than could be claimed for them during the years that followed the break up of the great Mughal Empire two centuries ago. I consider that we should watch with a very jealous eye any claims that may, from time to time, be advanced for anything resembling 'Extra-territoriality' in the Province of the North. I personally regret that any such principle was ever accepted or admitted when the various *sabon gari* were established. Its application should certainly not be further extended, unless in any particular instance the most weighty and convincing reasons can be adduced therefor: and I entertain the hope that, at no very distant day, it may be found possible altogether to abrogate it. That, at any rate, is one of the ends at which every Political Officer should consciously and consistently aim. In my view, the longevity of the Native Administrations of the Northern Provinces will in a

great measure depend upon the success or failure that may attend our efforts in this direction.

24. In conclusion, I would repeat that this minute, though addressed to Your Honour, is primarily intended for the guidance and instruction of the junior members of the Political Service of the Northern Provinces; and I should like to add that, before it assumed its final form, it had the incalculable advantage of being subjected to your expert comments, advice and criticism, and may now be taken as embodying views and opinions that are held no less strongly by Your Honour than they are by me.

1928: TWO SECRETARIAT DIRECTIVES

The extracts are taken from two circulars issued by the Secretary, Northern Provinces, Kaduna, to all Residents in the North, on 1 July and 23 November 1928. They were distributed to all Administrative Officers, as an open document. These circulars, along with the 1922 Minute of Sir Hugh Clifford and the Appendix to the 1934 Memorandum of Sir Donald Cameron, were reprinted by the Government Printer in June, 1936, as a pamphlet entitled INDIRECT ADMINISTRATION *and issued by the Secretariat, Kaduna, for the general guidance of Administrative Officers.*

A.

I am directed by the Lieutenant-Governor to inform you that His Honour has observed, particularly in the smaller Emirates, a lack of appreciation by Junior Officers of the correct procedure to be followed in dealing with Native Administration officials and indeed an inadequate knowledge of the working of Native Administration machinery in the chain of administration from the peasant through the Village and District Head to the Emir. Senior officers have acquired this knowledge by experience in the course of which many mistakes have been made. In the early days of the initiation and consolidation of 'indirect administration' many Emirates were found in an unreformed state and the process of reformation abundantly proved how easy it was to destroy the patient while trying to cure the diseases of the Native Administration body politic.

2. The younger Officers have not that experience and in the present state of progress reached by most of the Northern Provinces there is no need for them to acquire it as painfully and laboriously as their seniors, provided they can rely on the advice and assistance of the latter to enable them to understand the why and wherefore of the methods which have been evolved largely through the correction of mistakes of former days. A state of progress has been reached at which there is no room for what may be termed 'Amateur' or experimenting Administrative Officers content to work by the light of nature and to deal with each problem as it arises without taking advantage of the accumulated body of precedents and experience which now exists.

It is therefore with a view to the guidance of Residents and Senior District Officers in training their Junior Officers and especially Cadets that the following notes—additional to and to be read in conjunction with *Political Memoranda*—are prepared on points of procedure in which it appears that instruction is particularly needed.

They will be added to from time to time and embodied in any future revision of *Political Memoranda*. Suggestions from Residents as to their amplification are therefore invited.[1]

RESIDENTS' INSPECTIONS

3. (a) Residents should visit each Division of their respective Provinces from time to time and should satisfy themselves that the District Officer in charge thoroughly understands how he is to administer the Emirate, Division or other unit in his charge, and should make certain that he is not unconsciously undermining the authority of the Emir or the latter's confidence in him through ignorance of procedure and lack of insight, while expecting 'progress' in the Emirate. Such undermining may occur through excess of zeal in attempting to accelerate the march of progress by too direct action.

It is important that the District Officer should understand that real 'progress' comes from within the body politic and that to attempt to force the pace by direct action is calculated to kill initiative in the Native Administration. Moreover the bare exposition of improved methods of administration, accounting, agriculture, tax collection and so on is of little value, unless the Emir and the Native Administration officials are led by patient and often laborious explanations to assimilate these improved methods to themselves and to realize their advantages over the former methods. It has been found that informal conversations and discussions on matters not merely of local but of Nigerian and world wide interest have been much appreciated and have broadened the outlook of Emirs and Native Administration officials and increased their desire for progress.

EMIRS' REPRESENTATIVES WITH TOURING OFFICERS

(b) My circular No. . . . emphasized the necessity for touring officers—Departmental as well as Administrative—being accompanied by Emirs' representatives and the principles therein laid down should be adhered to and brought to the notice of junior officers. I am to remind Residents to impress on their subordinates the correct procedure in regard to interviews with persons representing respectively the various links in the chain of administration, from the Emir downwards, in order to avoid giving any one of them the impression that he is being 'short circuited'. . . . As a general rule a Village Head should only be interviewed in the presence of his District Head and both of them only in the presence of the Emir's

---

[1] One of these suggestions assumed the status of a public memorandum. It is cited at p. 189.

representative. A District Head should practically never be granted a formal interview except when an Emir's representative is present. A certain discretion must be exercised in hearing complaints of private persons against their superiors, whether Village or District Heads, but in most cases the Emir's representative should be present and such complainants should be encouraged to take their complaints to the Native Courts, District Head or Emir in the first instance.

So far as is possible direction and advice should be given to the superior and not to the inferior, i.e., through the Emir's representative to the District Head and so on down the scale. Only thus can the chain of responsibility be supported and insisted on. Chiefs are as a rule so little inclined to delegate authority to their subordinates that it is only by a strict adherence to this principle of making the superior responsible for the carrying out of instructions by the inferior that some idea of decentralization can be inculcated and an efficient administration be built up. . . .

POLITICAL MEMOS. AND CIRCULARS

(e) The Political Memoranda and file of Secretariat Circulars should be available in all offices for reference and study and Residents should take steps to ensure that junior officers read them.

B.

I am directed by the Lieutenant-Governor to refer to my Circular [*quoted above*] and to transmit for general information and guidance (a) the sub-joined extract from a memorandum addressed to his staff by the Resident Adamawa together with (b) a minute by His Honour.

Extract from Resident Adamawa's memorandum:

(a)
(i) 'The history of indirect rule is that it was introduced by Sir Frederick (now Lord) Lugard because he realized that he could not effectively administer the enormous area of the Northern Provinces with the utterly inadequate staff at his disposal, and that therefore he must enlist the assistance of the Native Chiefs. His policy was carried on by his successor Sir Percy Girouard, afterwards Governor of East Africa, and the details were worked out chiefly by Sir John Burdon (Governor of Honduras), Sir Charles Orr (Governor of the Bahamas), Sir William Gowers (Governor of Uganda), Mr. Temple, and especially the present Lieutenant-Governor, Northern Provinces, to whom, among other important matters, was due the creation of Native Treasuries, the most essential corollary to indirect rule.

(ii) 'The success of the Northern Nigeria system was so striking and the development of the Native Administrations was so rapid that the Colonial Office have adopted it as the basis of administration in every tropical African dependency where it is still not too late to introduce it. It is also being introduced into the Southern Provinces, where possible, with remarkable results, in Oyo and Abeokuta for instance.'

(iii) 'In addition to this, just before the war, in 1913, Dr. Solf, the German Colonial Minister, who had visited Northern Nigeria, gave orders that the Northern Nigeria system should be followed in the German Cameroons, and the German Resident at Dikwa (Von Raben) was sent to Kano to learn what he could in a week from the District Officer.'

(iv) 'Further, one of the few really successful Colonial Administrators produced by the French was General Lyautey who followed the principles of Northern Nigeria Native Administration in North Africa.'

(v) 'The most striking testimony to indirect rule is that after only eleven years of really effective administration when the war began in 1914, and during the whole period of the war when the country was denuded of troops, there was not one attempt by the Chiefs to regain by force what they had lost.

(vi) 'With reference to the printed instructions on indirect rule, which are being sent to you, there are some points which are rather commonly overlooked. These are: (a) 'If a Native Administration Official has offended he should not be sent to his Chief with a message that he must be punished and that he must be punished in a certain way. The fact should be put before the Chief, and he should be asked what action he proposes to take. If he does not award what you consider an adequate punishment, the escape of a subordinate official from just punishment is a minor matter in comparison with the major object. You must always remember that the Native Administration Officials are the Chief's servants and not yours. Unless these points are borne in mind you will inevitably produce in the Chief the *sai abinda ka che*[1] attitude which is the death knell not only of indirect rule but of any rule at all.' (b) 'No Native Administration Official should ever be forced on a Chief against his will or without his consent. There has been a recent instance where an Administrative Officer appointed his own Dogarai in a Division without any reference to the local Chief.' (c) 'No accused person should ever be sent to a Chief or Alkali with instructions that he shall be convicted and sentenced to a certain term of imprisonment, for not only is this against the canons of indirect rule, but it is also direct injustice in prejudging a case, and it naturally arouses in the native's mind the query why, if the British Officer concerned was so anxious to get a conviction, he did not try the case himself, with the conclusion that he must have had some underhand reason for not doing so.' (d) 'Where it is the custom for the people of a District to nominate a candidate or the District Headship for the Paramount Chief's consideration, an Administrative Officer should not use his influence on the electors in any way. The officer who has backed the District Head may make a comparative success of him for a time but when he is succeeded by another officer, or no officer is available for close

---

[1] i.e., of immediate acquiescence—at least orally!

supervision, trouble will begin if he is not the man the electors would have chosen.'

(vii) 'I am well aware of the strong temptation when things are going wrong to take the short cut by reverting to direct methods, but it is the long way round in the end, for it results in a *setback* to indirect rule. Direct methods are only occasionally advisable in places where indirect rule has degenerated into misrule, and crime is rampant, but such cases are rare and localized and direct methods should be dropped as soon as order emerges from chaos. . . .

(viii) 'It is not likely, in view of the results achieved, and of the backing of the policy by the distinguished officers mentioned above, that there could be anything wrong with the theory of indirect rule, and as regards qualifications for promotion and passing efficiency bars I put first the question whether an officer is imbued with the true spirit of indirect rule and make my recommendations accordingly.'

(b) Minute by his Honour:

(i) 'I think that the Resident Adamawa's memorandum [*quoted above*] forms a very valuable and helpful supplement to the printed circular which it was felt desirable to send out on the subject of Administrative method in dealing with Native Administrations.'

(ii) 'The pressure of economic development at the present time makes it increasingly necessary to utilize the productive and energizing capacity of all native institutions (which is very great) to the full, and to avoid arbitrary or empiric changes of method to which the people are not accustomed and which may produce discontent and dissatisfaction or ultimately inefficiency in the essential duty of keeping order.'

(iii) 'It remains true, as a Resident wrote in 1907, that: 'I need not dwell on the often stated truth that in a country of the size and with the population of Northern Nigeria the Government must utilize the existing native administrations to the fullest possible extent. In order so to utilize this most useful, and in many ways admirably organized, machinery it is essential that it should be permitted to work to a considerable extent on native lines, even at the cost of the loss of a certain amount of efficiency from a European point of view. There is a very great difference between ruling through native Chiefs on native lines and ruling, or attempting to rule, through them on European lines. . . . I take for granted that the policy of the Government is to supplement rather than supplant the pre-existing native administrations. This at any rate has been hitherto the declared policy. . . . In place of a small native state, with a Resident in an advisory position, interfering as little as possible in its interior economy as is consistent with seeing justice done, checking oppression and extortion, and gradually training the native admistration to stand on its own legs, there would be created, it seems to me, an enormous and unwieldy salaried native staff, for every action of which the Government would be directly responsible.'

(iv) 'But, it must be added, knowledge of how best to utilize for the common or general advantage the existing machinery of Native Rule, does not occur as a rule to a mind unaccustomed to deal with this type of administrative machinery.'

(v) 'Not only is practical experience of its working necessary, but if the standards of the past are to be maintained, officers must study native institutions and native social life, Muslim or otherwise, in terms of the vernacular, so that they are something more than alien officials imposing the will of Government on people who are virtually strangers to them in thought, and so that they become in a position to know in most subjects, without specific enquiry. what is the popular feeling or sentiment and what are the views of the ruling classes.'

1934: CAMERON'S POLICY OF INDIRECT ADMINISTRATION

The extracts are taken from the Memorandum THE PRINCIPLES OF NATIVE ADMINISTRATION AND THEIR APPLICATION, *written in Lagos on 13 July, 1934, by Sir Donald Cameron when he was Governor of Nigeria. Along with it was printed, as an appendix, a further minute not quoted here, on* THE POSITION OF ADMINISTRATIVE OFFICERS VIS-A-VIS DEPARTMENTAL OFFICERS AND OF DEPARTMENTAL OFFICERS VIS-A-VIS THE NATIVE ADMINISTRATIONS *composed by Cameron on 19 December 1932. In this he cited the most important paragraphs of a Minute by Sir Hugh Clifford in 1920, written when he was Governor, which was originally published in the* NIGERIA GAZETTE *of 21 November, 1920. Cameron, however, cancelled the subsequent footnote issued in 1926 which amended the 1920* MINUTE *by equating Administrative Officers with Residents, mutatis mutandis, in their position in the provincial hierarchy as the representative of the Lieutenant-Governor. This status Cameron abolished.*

PART I. PRINCIPLES

Definition of Indirect Administration

1. The system of native administration generally adopted in the Protectorate of Nigeria is known as 'Indirect Administration', and, based on several principles, is designed to adapt for the purposes of local government the tribal institutions which the native peoples have evolved for themselves, so that the latter may develop in a constitutional manner from their own past, guided and restrained by the traditions and sanctions which they have inherited, moulded or modified as they may be on the advice of British Officers, and by the general control of those officers. It is an essential feature of the system that, within the limitation and in the manner which will be discussed below, the British Government rules through these native institutions which are regarded as an integral part of the machinery of government (just as the Administrative Officers are an integral part of the machinery of government) with well-defined powers and functions recognized by Government and by law, and not dependent on the caprice of an executive officer.

Now firmly established elsewhere

2. The time is past when this system can be regarded as a sacred and mysterious art peculiar to Nigeria and understood only by a chosen few. Indirect Administration has become an everyday instrument of government and, after all, the conception is older

than Nigeria, as Lord Lugard has himself pointed out. The novel element in Nigeria, at the beginning of the present century, was the bold manner in which the doctrine was employed, that is, in using for the purpose the Chiefs of an alien race whose forefathers had invaded and conquered the greater part of Northern Nigeria but a hundred years before; Chiefs who now, in their turn, had been overthrown by British arms. It was a wise step—if I may be bold enough to record my judgement on such a matter—and for that reason the name of Lugard will always be associated with Nigeria. Probably the outstanding feature in that wisdom was the character of the office bestowed on those Chiefs; that of 'my Wakils or Governors' as Sir Percy Girouard afterwards described it. I am quite aware that it will be argued—by a few—that the conquering Fulani should not be regarded altogether as an alien race; but, even so, I do not think that I have ever heard anyone venture to assert that in the Hausa states the society is tribal. . . .

Reason for its adoption; existing conditions

3. The primary and compelling reason for the adoption of this system of Indirect Administration is not difficult to understand. Writing of the present day, I should explain the reason in this way: Nigeria is a large country and it has a large population. . . . The Protectorate is divided into twenty-two provinces and eighty-five divisions, each of the latter with its own staff of Administrative Officers. . . . Now, there are over nineteen millions of Africans in the Protectorate and the Administrative staff numbers but 347 including those on leave, a proportion of from one-third to one-fourth. It must be self-evident that not every tribesman can be reached directly by an Administrative Officer and it was therefore necessary to seek some other instrument to complete the chain of communication as between the Government and the people of this vast dependency. What more natural than that we should use for the purpose—if we can find them—the tribal institutions of the people themselves? I mean by the term 'tribal institution' the tribal authority which according to tradition and usage has in the past regulated the affairs of each unit of native society and which the people of today are willing to recognize and obey, if—I repeat the words again—if we can find it.[1]

Reason for its adoption; early conditions

4. The system was introduced in Northern Nigeria early in the century by Sir F. (now Lord) Lugard for the same reason, roughly

[1] Cameron, however, recognized that such authority would not normally be found in 'mixed societies of natives or where the tribal nexus' had disintegrated.

speaking. The number of officers available to administer the country more directly through an Administrative Service was altogether inadequate and there were no funds from which the staff could be augmented, conditions which continued for many years. As the system grew there was, naturally enough at first, a tendency to endeavour to place every unit possible under some Moslem Emir, a tendency which might well have been checked in later years when a much larger Administrative staff had become available. The 'pagan' communities in the Northern Provinces would probably, we now realize, have made greater progress if they had been developed in accordance with their own tribal institutions, however primitive, under the direct guidance of an Administrative Officer, instead of as a small part of a a much larger administration, under a District Head often alien to themselves interposed between themselves and the British Officer. Their own tribal institutions, moreover, based on their own decentralized and democratic system, afford them opportunity to express their own desires with great freedom, opportunity denied to them under the system described in the preceding sentence. In some cases pagan communities were placed under Moslem Emirs because, it was said, the latter had 'conquered' them before our advent: they had 'conquered' them to the extent that they had, as against other raiding chiefs, been strong enough to make a preserve of the particular pagan country for the purpose of slave-raiding. If it be correct, as it undoubtedly is, that the allegiance of a people to a tribal head, freely given and without external cause, is the essence of true indirect administration, we have in fact—although we seemed to have been oblivious of this—been in many instances administering pagan communities directly and not indirectly, and even then not through our own officers but through Moslem headmen. It is for this reason, in my considered judgement, that primitive communities in the Northern Provinces have made less progress in thirty years than comparable units in the South have made in three or four years.

Political objective must be defined

5. Returning to the present day, it seems to me that any system of administration of primitive people must be exposed to grave danger if the supreme authority has not formulated any governing policy as to the political development of the country as a whole. We must know, in short, where we are going and what are our aims. It is necessary that the Government should form some idea broadly of what the political evolution of Nigeria is likely to be and work towards that end. It is, of course, quite impossible for me to attempt to make any comprehensive forecast of the political evolution of the

country; that is a matter for patience and study over a number of years, and not for prophecy. But I think that it is permissible to postulate, even at this stage, that—at least for geographical and economic reasons—it is not likely that any part or parts of Nigeria will become separate, self-contained political and economic units, and that accordingly wisdom lies in the policy of treating the country as a whole, openly and without any mental reservations. That must be accepted as the settled policy of the Government and all our efforts in the direction of the development of the people from their own history and their own institutions should be governed by that central idea. It should be evident that if we did so frame our policy as to foster the development of the Northern Provinces as a separate political unit we should merely be seeking to revive a state of affairs that the amalgamation of Southern and Northern Nigeria in 1914 was specifically designed to terminate.[1]

Other advantages from the system

6. There are other advantages to the people, of course, to be derived from the system of Indirect Administration, many of them already manifest in Nigeria. Everyone will doubtless subscribe to the proposition that it is our duty to do everything in our power to develop the native politically on lines suitable to the state of society in which he lives. Our desire is to make him a good African, and we shall not achieve this if we destroy all the institutions, all the traditions, all the habits of the people, super-imposing upon them what we consider to be better administrative methods and better principles, but destroying everything that made the administration really in touch with the thoughts and customs of the people. We must not in fact destroy the African atmosphere, the African mind, the whole foundations of his race, and we shall certainly do this if we do not bring to the political application of the policy we have adopted a full understanding of its objects and an appreciation of the steps which we must take towards their fulfilment. When I write that our desire is to make the native 'a good African' I mean that he should be trained in accordance with his environment instead of being given a European veneer out of keeping with the conditions under which he must live in Africa, where his home and people are. We want to make him proud of being an African (just as a Canadian is proud of being a Canadian) on the basis of a true African civilization stimulated in the first instance by our own culture and example.

[1] This passage, of course, invites immediate comparison with the post-1946 constitutional proposals and developments.

Danger of impairing authority of Chiefs

7. It may be argued that so far as mere administration is concerned—and this is by no means the same question as the political training of the natives—we can achieve our object by adopting the practice of using the chiefs or other native institutions as our instruments, as our mouth-pieces through whom the orders of the Government are issued to the people; but with all the disintegrating influences which are at work to impair the authority of the chief over his people that authority will be undermined and completely disappear as certainly as it is disappearing in parts of tropical Africa, unless we take steps now to prevent its disappearance. As a consequence we should have destroyed the only foundations on which it is possible to build—and train.

Influence of British Officers

8. As I have already written, it must be remembered that it is quite impossible for us to administer the country directly through British Officers, even if we quadrupled the number we now employ. It has been well said, moreover, that 'a European officer cannot exert a personal influence on the characters of more than one or two hundred natives'. If the natives so affected should be, as they are where the Native Administration is retained as a real thing, in positions to influence other natives in their turn, then a Political Officer's influence is magnified by a natural process a thousand fold. If, on the contrary, they are not so placed, then whatever influence the Political Officer may have over the few with whom he comes into contact becomes a mere drop in the bucket and is lost in the mass.

Building on native institutions

9. In place of the alternative of governing directly through Administrative Officers and using the Chiefs merely as our mouth-pieces through whom we give our orders to the people, there is the other method of trying, while we endeavour to purge the native system of its abuses, to graft our higher civilization upon the soundly rooted native stock, stock that had its foundations in the hearts and minds and thoughts of the people and therefore on which we can build more easily, moulding it and establishing it into lines consonant with modern ideas and higher standards, and yet all the time enlisting the real force of the spirit of the people, instead of killing all that out and trying to start afresh. Under this system the native authorities become not only part of the machinery of Government but also a living part of it, and the political energies and ability of the people are directed to the preservation and development of their own institutions. This is a task which will provide in ever

o

increasing measure ample scope for those progressive Africans who genuinely desire to serve their own people. The training in the art of administration, in habits of responsibility and probity which the Chiefs and their Administrative staff receive through this medium must be of incalculable benefit to the whole body of persons concerned, provided always, of course, that in this and all other respects the Native Administration is in fact what we design it to be.

The real native authority according to the people's own ideas to be employed

10. This leads us to the very important point of the constitution of the Native Administration, or, more correctly speaking, the Native Authority. Emphasis must first be laid on the necessity, in seeking for the authority which according to tribal tradition and usage has regulated the affairs of the tribal unit with which we may be concerned, of assuring ourselves that the authority does in fact exist and is genuinely accepted by the people affected. If the latter are not prepared to accept the order of the so-called authority, chief or otherwise, unless we compel them to do so then, of course, the administration is not indirect and the Native Authority set up on such a basis is a sham and a snare. Pretence of any form in the administration of primitive peoples is a dangerous thing and I detest it from the bottom of my heart. It is not possible in civilized countries; you get found out by the people themselves. Moreover, if the authority has not the true spirit of the people behind it and is no more than a foreign and artificial intrusion imposed by ourselves, almost certainly in such circumstances the people will be kept in subjection and ignorance; indeed, they must be kept in subjection and ignorance if such an authority is to endure. But with the advance of education a people thus becoming enlightened cannot be expected to continue faithful to a Native Administration which is reactionary and oppressive in its tendencies, especially where, as in some instances, the Native Administration depends for its authority on fetish and superstition for the most part. The Native Authority that is not acceptable to the people and is maintained only because we impose it on them is therefore almost certainly bound to fail and it would be better to endeavour in the first instance to administer the people directly.

The people must be ready to recognize the authority

11. I am always careful, therefore, to enquire when any proposition is submitted to me for the purpose of constituting a Native Authority whether the people do in fact recognize the authority proposed and are ready to render obedience to it because it is in

accordance with their tradition and custom that they should do so; or because, having seen the benefits conferred on the people by a neighbouring Native Administration, they desire of their own accord to place themselves under the orders of a prominent man of their own society or under some other authority, and to obey those orders. I would add, at the risk of being thought tedious on this point, that it is ensnaring and dangerous in this connexion to proceed on the assumption that this or that must have been the tradition and custom of a people; that they must at some time have obeyed this or that authority of their own. The present generation is possibly quite ignorant of such tradition; it is they that are primarily concerned and we must be quite certain before constituting an authority on such a basis that they are going to recognize it and obey its orders.

If the native authority is not only accepted by the people but is also regarded by them as a real living force which they value owing to the reasons for its evolution and for the benefits, in the shape of justice and fairplay, which they receive under it, they themselves will supply the incentive to advancement, a point on which I shall have have something further to say.

The authority according to their own tradition

12. As I have written . . . above, we seek the 'authority which according to tribal tradition and usage has in the past regulated the affairs of each unit of native society and which the people of today are willing to recognize and obey'. If we are successful in our quest we use that authority as an instrument, as the instrument by means of which we can communicate—in an authoritative manner I might add—with the people of the unit. But it is a matter of paramount importance that in recognizing that authority and clothing it with legal sanction by appointing it to be a Native Authority under the law enacted for the purpose, we should in the first place regard it as the instrument which it is intended to be and retain that consideration steadfastly in our minds. Native Administration, indirect as well as direct, is a means and not an end, and our work but commences when the Native Administration is constituted as an instrument through which the people of the unit may be administered under the direction of the Administrative staff. Any tendency, therefore, to think that when after exhaustive inquiry 'the tribal institution' has in fact been identified (and recognized as a Native Authority) our work is at an end and that the Native Administration so set up can be left to work out its own salvation with a minimum of interference or even guidance on the part of the Government creates a danger to the system itself and should be checked. I trust

that it is not necessary for me to add that neither the Native Authority nor the Native Court is intended to be an instrument—I have used that term—for registering the wishes of an individual officer.

Education of the Native Authorities

13. It will be the primary duty and object of the Administrative officers to educate the Native Authorities in their duties as rulers of their people according to civilized standards; to convince them that oppression of the people is not sound policy or to the eventual benefit of the rulers; to bring home to their intelligence, as far as may be possible, the evils attendant on a system which holds the lower classes in suppression, so destroying individual responsibility, ambition and development amongst them; and to inculcate the unspeakable benefit of justice, free from bribery and open to all. The end to be sought is, in brief, just government according to civilized standards and the moral and material well being and the social progress of the people.

Supervision by Administrative Officers

14. We assume that we have the instrument, the proper instrument acceptable to the people affected; we are careful to remember that it is in the first instance an instrument—a means and not an end; and we have our programme for the general development of these institutions according to civilized standards as set out in the preceding paragraph. What is the next step? We can find the answer to this question readily if we pause to consider what the next step would be if we were administering the people directly instead of through an instrument, the Native Authority. The answer is that, as a minimum, there must be such a degree of watchfulness and supervision as will place the Government in a position to affirm at any time whether the rights of the people to justice and fair treatment under a British Administration are being fully assured and safeguarded and whether opportunity of development is also being fully assured to them. To achieve this great skill and tact and unlimited patience will be required, the degree of watchfulness and supervision varying naturally as between an organized Native Administration of standing and repute and a more recent creation of a petty order in a primitive society where those in authority are almost as ignorant as the people they are to serve. But whatever that degree of watchfulness and supervision may be we ought to be in a position to assure ourselves that the people are receiving fair and liberal treatment, not forgetting that an autocracy may need even more vigilance than may be necessary in democratic Bantu society as I knew it in East Africa; not forgetting, further, that, using again very

pregnant words, the allegiance of a people to a tribal head, freely given and without external cause, is the essence of true indirect administration, and that in the great part of Nigeria in which native society is not strictly tribal that allegiance should not be taken for granted. In these cases, as in all other cases, it is almost unnecessary to add, the incentive to obedience should be just government.

Failure to correct error

15. Lack of adequate supervision, because in the past a sufficiently high standard of supervision may not have been defined, is bad enough but even more serious is the deliberate policy disclosed in the tendency in the past to treat the petty Native Administrations of the Southern Provinces—I do not include in this expression the important Native Administrations of the Yoruba country and Benin —some of them not Native Administrations at all, in the same way as Administrations regarded as 'highly organized' and to refrain from correcting error because what has been known as the 'prestige' of the Native Authority would thereby be undermined. This tendency may be observed also in the Northern Provinces. It represents the serious mistake of attaching more importance to the machine than to the people it is designed to serve, and cannot be too strongly reprobated. A Native Administration under which the people are not receiving fair play generally can have no prestige which is worth upholding; and in my view the prestige which is sought for it will be far better secured by the intervention of the Administrative Officer in a manner that will show the people that while we are anxious to correct error and injustice we are at the same time ready to punish in our own Courts those who do not obey the proper orders of the Native Authority. It is a mistake also to believe that all possible cases should be taken in the Native Courts if the 'prestige' of those Courts is to be assured. There are cases which they ought not to take and some which many of them are not competent to take; and to try the Native Administrations which, after all, are but instruments in the administration of Nigeria, beyond their powers and their capacity must, surely, be unsound policy.

Progress in the Eastern Provinces of the South

16. But this is passing away, I hope, and I have no intention of imputing blame to Administrative Officers on this account. It is in a large part a heritage of the past; of the policy whereunder, when the Native Authorities Ordinance of the North was extended to the South eighteen years ago—quite a proper step in itself—Native Authorities were set up by a stroke of the pen in parts of the Southern Provinces composed of no more than placemen, persons with no

tribal authority whatsoever, put in by the Government to do work which they ought to have done themselves in the absence of real tribal authorities. I greatly admire the efforts which have been made to repair these mistakes. I have seen the results of the investigations which have been made in this connexion in the five Eastern provinces and they are of absorbing interest, reflecting the greatest credit on the officers responsible for the work. My own growing conviction is that the benefit to the whole of Nigeria would be almost incalculable if we could—as I believe we could—establish a more modern form of native constitution (in one of the Yoruba states as the most suitable in the first instance) modelled for the present on their own institutions, with a mixed Council in which the educated element of the people would be more adequately represented, and with the Resident exercising somewhat the same functions as he does in other British dependencies, i.e., openly as the adviser of the Native Administration and taking a directing interest in its day to day affairs.

New policy in Benin

17. As a beginning in this respect I introduced in Benin on the installation of a new Oba, a system whereby the Resident functions openly as the adviser of the Oba, sitting on his Council, and taking a directing interest in the day to day affairs of the Native Administration. The system has been extended to Ijebu-Ode, has been accepted by the Alake of Abeokuta (with a modification which is of no importance in principle) and will be further extended as opportunities occur. I sent the following message (now generally known as the Benin Minute) to the new Oba:—

I welcome the Oba-elect to the seat of his father and of his forefathers. I wish him well and I ask him to trust me and to heed what I am going to say. I am anxious—almost above all things in Nigeria—to make a success of the policy of administering the people through their own chiefs, but my experience here and elsewhere makes me doubt whether it will be possible to achieve this if we pursue the methods of the past. No sufficient attempt has been made in the past, I believe, to teach and train the chiefs in the very difficult art of administration. That is not our policy in the case of the Administrative Officer. We train him in England before he comes to the country at all, and we train him through many years before he is placed in such a responsible position as that of Resident. On the other hand, we have in the past taken the chief, quite untrained and quite uninstructed in methods of administration according to civilized standards, and left him to work out his own salvation as best he could, with the minimum of interference and guidance from the Resident or other senior Administrative Officer. I believe this to be a dangerous position from which no possible good can come; especially in these days when the people can express themselves and their grievances, when all the acts of Government, including those of the Native Administrations are, quite properly, open to public criticism, and when it is no longer possible to rely on fear and superstition in administering subject people. It is my sole desire, I repeat, to make a real success of the policy of Native Administration but I fear, as the words I have used in the foregoing remarks must disclose, that if some better methods for the training and guidance of the chiefs in the art of administration are not introduced, Native Administration through the chiefs cannot endure in the modern society in which we all now have to live in Nigeria, and must eventually crumble and fade away.

I propose therefore that for the future the Resident should exercise in Nigeria the same function as he exercises elsewhere in the British dependencies, that is, function openly as the adviser of the Native Administration and take a directing interest in its day to day affairs. He should sit with the chief and his council when it meets and advise them and direct them in the daily acts of the administration. The Council should meet at regular intervals as may be arranged with the Resident and the chief should obtain the approval of the Resident before issuing any orders that are not in accord with approved policy, that is, policy approved by the Resident. All orders will continue to be issued in the name of the chief in order that his authority may in no way be impaired in the eyes of his people; no direct orders to the people will be issued by the Resident or the Administrative staff, and the Resident will be directed to take the greatest care that the religious scruples and racial susceptibilities of the chief and his people are respected.

The Oba-elect must trust me when I say, again, that I am doing all this in order to strengthen his position; so that the policy of ruling through their Oba may continue and endure, gathering strength through the years to come. According as his administration gains strength in this manner, according as he is more and more able to stand by himself in administering his people in accord with civilized standards, so will the measure of control of the Resident be withdrawn, as it has been withdrawn in the other part of the British dependencies. . . .

Dangers of repressive tendencies and consequent stagnation

19. A student of Native Administration has written that he is 'at times disturbed by the widespread emphasis on the importance of preserving as much as possible of indigenous African life and custom'. 'The possibility is foreshadowed' he adds, 'of a new African feudalism which is prepared to be benevolent and paternal to the native so long as he will stay put and not raise envious eyes toward a full share in all that western civilization can give'. I am particularly attracted by these words because I have so frequently said both in Tanganyika and in Nigeria that a Native Administration which exists merely because the people are at present backward and ignorant and on that account are apparently willing to 'stay put' cannot and must not endure. If there is an attempt to keep the

people back and the Native Administration is consequently not so framed and constituted as to progress on modern lines alongside the Central Government of which it is but a part, but one of the instruments of that Central Government, then, naturally, the natives eventually refuse to 'stay put' and the edifice will crumble to the ground. Moreover, it is the avowed intention of the Government that the natives should not 'stay put'.

Publicity of our methods

20. A safeguard against stagnation of this nature and other doubtful methods of applying the policy of indirect administration lies, to my mind, in publicity. I am reluctant to make comparisons but it is my considered opinion that the Native Administrations of the Tanganyika Territory are, on the whole, more securely rooted and better equipped to stand up against assaults from the outside than are most of the Native Administrations in Nigeria, and I attribute this, for the greater part, to the fact that the former have from the date of their foundation been exposed to the full glare of public opinion, which must be and does act as a stimulus and a corrective. If the system of Indirect Administration is a real living, healthy growth, a thing generally desired by the people affected, it should not fear publicity. It seems to me, moreover, to be mere folly not to endeavour to enlist educated African opinion in support of a policy which we allege to be of such paramount importance to an African country.

Feudal autocracies

21. I have referred in the course of this Memorandum, with more particular reference to the Southern Provinces, to Native Administrations which are reactionary and repressive in their tendencies, in some instances depending for their authority on fetish and superstition for the most part. I am not unmindful of the difficulties which are presented where the Native Administration which we have created and recognized is based on a system of medieval polity dependent on the relation of vassal and superior, but I have deferred any more specific reference to this somewhat delicate part of the question in order to say here, in what appears to be its proper sequence, that the judgement that I have been able to form is that in some measure we have departed from the intentions and principles of Lord Lugard in this respect; particularly in drifting into the habit of mind—and I use the word 'drift' with intent—in drifting into the habit of mind that a feudal autocracy of this kind is the be-all and end-all of Indirect Administration. It would be a direct

contradiction in terms for me to say that it is the avowed intention of the Government that the natives should not 'stay put' and at the same time to say that I accept the view last stated that a feudal autocracy of this character is all that we are seeking. But we have made some progress in this respect in the last year or two. The policy accepted for some considerable time that the Moslem Administrations should be sheltered as far as possible from contact with the world was due no doubt to a feeling, however unformulated, that an unreformed feudal autocracy could not be expected to stand up against the natural forces of a western civilization that was gradually but quite perceptibly creeping further and further north in Nigeria; a curtain being drawn between the Native Administrations of the north and the outer world, so far as it was possible to maintain the integrity of that curtain. But we have advanced now to the stage that the curtain is being gradually withdrawn and, I hope, will be fully withdrawn within a comparatively brief period.

Feudal autocracies: doubtful whether training and supervision is sufficient

22. It is doubtful, however, whether even in the Native Administrations regarded as highly organized the amount of training in administrative work, of supervision and of guidance which the Resident and his officers can impart and exercise under the system as it still exists today can be regarded as at all adequate if we are really desirous of building well and securing the advancement of the people. I doubt sometimes whether we have done a great deal to impress on the minds of the Native Authorities concerned that the amelioration of the social and economic conditions of a people is one of the primary duties of an Administration and that the inspiration to improvement must come from within, from the Native Administration itself. Up to a few years ago every branch of activity, every department in the affairs of a Native Administration in the Moslem areas of the Northern Provinces remained in the hands of the Emir. In a few of them, recently, there has been some delegation of powers to members of the Emir's Council, one taking this department of the public service under his charge, another taking another department, and so on. It has been thought that this was quite an extraordinary advance, affording another reason for complacency. It is a great advance in one way but from the point of view of efficiency of administration according to civilized standards too much importance can be attached to it. The situation as it was belonged to the middle ages; it is a little better now by reason of this development but the necessity for close supervision and careful training in the difficult art of administration has not been diminished.

Possible very gradual reform

23. We are suffering in these respects, moreover, from the embarrassing heritage of the former practice of placing every pagan unit possible under a Moslem authority,[1] and from the effects of the unhallowed policy insidiously introduced during the latter half of the last decade of thinking of the Moslem Emirates in terms of the Indian States although, of course, the former have no element of sovereign power. The situation has for these reasons been rendered a difficult one and any system of reform must be a very gradual process. The question of the administration of pagans by Moslems should be examined as each vacancy occurs in the office of Native Authority in the large Emirates in which there are pagan communities. As to the rest of the problem my own view is that as opportunities offer the system of supervision by our officers should be made more evident and more effective following the principles of the Benin Minute[2]; and that an effort should be made to devise means that will allow the people to express themselves periodically, possibly through their Village Heads and Elders in conference with an Administrative Officer, the District Head and a representative of the Native Authority. It is a striking, but not a very comforting, reflection that the somewhat primitive people in the Ibo and Ibibio countries of the South are in this respect in a more favourable position than the peasantry generally in the North, with the deduction that the feudal autocracy with which certain minds have been quite content and sought to consolidate, is, after all, not the best thing from the point of view of the more humble folk who form the great majority of the people.

Types of tribal institution

24. I have written above that it is the policy of the Government to administer the natives through their own tribal institutions, explaining that I mean thereby the authority which according to tribal tradition and usage regulated each unit of native society before the advent of the British Government. Those units are of different sizes. One may embrace a whole sub-tribe such as the Egbas, ruled by one Head Chief with his traditional councillors and advisers; one may embrace only a clan (or even part of a clan) administered by one chief (i.e. he has no superior chief above him), again with his own councillors and advisers, or by a clan or sub-clan council; and a third may embrace nothing more than a few grouped villages

---

[1] Cameron drew attention to the need to separate the Gwoza peoples from the Dikwa Moslems as soon as possible. In the event, this was not achieved till 1960.
[2] See p. 202.17.

who for reasons of a common ancestry or other common heritage have agreed to work together under a council composed of their own village elders. Some of the Moslem Emirates are not true to the first of the classes enumerated above but for the purposes of this part of the Memorandum they are included in it.

25. Every unit, to be a unit, is in charge of an authority known to the people as their tribal head—a chief or a headman where the authority is not a council as described in the preceding paragraph—and every chief and headman has, as an integral part of the social scheme, his traditional councillors and advisers. He is not constitutionally an autocrat, and he and his advisers and the simple peasants know quite well the degree in which his powers are circumscribed by native tradition and custom. He knows equally well that if his people are harshly or unjustly treated they will leave him and join a more humane chief. This is a point of great importance and Administrative Officers should study it patiently and cautiously and endeavour to ascertain fully the nature and extent of the safeguards against oppression by a chief or headman, set up by native society through the ages in this manner for its own protection, safeguards which, I have no doubt, are still preserved, *e.g.* the chief who tries cases in his open court may be said to be for the most part only the mouthpiece of the court through whom its decision is promulgated. . . We seek to use the institutions which the people have evolved for themselves so that the latter may develop from their own past guided and restrained 'by the traditions and sanctions they have inherited'. Where the authority is vested in a council no question of the ascendancy of an autocrat should arise.

The Chief or Headman

26. Each such native unit is, in accordance with native custom, in charge of an authority—a chief or head man or a council. It had been alleged, it is true, that all that machinery of native government which existed before the European came to the country, or the greater part of it, had disappeared and ceased to function, indeed that in some places it has scarcely emerged; but the experience of the last few years shows clearly that such is not the case, that the machinery we are now seeking to use still in many places held a large share in the life of the people. There is a tendency sometimes to look for too much when we start to build up on autochthonous institutions in tropical Africa: I have heard it stated elsewhere, for example, that it is impossible to introduce any form of Indirect Administration unless one is able to find a potentate of the order and dignity of a king according to Western ideas.

Native institutions: how given legal status

27. These are the native institutions, which, in spite of neglect, had not ceased entirely to function, and we must now consider the manner in which they are brought within the ambit of our system of European directing rule. They have to be made part of our local constitution, they have to be clothed with the authority of the law, and this is effected by means of the Native Authority Ordinance whereunder such native institutions as the Government decides to recognize are given legal status by being declared 'Native Authorities' with certain specified powers. This is effected by constituting the 'office' of native authority for a specified area and appointing to the office so constituted the chief or other authority representing the native institution concerned. The first, the constituting of the office, is a constitutional act of high importance (unless the native authority is a subordinate one) and should not be delegated by the Governor, although he may delegate the power to appoint to the office except in the case of First Class Chiefs.

Recognition of Chiefs, etc. by the Governor

28. The chief or other authority representing the native institution comes to do so in a variety of ways which will be explained later, but appointment by the Governor, in the sense in which he appoints civil servants, is not one of those ways, though he may in certain circumstances refuse to accept a particular individual. The holder of a native office is either a hereditary chief, or a chief selected by the people for themselves, or a sub-chief, hereditary or otherwise, appointed by a Head Chief, or a native official appointed by the chief. The position is the same in the case of a council which is appointed to be Native Authority for we there declare that the holders of certain offices (e.g., the senior elder of A, the senior elder of B and so on) shall in association as a council be a Native Authority, the individuals who are members of that council being those who, in accordance with the principles here discussed, are the *de facto* holders (recognized by the Governor) of the separate native offices which, in association, are the council. In the case of hereditary chiefs we recognize *de facto* holders of the position as rightly entitled to it, and in the case of the head of a Native Administration or a sub-chief who is not hereditary, we accept the person who is declared by the people to be their choice, or who is appointed by the Head Chief, if there is one, after he has consulted the people affected. Upon a chiefship becoming vacant, we recognize similarly the person who, according to the laws of the tribe and the wishes of the people, is the rightful successor; such person is the chief, and his position does not depend on any act of appointment by the Governor,

though in extreme cases the Government may exercise its undoubted right of refusing to accept an individual who, on personal grounds, is not considered fit to occupy the position: in such cases the tribe would be required to make an alternative selection if necessary, i.e., if it were not decided to appoint the Senior Administrative Officer to fill the office of Native Authority for the time being. . . .

What depends upon the formal act of the Governor is the legal and constitutional status of the office of Native Authority, and in performing that formal act the Governor will prescribe the powers to be exercised by virtue of that office.

Limitation of the Powers of the Native Authorities

29. There are limitations to the powers of the Native Authorities . . . . the limitation lying in the fact that the Native Authorities are not independent rulers: they are merely the delegates of the Governor whose representative is the Resident. The Government reserves to itself the right to impose taxation, to make laws, to control the exercise of such subsidiary legislative powers as may be delegated to Native Authorities, to dispose (in the Northern Provinces) of such lands as are vested in the paramount power 'for the use and common benefit of the natives' and of course to raise and control armed forces. The disposal of the annual revenue of the Native Administration, the appointment and dismissal of important officers of the Native Administration and indeed all the important executive acts of a Native Authority, though emanating from itself, are subject to the guidance and advice of the Resident. It must be understood, moreover, that unless a chief (or other authority) has been 'clothed with the authority of the law' in the manner indicated above his orders are not lawful orders within the Statutes of Nigeria and cannot be enforced in any of the courts including the Native Courts. The idea that any chief can lawfully enforce his orders under the cloak of native law and custom although he does not hold office as a Native Authority is therefore erroneous. The new Native Authority Ordinance makes no provision for chiefs who are not Native Authorities.

Native Administration; forms of explained (Tribal Chiefs)

30. In the everyday language of the administration the Native Authorities are generally described as 'Native Administrations'. There are different forms of these Native Administrations, each constituted as was suitable to the particular native society and in accordance with its wishes. In the first place we may have the chief, the Superior Native Authority, who, with his constitutional advisers, is the fount of all authority within the unit. The Native

Treasury is the Treasury of this unit alone; the higher Native Court
—generally a court of appeal—is the court of this unit alone. The
Native Authority may delegate some of its authority to sub-chiefs
or headmen, often hereditary offices of some standing, and this is a
convenient course if there are areas at a distance from the chief's
headquarters.

Federation of Chiefs

31. In the second place, we may have Chiefs who administer clans
(or other sections) of the same tribe or kindred tribes and have
agreed, with the approval of their people, to form a 'Federation'
in order, chiefly, to pool their financial resources. Each Chief in
the Federation retains executive authority in his own unit, and is
appointed the Native Authority of that unit, but occasionally the
Chiefs sitting together in Council (which may itself be appointed a
Native Authority) may agree to pass an order or a rule (subject to
the approval of the Governor), applicable to the whole area em-
braced by the Federation. There is a danger in this practice if too
lightly applied in as much as in native society such orders or rules
of general application should be made by the executive authority
of the unit (i.e. its own Native Authority) with the advice and consent
of his councillors; and this wholesome safeguard in a democratic
society may be neglected if a Chief is allowed to assent to a measure
when sitting as a member of the Council, without consulting his
constitutional advisers. Administrative Officers should be careful to
see that constitutional usage in this connexion is not neglected.

Place of native court in a Federation

32. In this class of Native Administration (which, so far, has not
developed to any great extent in Nigeria) each Chief (Native
Authority) has his own Native Court, sometimes with inferior Courts
under it where the area of the unit is large, and the chiefs agree to
form a higher Court at the Federal headquarters which is generally
a court of appeal. In principle, in forming this higher Court each
Chief agrees that in his capacity as the chief executive of his own unit
he will within that unit engage to see that the orders and decisions
of the higher Court are duly carried out. It is therefore necessary
that where a higher Court is being formed in this manner the
Administrative Officer should be careful to see that this principle
is clearly understood by each of the Chiefs in the Federation, that is,
that in consenting to the formation of such a Court each Chief
thereby undertakes to give effect to its judgements within his own
unit of which he is the executive head. Where the authority is a

Council and not a chief . . . a federation can be formed on the same principles.

Federal Council not a superior Native Authority in the full sense

33. It should clearly be understood that the Federal Council is not a superior Native Authority in the sense that the Chief of a tribe may be a superior Native Authority; that it does not appoint the servants of each of the Native Authorities constituting the Federation, nor does it dismiss them. Far less does it appoint the successor to a Chief if a vacancy occurs in any of the units of Native Administration constituting the Federation; in such case the vacancy is filled according to the traditions and custom of the unit, in the same way as if no Federation existed.

President of Federal Council

34. In Native Administrations of this class the President of the Federal Council is generally chosen in rotation (quarterly or even monthly) from the Chiefs forming the Federation, but in some a permanent President has been appointed by the chiefs themselves. In one or two instances attempts have been made to regard the permanent President of the Council as a 'Paramount' Chief but the artificial nature of this pretension is as a rule soon disclosed. It has sometimes been thought, I understand, that a unit may withdraw from a Federation at its will and pleasure. I do not take that view. Once a unit has entered a Federation interests have been created of a general nature which should not be sacrificed at the whim of a Chief. A unit should, in my judgement, not be allowed to secede save for the gravest reasons and then only in the most exceptional cases. It will have a steadying influence on the Chiefs of a Federation to remind them, if necessary, that it will be difficult, if not impossible, gradually to develop native institutions by means of larger Native Councils if even the Federal Council cannot endure.

Tribal Councils

35. In a third class of Native Administration a Tribal Council may be formed of a number of petty chiefs, better described as Headmen, of the same tribe or kindred tribes, each with executive authority in his own unit (subject to the advice of his own Council of Elders), clothed with authority as a Native Authority. They sit as Chairman of the Council in rotation and pool the common resources in a common budget. If they cannot agree in regard to a Chairman the District Officer should himself act as Chairman. They have on occasion framed a general order or rule for the whole area served by the Council if appointed as a Council to be a Native Authority, but I

consider that in administrations of this kind it is for the present . . .
preferable that each Headman (Native Authority) should frame the
order or rule in his own unit, with the consent of his constitutional
advisers. In some cases a court of appeal has been appointed at the
Council's headquarters. Such a Council should as a rule not be
appointed to be a Native Authority unless it is to have executive
functions. Further, such a Council acting as an advisory and
financial body, and possibly forming from its members a Court of
Justice, may properly be designated a 'Native Administration'
although it may not itself, for the present, have been appointed to be
a Native Authority.

Clan and Village Councils

36. In a fourth class of Native Administration we have the
Councils of the Clans, Sub-Clans and Village Groups which are
being constituted after careful research by the Administrative staff
in the Eastern Provinces of the South. These Councils are not all
of a type but, speaking generally, it may be said that each village
through its 'headman' (however nominal, generally the senior elder)
and elders, or a selected number of them according to their own
customs, is represented on the Council which is appointed to be
the Native Authority. It seems unwieldy and topheavy, especially
where the people are illiterate and all the elders of all the villages
in the Group have a right to a seat on the Council (Native Authority)
but it is strictly in accord with native tradition in the early years of
their society, and each Council is fashioning itself and the corporate
spirit is clearly functioning in many instances. In some cases an
executive committee answerable to the Council is appointed and it
will be interesting to see how this system will function. The members
of such a committee should be appointed for a definite, brief, period.
There is no doubt, and perhaps this is the most important consideration of all, that the Native Courts constituted on a parallel basis
command the respect of the people and are already highly prized by
them as a welcome substitute for the Court of the 'Warrant Chiefs'.
Moreover, in some of the most unlikely areas (judged by their
history) the Councils have had the will to suppress disorder and
crime and have met with some success in doing so. The Councils
described in this and the preceding paragraph afford the people
opportunity to express their own desires with great freedom, and in
several native communities there is a marked disposition to appoint
men of some education to the Councils. . . .

Form of Native Administration not to be stereotyped

37. No attempt has been made, nor should it be made, to stereo-

type the various Administrations and force them into one pattern or another. It suffices if, in each case, the Native Administration is in accordance with the wishes and traditions of the Chiefs and people, and adequately fulfils the object of its existence, that is, the discharge by the local native authorities of the functions of local government in native affairs to such extent as circumstances may permit in each case and with due regard to expansion in the future.

Effective administration not possible without delegation of Authority

38. Particular care should be taken to consult the Head Chief of a unit where there is one, and to explain to him the need for delegation of authority, and the manner in which such delegation is effected by the Ordinance, while retaining unimpaired the power of the superior authority. It should be explained that though delegation must be exercised with care in proportion to the standing and ability of the sub-Chiefs and Headmen, without it effective administration is not possible, and it should be made clear that by consenting to the establishment under the law of the offices of subordinate Native Authorities the Chief is not surrendering in the smallest degree whatever control he may now enjoy over the appointment of individuals to those offices, or the manner in which they exercise their functions.

The Governor establishes the Office of a Native Authority

39. Thus the Governor establishes by a formal instrument under the law certain offices to be executive institutions for a particular area, institutions to which, in accordance with the policy of Indirect Administration, is entrusted the administration of the people whom they represent, subject to certain limitations and obligations, as explained in this Memorandum; just as under closely related legislation he establishes, in the form of Native Courts, complementary judicial institutions. The Native Authority Ordinance makes provision for the limitation in particular instances of the powers which may be exercised by virtue of the establishment of any office to be a Native Authority, for it may be found that there are Native Authorities to whom in the beginning it would be unwise to entrust full powers; and, as has been explained above, for a general control of subordinate authorities by their superiors; but it is not concerned with the individual who may occupy an office, further than to require that he be recognized by the Governor as the person holding a particular native office and appointed in that capacity to fill the office of Native Authority.

P

A Native Administration may be evolved at present day

40. Although in general Native Authorities will be established Chiefships, or a federation of such Chiefships, or clan or other councils as already described, it is also possible, where none such exists, for an Authority to be evolved at the present time in mixed areas, i.e., where there is a mixture of tribes, either in the form of a Council of the Heads of families, clans, settlements, or villages, or by the selection by the people of their own volition of an individual to be their chief. This form of Native Administration is not tribal and is really more 'local Government' than 'Native Administration'. Particular care is necessary in dealing with any such development to ensure that the authority proposed is in conformity with the general structure of the native society concerned, is desired and will be respected by the people, and that the proposal is not due to the selfish place-seeking of ambitious individuals. The individual members of such an authority must hold their positions by virtue of hereditary right, or of selection by the people in some manner understood by them, and Administrative Officers should not concern themselves with the methods of selection further than to make sure that they conform to these requirements and that the individuals so selected are such as the Government may accept; in particular, 'elections' on European lines should be avoided.

Native Authorities given powers of subsidiary legislation

41. Section 16 of the Native Authorities Ordinance gives to Native Authorities, subject to the control of the Governor, a power of subsidiary legislation upon a very wide variety of subjects. . . . It is intended primarily to enable native law and custom to be crystallized, when it seems desirable to do so, in the form of recorded rules, and to permit of the development and expansion of their own law by the Native Authorities to meet the changing needs and advancing civilization of their own people. That power of legislation, and the concomitant power to impose fees for particular purposes, are not intended to open the way to the substitution for native law of something which the British Officer thinks is better for 'it is idle to make an improvement if the laws precede the capacity of the people, for whom they are made, to appreciate them'. The Government therefore only interferes to suppress that which is repugnant to European ideas of justice and morality—for example, poison ordeals, the more objectionable forms of witchcraft, the killing of twins, or of dependants at the death of a Chief: for the rest, if the customs of native society weigh heavily on its members and they suffer by reason of their own institutions, they will be the more ready to effect real reform from within, and for that purpose this power of

legislation is given. Its exercise should be permitted only for political reasons in the interests of the people on the lines described above.

Making of rules and orders by Administration

42. It may also happen that in the details of administration it will be found desirable to impose fees for certain services, such as the registration of marriages and their dissolution, or the establishment and maintenance of markets; or to regularize by a general rule the performance of communal services such as the clearing of roads or of tsetse bush; and rules to this end may also be made. It is not intended to permit the addition to the existing taxation paid by natives of a multitude of irritating petty fees, for the broad principle upon which a direct tax is justifiable and intelligible to natives is that in one payment the subject renders all that is due from him to his Chief and the Government for the period concerned, a payment which represents at one time the bond of duty from him to the Governor and to his own Chief.

Dependence of Native Administration on Administrative Officers in administrative and financial matters

43. It is natural that in the early stages of Indirect Administration newly formed Native Authorities will naturally incline to lean on Administrative Officers whose orders they have so long been accustomed to await and to whom they have looked for guidance in all matters. While it is not desirable that they should be trained to act in complete independence of the Administration, the need for fostering the self-reliance of the Native Authorities and their gradual emancipation from direct control and dependence in small matters must constantly be kept in view. It is believed to be the habit of some Native Authorities to cloak all orders in the form of a Government instruction, partly the better to ensure observance and partly to evade odium for an exacting order. It is apparent that this tendency will be accentuated if the Native Authorities are frequently induced to issue orders which they do not appreciate and to which they are possibly at heart opposed. Where it is unavoidable that the Administration should obtain the issue of particular orders Administrative Officers should seek to persuade the Native Authorities to take the necessary steps, refraining as long as possible from giving them direct instructions.

The Ordinance to be used for the purpose for which it has been designed

44. The ordinance endeavours to embody the principles of Indirect Administration, to provide for the local government of

natives indirectly through their own authorities and not directly
through the Administrative Officers, to preserve and permit of the
future development of the administrative machinery which has been
created by the natives themselves, and the institutions which have
grown out of their own traditions or may be evolved by them in the
future; and so in effect to assist the native to develop that civilization
which he can develop. The Governor looks to all Administrative
Officers loyally to make use of the Ordinance for these objects, and
in particular to exercise their own powers under it with the utmost
circumspection, bearing in mind constantly that the conditions
under which they may take action . . . are not a mere formality but
are intended to restrict direct action by the British Officer to cases
of genuine necessity (in particular to redress injustice or other
wrong), for such action is in itself a violation of the principle of
Indirect Administration. It is, of course, the duty of an Administrative Officer to advise a Native Authority to make any order which
may be lawful under the Native Authority Ordinance, if he considers that it is in the interests of the people that the order should be
made; and if his advice is neglected he may then, under the Ordinance, order the Native Authority to make the required order. He
may convey his instructions to a Native Authority verbally or in
writing; it is not necessary that they should be drawn up in formal
manner in the same way as orders which he may have to make under
the Native Authority Ordinance in case of default by a Native
Authority.

Native Authorities and their employees distinguished

45. The Governor establishes, as has been explained, the office
of Native Authority: that office . . . normally consists of a hereditary
tribal chief, invariably in association with certain elders and other
persons who occupy positions of dignity and responsibility, or of
some other authority. Subordinate to that office there may, it has
been seen, be others of importance whose offices may if necessary
similarly be established as (subordinate) Native Authorities, and in
such cases the holder of those offices must be dealt with through the
principal authority but subject to the same limitations as to recognition, dismissal, prosecution, etc., as in the case of the Head Chief,
though the Governor may delegate his powers in this respect. The
holders of offices not so declared to be 'Native Authorities' are
merely employees of the Native Administration.

The Native Authorities an integral part of the machinery of Government

46. The prestige and influence of the Native Authorities can best

be upheld by letting the peasantry see that the Government itself treats them 'as an integral part of the machinery of the Administration'. That there are not two sets of rulers, British and Native, working either separately or in co-operation, but a single Government in which the Native Chiefs have well defined duties and an acknowledged status side by side with the British Officials. Their duties should never conflict and should overlap as little as possible; they should be complementary to each other, and the Authority itself must understand that it has no right to its place and powers unless it renders proper service to the State. It is obviously desirable that Government should be called upon as rarely as possible to intervene between the Native Authority and the people for if a Native Authority has lost prestige and influence to such a degree that it has to appeal to Government to enforce its orders it becomes not merely useless but a source of weakness to the Administration. This does not of course mean that any community may by appealing to Government throw off its allegiance to a Chief, or that mere unpopularity which may be due to the exercise of very necessary discipline, forms any grounds for the deposition of a Chief.

Education of Native Authorities in art of Administration

47. In order that Native Authorities may find adequate scope for their energies, take keen interest in their duties, and command that respect and obedience of their people, it is essential, provided that the general supervision by the Administrative staff is adequate and the latter is aware of what is going on, that they should in the exercise of their legitimate powers be given the greatest possible latitude and support compatible with their capacity and the position they occupy in relation to the Central Government. We should endeavour to give them an interest and an object beyond the routine performance of their duties, to interest them, to engage their sympathies and active co-operation in our efforts to promote the welfare and progress of their people; for their primary duty is to their people and by the manner in which they fulfil it they will be judged. At the same time it will be the primary duty and object of the Administrative Officer to educate the Native Authorities in their duties as administrators according to a civilized standard; to impress upon them the advantage of delegating the control of districts to subordinate chiefs and headmen and of trusting and encouraging those subordinates, while keeping a strict supervision over them, to see that there is no favouritism in such appointments; and to inculcate the unspeakable benefit of justice, free from bribery and open to all. So long as they prove themselves loyal and capable it is through them that the people will be governed and it is the desire of the Government to

uphold their authority and prestige in every legitimate way, and to encourage initiative and a sense of responsibility. Suggestions for reform or progress should always be encouraged and all orders to subordinates should be given by British officers through the responsible chief.

Subordinate Authorities to be dealt with through the head Authority

48. When an Administrative Officer interviews a native subordinate his superior should if possible be present. An officer on tour should be accompanied by a representative of the Native Authority and make him the mouthpiece of any executive orders given to Headmen and other officers of a Native Administration. The chain of responsibility from the Village Headmen to the Native Authority will in this manner be maintained. Such executive order must of course be distinguished from orders which in case of default by the Native Authority may have to be given by the officer to the Native Authority under the Native Authority Ordinance. . . .

Attire and badge of Office of Sub-Chiefs and Headmen

49. Chiefs and headmen who are not the Head of Native Administration but subordinate to a superior authority may be permitted to wear such distinguishing dress or customary badge of office as the Native Authority concerned, with the concurrence of the Resident, may approve. Customary badges or other emblems in this sense should be bestowed by the superior authority and not by the Government, and if occasion requires it is the superior authority which should withdraw any such privilege.

Chiefs not the salaried servants of the Government

50. It must be understood that chiefs are not salaried servants of the Government although they are part of the machinery of Government, and provided, therefore, that their work is generally satisfactory, their minor delinquencies should be made the occasion for guarded rebuke rather than punishment. Officers will note the revision in this respect of the wording of memoranda previously issued several years ago, on the general ground that no opportunity for gentle instruction of the native should be lost whether he be chief or peasant. It must constantly be kept in mind in this connexion, however, that there is sometimes a temptation to look for too high a standard in the native chief. The centuries which lie between ourselves and the native in point of development cannot be bridged in a generation or two. We are not entitled to put the whole tribal system on one side, to depose a chief, or to refuse to recognize the lawful successor to an office, merely because we do not find in the person

concerned standards which might be expected in the best sections of English public life. From the point of view of capacity especially it should be remembered that it is not always possible to obtain a successor who is much better than the holder of the office (and at the same time as acceptable to the people), and that experience has sometimes shown that a chief who has been condemned by one Administrative Officer as useless and incapable has been made an efficient chief through the patience of another Administrative Officer. As regards abuses it must be remembered that abuses are inevitable, but the power of supervision exists and must be exercised, and we are using in this scheme of Native Administration an instrument which is being carefully and patiently fashioned for our purpose. Moreover, the native should be afforded opportunity to voice his grievances and as a rule in most parts of the country will come readily to lay his complaint to his Administrative Officer, provided he knows at what times and places he will have ready access to him. It is for this reason important that Administrative Officers in their stations should be easily accessible to natives, that district travelling should be systematically organized, and that any tendency to inconsequent movement should be corrected. An officer who comes and goes hurriedly in a motor car will not hear much that he ought to hear and that he would hear were it known beforehand that on a certain date he would be at a certain place. Administrative Officers must of course, at once step in to put a stop to abuses, and if no other course is possible the deposition of the delinquent chief may eventually be necessary but it should be regarded as an extreme step only to be recommended when all other means have failed.

Important Chiefs' neglect of duty or commission of offences

51. It will, however, happen on occasion that important chiefs may fail to comply with reasonable requests, or be unduly dilatory in fulfilling promises; such cases should first form the subject of protest and, if this is unheeded, of report of the Resident. More serious offences such as embezzlement of the funds of the Native Treasury, extortion or other criminal offence, refusal or neglect to carry out the awards of the Native Courts, or improper interference with them, should at once be reported for instructions as to the course to be taken. Important chiefs, and persons holding high rank in a Native Administration, should not prior to trial be kept under detention in the common prison or elsewhere unless such extreme measures are necessitated by a very serious political crisis, in which case they should if possible, be sent immediately under strong guard to Provincial Headquarters.

The remedy of private persons against a Chief

52. The following paragraphs dealing with the punishment of chiefs have reference, as regards the Courts, only to cases in which the Government is dissatisfied with the conduct of a chief. The remedy of private persons against a chief in a court of law remains of course unaffected as does the traditional authority of a Head Chief over his subordinates.

Native Authorities to be dealt with as prescribed in the Ordinance

53. A Chief in his capacity as a Native Authority within the meaning of the Native Authority Ordinance should if his actions are such as to make him liable to prosecution under that Ordinance be dealt with as prescribed therein, subject of course to the limitations imposed by the Governor's instructions for political reasons on the use of the punitive sections of the Ordinance against Chiefs.

Trial of important Chiefs

54. If it becomes necessary to bring an important chief to trial the approval of the Governor for his suspension should first be obtained, as it is desirable that, if it is decided to prosecute, such chiefs should be suspended before being put up for trial. It must be realized that conviction in a criminal court of a serious offence will usually necessitate deposition and that the deposition of a chief with its break in the continuity of succession is a step which should only be resorted to when no other course is possible. It should be remembered that the successor of the deposed chief may be likely, given the same circumstances, to act in the same way, and that the deposed chief himself, unless his punishment is such as to result in his removal from his area for a very long time, becomes an embarrassment to the Government and a rallying point for the malcontent and the agitator. Moreover, the deposition of an important chief is a very grave disturbance of the tribal organization which can only be justified by absolute necessity. If, however, it is decided to proceed to trial the machinery of the High Court, which includes any Magistrate's court having jurisdiction in the matter, should be employed, and not that of the Native Courts; the principle being that in these extreme cases the Government makes clear to the people the power which it possesses to deal with the wrongdoer however highly placed. Where an important chief has to be deposed as the only and proper course left to the Governor the latter should be prepared to vest the powers of the chief in an Administrative Officer for the time being instead of putting in a weak or unacceptable native substitute. . . .

Offences by minor Chiefs

55. In the case of minor chiefs and headmen the general principle to be followed is that the Head Chief, where there is one, should deal with all those under his authority, subject to the guidance and advice of the resident where the person concerned is a sub-chief or important headman. Where there is no Head chief, minor chiefs and headmen (and officials of the Native Administrations) who commit serious offences for which they are liable to arrest may be arrested if thought desirable by the Resident, who may, if the law admits in the particular case, exercise his discretion as to whether complaint should be made to a Magistrate's court or to a Superior Native Court; or the case may be reported with a view to the removal of the chief (if he is one for whose removal authority is required) and his replacement by a better man. This last provision refers of course only to hereditary chiefs or sub-chiefs of some standing and not to persons whose appointment and dismissal have always been in the hands of a chief, whose authority in this respect remains unaltered, and who may be left to deal with his subordinates, either by executive action or through the Native Court, subject, of course, as in all cases, to any advice which the Resident may deem it necessary to give him.

Minor causes of complaint

56. Minor causes of complaint such as negligence to carry out orders, etc., may in the case of these less important chiefs best be dealt with by the appropriate Court of the Native Administration (if there is one) and, if repeated, by reduction of salary, by fine, or deprivation of office. Where there is a Head Chief action will normally be taken by him, whether of his own motion or at the request of the Resident or District Officer, but if there is no Head Chief through whom the minor chief can be dealt with, small fines in the form of deductions from salary may be imposed by the Resident on minor Chiefs in receipt of a salary, where warnings have no effect: any part of a salary so withheld remains of course in the Native Treasury.

Minor Chiefs may elect to be tried

57. The object of dealing with minor offences in this manner is to save the chiefs concerned from the humiliation, and consequent loss of influence, incurred by a public trial, but if the offence is one amenable to the law, and not mere obstructive negligence or incapacity, they should be offered the option of trial before fine or removal from office.

Punitive Authority to be sparingly exercised

58. The foregoing provisions for the punishment of chiefs and headmen and important members of the Native Administration are intended to govern such action when it becomes necessary, but it must not be forgotten that, as already stated, chiefs and headmen are not mere employees of the Government and that the constant exercise of punitive authority means the destruction of their influence; that advice and sympathetic guidance are far better tools in the hands of the Administrative Officer. Moreover an officer who finds himself constantly at variance with his chiefs and disposed to punish them, will do well to pause and reflect if the wrong is all one side, for it may be on occasion that in his own actions in dealing with his chiefs he will find the key to his difficulties. A small measure of willing service by a native even though his methods may not be perfect is worth far more than apparently more extensive results obtained under a policy which aims at a servile obedience to the order of an Administrative Officer by a chief headman who scarcely understands those orders.

Means to be employed when there is no chief

59. Although normally a Native Authority may be a hereditary tribal chief, with his elders, it is often impossible to find a chief, who is really recognized as their superior by his fellow chiefs, to place over a Native Administration, and in such cases since it is impossible for every petty unit to form an Administration of its own (even in the form of a petty Council) recourse has to be had to various expedients, or to co-operation with other people in the evolution of some other form of Native Authority. Of the expedients which have been tried, the most promising is that of a council of chiefs (or other authorities) from tribes of the same or kindred stock, even though each authority retains executive authority in its own area.

Councils of several kinds

60. Such councils need careful handling, however, for they are of several kinds and care must be taken that they are not confused, for to do so may cause serious difficulties. The most elementary form is a council of authorities which may be no more than a deliberate body; or the authority may pool their funds and co-operate only to the extent of occasional meetings, at which as a rule the District Officer should preside, for the administration of their common resources. The greatest practical difficulty in the case of these councils arises from the absence of an appropriate central executive, especially when the council consists of a considerable number of authorities, for though normally each member of the council

retains its executive authority in its own area it is unavoidable that certain executive functions must be discharged by the council as such, especially in connexion with the Native Treasury. In these circumstances if a native with previous administrative experience is employed as Court and Treasury clerk at the Council Headquarters, he is naturally apt to concentrate all real power in his own hands, especially as the members of the council may all be illiterate. In some cases it has been found possible for the president of the council (if there is a president, either permanent or in rotation) to act in this sense as its executive officer in between meetings and in some cases an executive committee has been appointed. Where either course is impossible, the next best arrangement is for these duties to be carried out in the District Office under the personal supervision of the District Officer, the council paying the necessary clerical staff. As the present Councillors come to be replaced by educated men and the council system becomes firmly established, this arrangement can be modified in whatever way circumstances may suggest.

Councils to choose their Presidents and to be Courts of Appeal

61. Every council of whatever kind should be allowed to choose its own president, and should if the law and the circumstances of the case permit be a court of appeal for all the Native Courts in the area over which it, or its members severally, have jurisdiction. If the council is a federation of authorities each will administer its own area; and if it is itself a Native Authority over the whole area it will appoint such subordinate officers as may be 'central' officers of the administration (as opposed to officers of the authorities in their own respective areas).

Amalgamation of small units into neighbouring larger units

62. At times it will happen that there is a more powerful and vigorous authority in a district whose area is surrounded by smaller units, numerically and financially weak and barely able to maintain themselves. Provided such units are of the same, or a kindred tribe, or at any rate show a disposition favourable to amalgamation, it is highly desirable that they should be induced gradually to group themselves under their more powerful neighbour, but such grouping of units must have the full concurrence of the people concerned (who must not lose their political identity and right of regulating their own affairs generally) and must not be forced upon them by the Administrative staff. If we force on them a system which is not in accord with their traditions and which they do not like we are creating an artificial administration which cannot endure and is for that reason highly dangerous. A Native Authority is not, how-

ever, artificial because progressive and not in accordance with conditions as we found them. Consolidation by petty authorities of the same, or a kindred tribe under a superior authority—whether chief or council—is not artificial if accepted and desired by the people.

Native institutions to be preserved and their evolution left to the people

63. The foregoing paragraphs should be sufficient guidance for Administrative Officers in deciding upon the form of Native Administration which is best suited to the circumstances of their district: it is realized that they are somewhat general in form, but it is not possible, or indeed desirable, to be more particular, for we have in the country an infinite variety of conditions, and tribes and communities of very different degrees of political organization. The great aims to be followed throughout are those of building on the existing organization and ideas of the people, of leaving it to the people themselves, assisted by sympathetic advice, to devise and develop their own local institutions according to the standards of modern civilization, and of resisting the temptation to play the part of 'King-maker' or constitution maker; many ideal states have been devised by theorists for mankind, but the only true political development proceeds from within by evolution.

Free movement of Natives

64. It should clearly be understood that native custom may not be invoked to prohibit, restrict or regulate the movements of natives from one area to another. . . .

Responsibility of Native Authorities for maintenance of peace and order in their area

66. The maintenance of peace and good order among the natives, and the protection of property in rural areas, are the most important functions of the Native Administrations, and in so far as natives are concerned organized and experienced administrations should be encouraged to discharge those functions without the assistance or intervention of the Police. Normally, native police constables should not be sent into the area of a highly organized and responsible Native Administration and police posts should not be established therein; but the first consideration is the safety of life and property and the apprehension of offenders, and Residents should see that such arrangements are made by District Officers in consultation with the responsible police officers as will most effectively achieve that object, while at the same time preserving the essential responsibility of the Native Authorities for the general maintenance of law and

order in their areas. Subject to the consent of the Resident, a District Officer may even in less highly organized native administrations give a general direction that without his prior consent Government native police may not enter the area of a Native Administration except in case of direct emergency or in actual pursuit of an offender, but if such a direction is given the circumstances of every case in which permission is refused must be reported for the information of the Governor. European police officers should in the less highly organized Native Administrations be at liberty to travel freely wherever their duties may require them and the Native Authorities should render them all assistance. Police officers should, of course, keep District Officers informed of their intended movements and of any action they may find it necessary to take in a Native Administraarea in discharge of their duties.

Scope and intention of the Memorandum

67. This Memorandum is intended as a general exposition of the principles upon which the policy of Native Administration which has been adopted in Nigeria is based, and as a guide in a broad way to the application of those principles. It is fully realized that owing to local conditions it may not in all cases be possible to apply the principles in the same manner or in the same degree, and the Memorandum must therefore not be interpreted in too narrow a manner. The intention is none the less that the essential principles, which should be clear to all who study the Memorandum carefully, should be retained, and with as little variety as possible in their application to the great diversity of conditions and people confronting Administrative Officers throughout the dependency. . . .

1939: THE BOURDILLON MINUTE

The extracts are taken from the MINUTE ON THE APPORTIONMENT OF REVENUES AND DUTIES AS BETWEEN THE CENTRAL GOVERNMENT AND THE NATIVE ADMINISTRATIONS *composed by Sir Bernard Bourdillon in 1939 when he was Governor of Nigeria. Its origin was the novel proposal submitted to His Excellency by the Chief Commissioner, Northern Provinces, to adjust the apportionment of tax between Government and the Native Authorities according to the needs of particular Native Treasuries in balancing their budgets. This request was made in January 1936, but the Minute did not take final shape until 1938. It was thus the product of extensive consultations and prolonged thought, and became the first comprehensive and authoritative review of Native Administration finance in relationship to that of Government.*

. . . . Apart from comparatively modest sums derived from court fees, interest on investments, and a few miscellaneous sources of revenue, the major part of the income of Nigerian Native Administrations consists of a percentage of the direct taxes (never less than fifty per cent) allotted to them by the Governor under the Native Revenue Ordinance. In September, 1935, the Chief Commissioner, Northern Provinces, applied for an increase in the allotment made to the Bussa and Kaiama Native Administrations on the ground of their poverty. The request was granted, with some reluctance, and the Chief Commissioner having successfully inserted the thin end of the wedge went on to assume that in principle the Government was prepared to assist the poorer Native Administrations in this way. . . .

2. That assumption (that in principle the Government was prepared to assist the poorer Native Administrations by granting them higher percentages of the tax) ran counter to the proposals approved by the Secretary of State in 1927, but not to Sir Donald Cameron's forecast of his own future policy. I had no hesitation in accepting the latter, and rejecting a policy which had regarded the state of development of a Native Administration as the sole criterion by which to decide how much revenue it should receive. This 'to him that hath shall be given' policy was obviously the surest method of securing inequality of development, both political and economic. The risk of such unequal development is inherent in any system which, like our Native Administration system, pours a considerable portion of the revenue of the country into local watertight compartments, and the system by which the revenue is apportioned between those compartments must take that risk into account, and endeavour

to minimize it. The assumption made by the Chief Commissioner, Northern Provinces, was obviously a step in the right direction, and I had no hesitation in accepting it. The distinction between fully organized and partially organized Native Administrations was therefore abandoned as a criterion of claim to a higher percentage of tax. A distinction was drawn instead between those Native Administrations which were well enough off already to bear their fair share of expenditure upon public works and social services and those which were not, and it was laid down that applications for increased revenue from the latter should, as a general principle, take precedence over similar applications from the former. One exception to this general principle was to be the case of applications for increased revenue to cover the cost of services hitherto performed by the Central Government which it is desired that a Native Administration should take over. I found it necessary at the same time to lay considerable emphasis on one point the importance of which appeared not to have been sufficiently recognized hitherto. The point was this: if a demand is made by a Native Administration for increased revenue to meet the cost of new services, the Government must, before meeting the demand, satisfy itself that the services in question are of such a nature that the undertaking of them is warranted by the budgetary position of the country as a whole.

3. And now let me go one step further. This consideration applies not only to fresh expenditure to be financed by increased revenue, but to all expenditure by Native Administrations. I do not mean to say that the Kano Native Administration should have been forbidden to build its new offices because, for example, the Bauchi Native Administration was unable to build new offices of a similar standard. But I do mean to say that if the Kano Native Administration had contemplated putting up extravagant and expensive buildings which, although within their capacity, were obviously such as the country as a whole could not afford, they would have had to have been told to revise their ideas. The point that I wish to establish beyond doubt is that when it is a question of embarking on a new project of any magnitude or upon a considerable extension of existing services the deciding factor is not whether the Native Administration can afford it but whether the Nigerian Government can afford it. There has not always been agreement upon this point, a decision upon which involves a consideration of the nature of the direct tax. I will not recapitulate the controversy which took place in this connection in 1926–28. It is enough to say that in the latter year the Secretary of State definitely laid down that the tax is not levied by the Native Authorities with the approval of the Governor, but by the Governor himself. It follows from this that the Governor,

when he takes action under the Native Revenue Ordinance, is not deciding how much revenue shall be collected from the Native Administrations, but how much shall be allotted to them. To put it another way, he is not deciding how much each Native Administration shall contribute towards the expenses of the Central Government, but how much the Government shall expend through the agency of each Native Administration. In theory it is not in the least necessary that the amount allotted to each Native Administration should bear any relation at all to the amount of tax collected by that Native Administration. In practice it is not only convenient but highly desirable that the amount should be, as it is now, a definite proportion of that tax. It is clearly an incentive, and a necessary incentive, to efficiency in tax collection, that the amount which a Native Administration has to spend should depend upon how much it can collect, and a direct connection in the mind of the tax-payer between the money which he pays and that which is expended locally for his benefit makes an enormous difference to his readiness to pay.

4. From this consideration of the nature of the direct tax it is clear that the Government must always retain the right, in times of emergency, to reduce the percentage of tax handed over to the Native Administrations, as was done in 1932. The larger portion of the revenue which the Central Government administers itself is derived from indirect taxation, the proceeds of which are subject to very much greater fluctuation than are those of the direct taxes. It follows that a depression hits the Central Government much harder than it hits the Native Administrations. In times of stress it is obviously out of the question for the Government to continue, for any length of time, to practise a more stringent economy in the expenditure of the money of which it retains direct control than in that of the money which it hands over to the Native Administrations. The Government may, for a year or two, be able to maintain its services unimpaired by rigid economy and by drawing on its reserves. But once retrenchment becomes necessary, the question as to what services should be reduced must be looked at from the point of view of the country as a whole, not from that of the respective capacities of the Central Government and the Native Administrations on the basis of their existing incomes. In these circumstances it may become necessary for the Governor to allot to the Native Administrations something approaching more nearly to a constant proportion of the whole income of the Government than. . . .

5. So far, the examination of the assumption made by the Chief Commissioner, Northern Provinces, and mentioned in the first paragraph of this memorandum had led to the establishment of

three principles: (i) that, when the Government can afford to increase the share of its income which it allocates for expenditure by the Native Administrations, the demands of the poorer Native Administrations should receive prior consideration; (ii) that the decision as to whether a new project should be undertaken by a Native Administration must depend ultimately, not only upon the capacity of the Native Treasury, but upon that of the Nigerian exchequer; (iii) that, with the object of maintaining a proper balance of expenditure over the whole country in times of financial stress, the Government must retain the right to reduce the proportion of direct tax allocated for expenditure by the Native Administrations.

6. The establishment of these three principles enabled the Government to deal with outstanding demands from the poorer Native Administrations for increases in revenue, and a number of adjustments in the percentages handed over to Native Administrations have been made, with the result that we are definitely nearer than we were before to an equable distribution as between the various Native Administrations. I still felt however that it would be desirable if possible to go a little further. The allocation of revenue between the Central Government and the Native Administrations was obviously bound up with the allocation of duties, and it had become apparent to me that existing practices in this respect differed widely, not only as between the Northern Provinces and the Southern Provinces, but inside these two areas. It appeared to me that in the past the distribution of duties had been rather haphazard, and that the general tendency had been for the distribution of duties to depend on the allocation of revenue rather than the reverse, which seemed to me wrong. It was obvious that one could not hope to find a formula which would apply exactly both to the large Emirates of the North and to the petty village councils of the Eastern Provinces, and that, in the application of any general principles which might be laid down, there must be great elasticity. I could not however discover that any general principles had ever been formulated, and it seemed to me desirable that the possibility of formulating them should be examined. The inquiry into this possibility has taken a long time and involved a good deal of work; the results are, I fear, somewhat nebulous. But I think that they are worth recording. Not only will they act as a rough guide to Chief Commissioners and Heads of Departments, but the search for them involved the consideration of a fundamental issue, concerning which, although much has already been written about it, I shall venture to record a few observations.

7. The issue to which I refer concerns the status of Native Authorities. Rather to my surprise, I found that some differences of opinion

Q

existed on this point, and it was quite clear that unless those who were seeking for principles to govern the distribution of duties were at one upon this fundamental issue, they would be approaching their problem from a number of different angles.

8. To begin with, I found myself faced with a suggestion that in speaking of 'the unhallowed policy insidiously introduced during the last half of the last decade of thinking of the Moslem Emirates in terms of Indian States', and that, in stating that the former have no element of sovereign power, Sir Donald Cameron had reversed the policy of Lord Lugard. Miss Perham has effectively countered this suggestion in her *Native Administration in Nigeria*, and a private letter[1] from Lord Lugard himself confirmed my opinion that the suggestion was not warranted by the facts. . . .

9. It was next suggested to me that the Native Authorities should be regarded as 'Local Authorities', that a basic percentage of the tax should be allotted to them, and that any allocation above that percentage should be regarded as a grant-in-aid. In this connection I observe that Lord Hailey, in his *African Survey*, at page 539, has written: 'There is, indeed, in some territories, a tendency to use them' (i.e. the Native Authorities) 'as a convenient agency for carrying out functions which are not even those of local self-govern-ing institutions, but would normally be discharged by the general administration'. In so far as Nigeria is concerned there is a good deal more than a tendency in this direction—it is an accepted, indeed an integral, part of the policy of indirect rule; Native Authorities are, for example, statutorily responsible for the maintenance of order and good government within their areas. Another reason why the Native Authorities should not be regarded as 'Local Authorities' is that they possess no measure of financial autonomy. It is of the essence of our policy that they should be given financial responsi-bility, increasing *pari passu* with, or even slightly in advance of, their capacity, but it is at present no part of that policy to give them the financial autonomy normally exercised by local self-governing bodies or (to return for a moment to the 'unhallowed policy') by units in a federation.

10. I was tempted for a time to accept, as an adequate definition of the status of the Native Authorities, the expression 'Agent of the Governor',[2] which had been used by both Sir Percy Girouard and Lord Lugard in respect of the Northern Emirs. But the Northern Provinces Residents' Conference pointed out, quite rightly, that this term only reflects one aspect of their status, the legal, and ignores the historical and traditional aspect. I agree, but in order to correlate the

[1] See Foreword, p. II xi.
[2] Already met with as 'Wakils', *passim*.

two aspects, I would put it in another way. The *Oxford English Dictionary* defines 'authority' as 'Power or right to enforce obedience'. Now in the case of a mere agent both the power and the right are derived from the appointer of the agent. In the case of a Nigerian Native Authority, be it a Moslem Emir, a Yoruba Chief or a Pagan Council, while the right to enforce obedience is wholly derived from the Government, the power to do so is partly so derived and partly inherent. The appointment of a mere agent is an act of appointment and nothing else. The appointment of a Native Authority is an act both of appointment and of recognition. To say, as Sir Donald Cameron said, that the Moslem Emirates have no element of sovereign power is not to deny them that inherent authority which they undoubtedly possess, in common with all other Native Authorities, and the possession of which is, in fact, the reason why they are selected for appointment as Native Authorities.

11. My final conclusions were expressed in an address to the Northern Provinces Residents' Conference in 1937, in the course of which I spoke as follows:

The Emirs, in common with all other Native Authorities, are indigenous institutions which the Government has recognized and to which it has assigned definite powers and allotted definite duties, these being in the Native Authority Ordinance and the Native Revenue Ordinance. They are an integral part of the machinery of Government—a machinery which has been designed with the very definite aim of educating the people of the country politically and administratively in order that they may gradually take a larger and larger part in the management of their own affairs. In pursuance of that aim it is the intention of the Government to continue to uphold the authority of the Emirs, and to add to their responsibility as their capacity for administration grows.

This is not, perhaps, a very precise definition, but for the purpose of this memorandum what is needed is a definition which will fit all types of Native Authority. There is, to my mind, a definite danger in attempting at the present stage of their development, to define the status of Moslem Emirs, Yoruba Chiefs or Eastern Clan Councils too closely. Their position is not necessarily static, and by attempting to define it closely in theoretical politico-scientific terms, we run some risk of committing ourselves to certain lines of development which future experience may show to be undesirable.

12. While we have not arrived at any very precise definition of the status of Native Authorities, we have nevertheless established four points, each of which has a corollary which we may find useful in determining the nature and scope of the duties which can properly be entrusted to Native Administrations:

(i) they are not autonomous bodies on the lines of units in a

Q*

federation or local self-governing bodies. The corollary to this would appear to be that there are no specific duties which the Government must assign to them as a matter of right.

(ii) they are not 'local authorities' and their duties need not be limited to those normally performed by such authorities. The corollary is that from the purely constitutional point of view there is no class of duties which it would be improper to entrust to them.

(iii) they are more than mere agents in that they have a certain inherent authority. The corollary is that they should be entrusted with those duties which that inherent authority makes it easier for them than for the Central Government to perform. Two such duties, which have in fact been assigned to them by statute, are the maintenance of order and good government and the collection of taxes.

(iv) they are an integral part of the machinery of Government, and that machinery has been designed with the very definite aim of educating the people of the country politically and administratively. The corollary on this is that the Native Administrations must be given plenty of work to do, and their responsibilities increased as their capacity grows. This increase of responsibility can of course be qualitative as well as quantitative. It is only in the latter sense that it concerns us at the moment.

13. I have suggested that there is no class of duties which, from the purely constitutional point of view, it would be improper to entrust to the Native Administrations. But from the practical, as opposed to the theoretical point of view, there are certain departments of the Government in which centralization is essential and the whole of whose activities must be directly controlled from the centre. These are, in alphabetical order, Customs, Marine, Military, Mines, Port, Posts and Telegraphs, and the Railways. . . .[1]

14. With regard to the remaining departments it is scarcely necessary to say that the control of policy must remain entirely in the hands of the Central Government. But, as the competence of the Native Administrations increases, they should be increasingly taken into our confidence, and their advice and opinions asked for, on questions of policy.

15. We are now in a position to examine, in the light of the conclusions already reached in this memorandum and the corollaries to those conclusions stated above, the problem of the distribution of duties as between Native Administrations and the Central Government. Let us first begin by deciding which duties clearly belong to

[1] A similar division of functions was to be followed, a generation later, in separating 'Federal' from 'Regional' responsibilities under the Macpherson Constitution of 1954.

the Central Government. These may be briefly described as the control and financing of all central institutions, works and activities and of those which serve more than one Native Administration or more than a comparatively small group of Native Administrations....

16. Having got thus far we are left with the duties below the line, which again should not be difficult to determine. Clear examples are dispensaries, maternity centres, rural African hospitals, elementary and higher elementary schools, agricultural 'extension' work and local demonstration and experimental farms, local roads, fuel plantations. These and other below the line duties should be classed as duties which may be assigned to Native Administrations. We have now two classes of duties, Central Government duties, and potential Native Administration duties, and it remains to lay down, if possible, the principles that should govern us in deciding when the latter should actually be taken over by the Native Administrations. But before proceeding to do this, I would refer to two duties which fall on the Government in connection with the duties of the Native Administrations themselves.

17. The first duty is that of providing expert advice and supervision in connection with the technical activities of the Native Administrations (including education). A considerable number of Departmental Officers spend their whole time supervising and directing Native Administration activities. Considerable difference of opinion has existed as to whether these 'seconded' officers, as they are termed, should be paid for by the Central Government, or whether the Native Administrations concerned should refund their salaries to the Government. This latter practice, initiated I believe during the depression, was welcomed by a good many of the Northern Provinces' Residents, on the grounds that much more interest would be taken in the activities of these officers if the Native Administration was responsible for their pay. I believe this idea to be entirely erroneous, and most of those who held it have, in fact, discarded it. Two years ago the Northern Provinces Residents' Conference unanimously advised that the practice should cease, and it is now in abeyance. After weighing the arguments on both sides, I have decided (for reasons other than those urged by Residents) that it should not be revived. I do not believe that these officers were ever looked upon by the Native Administrations as 'Native Administration officials'. They are practically all Europeans, and they have always been regarded as Government officials. The decision that the Native Administrations should pay their salaries was acquiesced in rather than desired. In the present state of development it is, and for a long time will be, the clear duty of the Government to assist the Native Administrations in the performance of the

duties allotted to them by providing expert advice and supervision, which advice and supervision must be directed by the Government itself. A suggestion that the Native Administrations should pay the salaries of Administrative officers would, I believe, be regarded by the Emirs with amazement. As in the administrative field, so in the technical, they welcome that advice and supervision which it is the duty of the Government to provide. In course of time, as the Native Administrations develop, it should be possible to restrict Government supervision considerably, and to put higher in the scale the point at which such supervision ends. But for the present, as a general rule, all departmental officers whose duties are wholly or to a large extent supervisory should be under the control of and have their salaries paid by the Central Government, as well, of course, as those in charge of Central Government works or institutions.

18. To this general rule there is one general exception. Departmental officers who are engaged solely in the direction of revenue-earning projects should be paid for by the Native Administrations. The Government retains the obligation to advise in regard to these projects, but it is clearly right that the Native Administration should pay for the whole staff employed upon them. Such projects include water and electricity undertakings, and Native Administration Forest Reserves. It is not necessary that the project should be at the moment self-supporting, but it must be potentially so.

19. There is another possible exception to the rule. A large Native Administration may have a big enough works programme to demand the whole time services of a supervisory Public Works Officer. The question whether he should be paid by the Native Administration or the Government should be determined separately in each case in the light of other circumstances.

20. Further, I wish to make it quite clear that the general rule is not a law of the Medes and Persians. We should always be prepared to modify it in particular instances, for good reason shown.

21. The second of the two duties of the Government is that of providing facilities for the training of Native Administration staff. The problem of providing this staff is of the greatest importance; in fact it would be no exaggeration to say that it is absolutely vital to the progress of the country. While it is reasonable to expect the Native Administrations to pay for the subsistence of their men while under training, the training must be supplied and paid for by the Government. In this connection I cannot avoid a reference to the necessity for the Native Administrations to provide salaries and terms of service sufficiently attractive to induce a sufficient number of men to offer themselves for training. At the moment the different rates paid by the different Native Administrations, and the inferiority

of these rates of pay to those given by the Government, coupled with the absence of incremental scales and pensions,[1] is producing a very serious situation, particularly in the North.

22. And now let us go back to the problem referred to that of deciding which of the potential Native Administration duties should in fact be handed over to a Native Administration. Here, it seems to me, there are three clear principles to guide us, and I am grateful for a felicitous suggestion that they should be named Competence, Consent and Cash.

(i) *Competence*—It is clear that we must not hand over to a Native Administration a duty in the performance of which it is capable of taking no intelligent interest and no intelligent part. Subject to supervision and advice which will vary considerably in degree in different cases, the Native Administration must be able to take a real and considerable part in the practical side of any activity which it is permitted or required to undertake. . . .

(ii) *Consent*—It is a matter of common experience that the Native Administrations perform most effectively those duties in which they are most interested, and it is useless to thrust upon them duties which they actively dislike. But this does not mean that we must absolve them from all the unpleasant duties of Government and only entrust them with those which will make them popular with their own people. We shall have frequently to persuade them, as we did the Benin Native Administration in the case of their Forest Reserves, that it is to their advantage and that of their people that they should undertake duties which involve a good deal of odium. But they must be persuaded, not compelled, to undertake them.

(iii) *Cash*—It is obvious that we cannot entrust to Native Administrations duties which they have not the funds to perform. If extra funds are necessary, we must provide them if we can afford to do so, by increasing the percentage of tax allotted to the Native Administration in question. In the case of capital works, whether revenue producing or not, it is in full accordance with the definition of Native Administrations as integral parts of the machinery of Government that the Government should, if it can afford to do so and the Native Administration cannot, bear part, or even the whole of the cost. It is also perfectly legitimate for a Native Administration with an ample development reserve but no surplus income to provide part of the capital cost of an undertaking which is to be run by the Government. But whether the extra money to be provided is recurring or non-recurring, we must always be guided by the consideration . . .

---

[1] Salary scales, as we know them today, were not introduced by Native Administrations till after the 1939–45 War. Today N.A. Staff Regulations are very comprehensive.

whether the services to be undertaken are such as the country as a whole can afford. And here I should like to observe, in parenthesis, that I dislike the use of the expression 'grant-in-aid' as applied to Native Administrations.[1] The Native Administrations are part of the Government, which already provides them with the bulk of their income. To describe any addition to the amount which the Government spends through their agency as a grant-in-aid is clearly incorrect.

23. I will now attempt to summarize the conclusions at which it has been possible to arrive. A consideration of the status of Native Administrations leads to the conclusion that from the purely constitutional point of view there are no duties that we are obliged either to hand over to them or to refrain from handing over. We have a very free hand and need be guided only by considerations of good government. Starting from this point we have established the following conclusions, which are summarized in a slightly different order to that in which they have been considered *in extenso* in this memorandum:—

ALLOCATION OF FUNCTIONS

1. The duties which must always belong to the Central Government comprise the control and financing of all Central institutions, works and activities and of those which serve more than one Native Administration or more than a comparatively small group of Native Administrations. This covers the whole of the functions of certain departments.

2. The duties which come below this line in the remaining departments must be regarded as duties which may be assigned to Native Administrations.

3. In deciding whether they should be so assigned, the Government must be guided by the three considerations of the executive ability of the Native Administration to undertake them, its willingness to do so, and its financial capacity to do so.

4. In connection with duties assigned to Native Administrations the Government retains two duties, firstly that of providing expert supervision and advice, and secondly that of providing facilities for the training of the necessary Native Administration staff.

ALLOCATION OF REVENUE

1. The Native Administration system, which pours a considerable portion of the income of the country into watertight compartments, involves a considerable risk of uneven development. The system by which the amount of revenue which is poured into each of those

---

[1] Yet it has aggressively persisted, to this day.

compartments is regulated must take that risk into account and endeavour to minimize it.

2. Once it has been decided that a particular service can properly be performed by a Native Administration, the question whether that service should be undertaken at all, and if so how much money should be expended on it, depends ultimately, even if the Native Administration can afford to finance the service without being given any more revenue, upon the financial capacity of the country as a whole.

3. In order to maintain evenness of development in times of financial stress, the Government must be prepared, if actual retrenchment becomes necessary, to cut down the shares of tax allotted to Native Administration.

1947: THE LOCAL GOVERNMENT DESPATCH

The extracts are taken from DESPATCH BY THE SECRETARY OF STATE FOR THE COLONIES TO THE GOVERNORS OF THE AFRICAN TERRITORIES, *dated 25 February, 1947. The Colonial Secretary at that time was the Rt. Hon. Arthur Creech Jones, who is also the author of the second passage quoted here. This is taken from his paper 'The Place of African Local Administration in Colonial Policy', appearing in the* JOURNAL OF AFRICAN ADMINISTRATION, *vol. 1, no. 1, June 1949, pp. 3–5.*

A.

Sir,

Since I took office as Secretary of State in October I have been considering some of the basic problems of African administration, and I think it right that I should now address you on this subject, since our success in handling these problems and the extent to which we can secure the active co-operation of the Africans themselves may well determine the measure of our achievement in the programmes of political, social and economic advancement on which we have now embarked. I believe that the key to success lies in the development of an efficient, democratic[1] system of local government. I wish to emphasize the words efficient, democratic and local. I do so, not because they import any new conception into African administration; indeed these have been the aims of our policy for many years. I use these words because they seem to me to contain the kernel of the whole matter; local because the system of government must be close to the common people and their problems, efficient because it must be capable of managing the local services in a way which will help to raise the standard of living, and democratic because it must not only find a place for the growing class of educated men, but at the same time command the respect and support of the mass of the people.

2. In African administration the term local government must not be interpreted narrowly; it covers political questions such as the functions of native authorities, the composition and method of appointment of councils and the constitutional position of chiefs; financial questions such as the working of native treasuries and the relationship between central and local taxation; judicial questions such as the operation of native courts and the development of African

[1] Later altered to 'representative'. See p. 245.

law, both traditional and statutory; and economic questions such as the control of land usage and the evolution of systems of land tenure. . . . In urban areas the special problem arises of developing municipal government, or in some places, associating Africans with non-African communities in municipal government where it already exists. In rural areas local government bodies may be native authorities, large or small, or local native councils, as in Kenya. Where native authorities are large and responsible for hundreds of thousands or even millions of people, the problem is one of building up a system of local government below them in close touch with the people themselves; where they are too small to be effective, the problem is one of securing fusion or federation of existing units. The general policy must be applied differently in different areas; the broad aim of securing an efficient and democratic system of local government will, however, be the same everywhere.

3. The African Governments are now beginning to put their ten year development programmes into execution. The stage has been reached when paper plans must be translated into action, and it is in the townships and villages, among the people themselves, that much of this action must take place. There are many development schemes where success, in whole or in part, depends on the active co-operation of the people, and that co-operation can best be secured through the leadership of local authorities. Without an efficient system of local government the great mass of the African population will derive only partial benefits from the monies voted for development by the Colonial Legislatures and the grants made under the Colonial Development and Welfare Act.

4. Local government has an equally important part to play in the sphere of political development. Since 1940 much progress has been made in the granting of increased responsibility to Africans in the central political and administrative machinery of government. In Nigeria and the Gold Coast Africans have been brought onto the Executive Councils and there are now African unofficial majorities on the Legislative Councils. In all the East African territories African members have been appointed to the Legislative Councils for the first time, and such appointments will before long be made in Northern Rhodesia and Nyasaland. Everywhere Africans are playing an increasing part in the making of policy by their service on boards and committees. For the most part these positions of responsibility are necessarily being filled by men from the educated minority, and in present circumstances almost all the leaders of African society must be drawn from this class. But this very situation, inevitable as it is, carries with it one danger for the future, in that it may result in the creation of a class of professional African

politicians absorbed in the activities of the centre and out of direct touch with the people themselves. The problem is fully recognized by the African Governments and is being met in some Territories by the establishment of regional or provincial councils, through which a chain of representation from the people to the Legislative Councils can be secured. The Native Authorities, as the organs of local government, are the most important link in this chain. In countries where literate systems of voting cannot yet be used for the purposes of election, local government bodies must normally provide the electoral machinery so as to ensure that the representatives of the people on provincial, regional and central councils are chosen by the people in accordance with methods which they themselves accept and understand. Local government must at once provide the people with their political education and the channel for the expression of their opinions. An efficient and democratic system of local government is in fact essential to the healthy political development of the African Territories; it is the foundation on which their political progress must be built. But the rate of political progress cannot be regulated according to a pre-arranged plan; the pace over the next generation will be rapid, under the stimulus of our own development programmes, of internal pressure from the people themselves, and of world opinion expressed through the growing international interest in the progress of colonial peoples. If local government is to keep pace with political progress and to exert its due influence on that progress, the Native Authorities must adapt themselves rapidly to the needs of the modern world, and the African Governments will have a major part to play in encouraging that process. In many parts of Africa the development of local government bodies has been held back by the lack of education and the ill health of the people. Where conditions are still primitive they cannot be transformed except through a laborious process of evolution. The political development of the Territories will, however, forge ahead in spite of conditions in the more backward areas, and, if this development is not to be one-sided, it is necessary that local government should everywhere progress as rapidly as possible to the stage at which it can play its effective part in the development of the Territories.

5. I do not intend in this despatch to attempt any general statement of my views on the means by which the policy of local government should be carried forward. Indeed I have not yet reached any final conclusion whether such a statement of policy is required at the present time. It is, I know, widely held that conditions in the African Territories are so diverse as to make difficult, if not impossible, the laying down of any general principles of policy which

would be of practical value. As at present advised I do not myself share this view and I believe that at the appropriate time there would be much advantage in producing a statement dealing not with the detailed applications of policy, which vary from territory to territory, but with its objectives, which are common to all territories, and the manner in which those objectives could best be approached. Such a statement would, however, demand the greatest care in preparation and I should wish its terms to be discussed with officers having up-to-date practical experience of the work of African administration in the field. As you know I am arranging to hold a summer school on this subject at Cambridge in August, which I hope will be as representative of the Administrative Service in Africa as the importance of the subject deserves. I intend that the minor aspects of local government should be discussed at the summer school and in particular I hope that attention will be given to the following points:

(i) Means of securing an effective place in local government for those Africans who are best qualified to be real leaders of the people.[1]

(ii) Means of developing real financial responsibility in local government bodies both in relation to the raising of taxation and the control of expenditure.

(iii) The division of functions between local government bodies and the Central Government and the place of local government bodies in political systems of the territories.

(iv) The functions of local government bodies in relation to the control of land usage and the conservation and development of natural resources.

(v) The bearing of African legal systems on social and economic development and their evolution in relation to European law.

(vi) The development of local government for Africans in urban areas.

6. I shall be in a better position after the summer school has taken place to consider whether any statement of policy is required and, if so, what form it should take and whether it should be confidential or for publication. I should not of course regard the exchange of views at the summer school as substitute for consultation with Governors, and at the appropriate time I should wish to obtain Governors' views on these points. Meanwhile I shall take the opportunity in this despatch to address you on certain questions of machinery which I regard as essential to the successful formation and operation of any policy of African local government. I believe that the knowledge of the subject which undoubtedly exists through-

---

[1] The Gibbons Report on Local Government in East Africa and Eastern Nigeria put paid to this pious hope.

out Africa must be made more readily available to all concerned, so that it may exercise the right influence on the formation of policy. For this purpose we must provide for a much more effective and continuous exchange of information between individual African Governments and between the African Governments as a whole and the Colonial Office; and equally the machinery both of African Governments and the Colonial Office must be so devised that policy with regard to local government for Africans can be kept constantly under review. At the same time, in recognition of the predominant part which the district staffs play in the execution of policy, means must be found of ensuring that they are enabled to devote the majority of their time and attention to this vital work. . . .

14. The District Staffs.—The principal instrument for putting into effect the policy of African local government is the District Commissioner and it is vital to the success of this policy that the best possible use should be made of his services. I wish to make known to the Service generally my deep concern for the welfare of all staff working in the field. Since I am here discussing the problems of local government, what I say is necessarily addressed to the position of the Administrative Officer, but the principle applies equally to all technical field staff and I should like this to be clearly understood. . . . I regard it as of fundamental importance, and I know that Governors agree, that District Commissioners should be given by Governments the widest possible latitude within the general framework of policy to press on with the development of local government in their district and that full scope should be given for the exercise of individual energy and initiative. For this purpose it is necessary that the district staffs should be kept fully and continuously informed of the broad lines of Government policy within which they must operate; that they should be relieved of the mass of routine which at present often makes it difficult for them to devote enough time and attention to their true work of local government; that every effort should be made, even at some sacrifice of convenience, to leave them in their posts for sufficiently long periods to enable real progress to be made during the term of office of each District Commissioner; and finally that one-man districts should be avoided so that regular touring may take place. I am aware that these problems have been engaging the attention of African Governments for many years. What I have to say is not new. I say it because I believe that the time has come to make renewed efforts to solve these problems of machinery, so as to ensure that the district staffs are in the best position to deal with the exceedingly difficult problems which lie ahead of us in Africa in the immediate future.

15. You will have appreciated from the preceding paragraphs the

importance which I attach to keeping the district staffs fully informed of developments both inside and outside the Territory. I suggest that this could be achieved in the following ways:

(a) By providing officers in the field with information regarding current developments in the policy of the Government concerned both while policy is still being formed and after decisions have been taken. Written information should be supplemented by personal contacts between headquarters and the district staff and it should be the special responsibility of the Secretary for African Affairs, or the equivalent officer, to maintain these contacts by frequent touring.

(b) By means of periodic conferences which are a regular feature in some Territories already and undoubtedly fulfil an extremely valuable function.

(c) By arranging for Officers to attend courses, etc., while on leave in this country.

(d) By arranging visits for officers to other British Territories in Africa and to foreign territories.

(e) By encouraging the production of local periodicals whether on an official basis or on the initiative of individual officers or departments.

(f) By ensuring the distribution of important Government publications, e.g., White Papers, etc., published in the United Kingdom.

(g) By ensuring that all important publications affecting their work are made available officially to the district staffs and that they are kept up to date in the general literature of their profession. Arrangements should be made to circulate to them a list of recent publications on all matters affecting their work. In order to assist Governments in this I am examining the possibility of circulating book lists regularly to all Colonial Governments.

(h) By arranging that the district staffs have the means to keep abreast with world affairs and new ideas by means of station or office libraries and central or provincial lending libraries. Library facilities should be renewed and where necessary supplemented.

16. Finally I come to the actual work of District Commissioners and to the complaint which has been heard on all sides for many years, that the district staffs have become increasingly over-burdened with minor routine matters which make it impossible for officers to devote sufficient time and attention to their proper function of local government. You will, I am sure, agree with the view I strongly hold that the development of African local government should be the principal function of district staffs, and I should be glad if this could be laid down emphatically for the guidance of all your officers.

This does not of course apply to officers in towns or settled areas who are deputed to deal with the affairs of the non-African communities; nor is it intended to mean that in mixed areas the affairs of these communities should receive less than the attention which they deserve. I do, however, again wish to emphasize that work connected with local government is of greater importance than the submission of returns or the writing of routine reports. I am not suggesting that routine work should be neglected or put aside, but I do consider that it should be subjected to careful scrutiny by Governments to ensure that demands made on District Commissioners by the Secretariat and departments are fully justified and that less important items may, where possible, be eliminated. If any question of priority arises between the two functions, the work of local government must in my view take precedence over all but absolutely essential routine work.

17. Routine work must nevertheless continue, and to help the district staffs to deal with it I suggest, in the first place, that Governments should examine the possibility of increasing the mechanical aids to work at district headquarters and in particular that attention should be given to the increased use of typewriters, stenographers and even possibly dictaphones in the larger centres. I believe that it would be useful for any Government which has not recently done so to entrust one of its officers with the task of examining the possibility of adopting arrangements to increase office efficiency in the districts. Secondly, and far more important, I consider that arrangements should be made to relieve District Commissioners, and District Officers or Assistant District Commissioners, of the personal responsibility for the handling of routine work. In my view the aim should be to provide every district office with a competent office manager who, while coming under the authority of the District Commissioner, would himself be responsible for such matters as the local Treasury, the issue of licences, the handling of cash, the preparation of returns and such other matters as could be delegated to him. This office manager should himself be recognized as sub-accountant for the district so that he and not the District Commissioner himself could carry the financial responsibility. Such posts should be filled by Africans whenever suitable Africans are available; and, where they are not at present available, by Asians or by Europeans whether male or female. It may be that as a result routine and financial work might in some cases be handled with slightly less efficiency than when dealt with by Administrative Officers themselves, but this could be offset by establishing a system of travelling inspectors of the work of these office managers. In any case, any loss of efficiency involved in the change at first would, in

my view, be more than balanced by the advantage of freeing Administrative Officers for the exercise of their proper functions. In permitting highly trained and highly paid Administrative Officers to devote large parts of their time to dealing with minute details of routine administration, I consider that we are acquiescing in an arrangement which is most uneconomical and I feel sure that this state of affairs must be brought to an end at the earliest possible moment. I wish to make it clear that I attach great importance to this point; indeed I regard it as essential that steps should be taken without delay to relieve Administrative Officers of routine work and to ensure that they are able to devote themselves primarily to travelling extensively throughout their districts and to the problems of political, economic, and social development and above all to the development of local government. . . .

B.

The broad lines of present policy in the British non-self-governing territories overseas have for the most part been clearly defined. The problem of applying that policy in the varying circumstances of each of the territories is a constant one. Moreover, British policy itself, in many respects, is not a constant conception; it has, over the last generation, been modified in the light of changing conditions and influences in the world.

The essential and permanent objective of British policy is to bring forward the African territories to self-governing responsibility within the Commonwealth. To that end, an evolutionary process towards more liberal, representative[1] and responsible political institutions is going on. Progress, however, depends on developing in African communities a sense of community obligation and social responsibility and service. In this, local government plays a conspicuous part. It is the broad base throughout the whole community on which responsibility and community requirements can grow. It is through these organs of government that the African may acquire experience in civic responsibility and handling his own affairs, factors essential to his effective work in the central political institutions of his territory.[2]

We have moved a long way since Lord Lugard popularized the conception of indirect rule, a policy which fully recognized the structure of African society and which accepted and tried to govern through the indigenous institutions. Sometimes, of course, institu-

---

[1] Cf. footnote p. 238.
[2] In the event, most politicians moved straight to the 'centre' without the envisaged apprenticeship in 'local' government administration.

tions of native authority had to be artificially created but, broadly, the system suited the needs and met the wishes of African society in the early stages following its adoption. It was democratic in the sense that it left the affairs of the local communities in the hands of the chiefs and rulers recognized by the people themselves. The essence of the system was the continuance of the old way of life insofar as it was not contrary to British conceptions of natural justice. Apart from the desire to eliminate certain objectionable practices, it was, broadly speaking, a static policy, or one which moved only at the speed of the societies for which it was designed. It could not, in the nature of things, remain permanently suitable when new economic, political and social changes began to work and modify the authority, habit and ways of life of the whole community. Inevitably, new influences began to appear and elements in the community to demand services, development and responsibility as exist in the modern world outside their own territories. We are now called to apply a new yard stick to an awakening African society. We use the word development to describe the new process. Development or progress, planned and inter-related change and improvement in all fields, economic, social and political, are the keynotes of our present policy.

All this necessarily involves adjustment in conceptions of political structure and responsibility. It means a marked change in approach to indirect rule. The principle of working through the native peoples and their institutions, new or old, cannot be abandoned; but it must be recognized that development is only practicable if it is grafted on to the growing aspirations of the African people and enjoys the co-operation of the more dynamic and flexible expression in the changing conditions of today. It is less that policy should be restrained by the old, almost universal conservatism in African society which served as the basis of the indirect rule policy; but that it should meet the desire for change and improvement on the part of the African people themselves. Local government machinery is required for the administration of plans for progress in the economic and social fields, while an outlet is required for the growing political consciousness of the ordinary people. For these purposes the unmodified traditional machinery is inadequate; and, wherever possible, it must be adapted to the new needs of local government and administration. It is no longer a question of maintaining the *status quo*, where its use no longer meets the wishes of the people; but clearly it must be an object of policy, where the people are developing their own ideas of progress, to help them to build up institutions which satisfy their wishes and are adequate for more modern needs.

This new policy has not, of course, just now been 'discovered'; it has developed over a period of years as the need for development in all fields and the growth of African aspirations has been studied and appreciated. It is the result of a natural organic growth which has quickened in pace as it developed and which owes much to the many far-sighted administrators who guided it through the various stages of native administration to present conceptions.

The burden of translating the new policy into reality is a co-operative one between the leaders of the people and the officers of the administrative and technical services in the field. It necessarily makes greater demands on the skill, patience and knowledge of Colonial officers than before. Indirect rule, which took as its object the preservation of tribal institutions, required officers with a sympathetic interest and a good knowledge of African society and institutions. In consequence, great importance attached to the study of anthropology.[1] But the qualifications and knowledge needed to carry out the new dynamic and constructive approach and to build up the local political and administrative institutions required, cover a much wider field. Not only is it necessary to have this anthroplogical knowledge and to know how society is organized, but it is also necessary to foresee clearly what is happening to African society by the play of modern influences and forces and to appreciate the sort of society that is desirable to people and government alike and how to achieve it. This requires close study of the changes which are taking place in African society, the rise of new classes, the decay of old customs, the problems of urban populations and the effect of new factors such as education, organized labour, money economy and cash crops.[2] It requires also a knowledge of contemporary political and social developments in Africa and the wider world, and of the experience and techniques developed to meet similar problems both in and out of Africa. In particular, administrators in Africa may now usefully draw on the great fund of knowledge in the history and practice of local government and social administration which is available in the United Kingdom.

At the same time as new local institutions are being planned and created, African societies require some guidance in their adjustment to sweeping social and economic changes. Their customs in regard to marriage and inheritance, for example, must be carefully adapted to values and circumstances vastly different from those in which

[1] Cf. Note 118, p. 40. Cf. also A. I. Richards 'Anthropology on the Scrapheap?', *Journal of African Administration*, January, 1961.

[2] Since this was written, the intervening fifteen years have witnessed an unparalleled flood of specialized studies and monographs centred on the general theme of 'change and continuity in African society in transition'.

they originated. Changes in traditional land-holding systems also give rise to grave problems of adjustment. Land-tenure customs must be modified to allow better land use, soil conservation and more productive farming methods. In many places methods of land registration need to be worked out; while subdivision and fragmentation of holdings, and transfers of customary rights need thorough investigation. All these questions are only a few items in a long catalogue.

Experiment, experience, knowledge and thought must solve these problems. Past efforts in these fields have brought rich stores of experience and knowledge. But much has been unrecorded, uncommunicated or unstudied, because it remains in the minds of men or in local records. Discoveries in administrative and political techniques at times have spread so slowly from province to province, and even more slowly from territory to territory, that often before they were applied the circumstances for which they were fitted were beginning to disappear.

As the speed of African change hastens, no one can afford to disregard experience gained or to allow new ideas to pass unnoticed. Police and practice must both be reviewed continuously to keep in step with change, and indeed to anticipate its direction. . . .

DATE DUE